PAUL
UNBOUND

Prometheus Bound, Dirck van Baburen, 17th century

PAUL UNBOUND

Other Perspectives on the Apostle

MARK D. GIVEN

EDITOR

HENDRICKSON PUBLISHERS

Paul Unbound: Other Perspectives on the Apostle
© 2010 by Hendrickson Publishers Marketing, LLC
P. O. Box 3473
Peabody, Massachusetts 01961-3473

ISBN 978-1-59856-324-5

Printed in the United States of America

First Printing — January 2010

Cover Art: Pittoni, Giovanni Battista (1687–1767) St. Paul.
Location: Cassa di Risparmio, Ferrara, Italy
Photo Credit: Alinari / Art Resource, N.Y.

Library of Congress Cataloging-in-Publication Data

Paul unbound : other perspectives on the Apostle / edited by
Mark D. Given.
  p. cm.
Includes bibliographical references and indexes.
ISBN 978-1-59856-324-5 (alk. paper)
1. Paul, the Apostle, Saint. I. Given, Mark Douglas.
BS2506.3.P3843 2009
225.9′2—dc22
                           2009020512

Contents

List of Figures

List of Contributors

Warren Carter

Professor of New Testament, Brite Divinity School, Texas Christian University, Fort Worth, Texas

Charles H. Cosgrove

Professor of New Testament Studies and Christian Ethics, Northern Seminary, Lombard, Illinois

A. Andrew Das

Professor, Niebuhr Distinguished Chair, Elmhurst College, Elmhurst, Illinois

Steven J. Friesen

Professor, Louise Farmer Boyer Chair in Biblical Studies; Fellow, Institute for the Study of Antiquity and Christian Origins, University of Texas at Austin

Mark D. Given

Associate Professor of Religious Studies and Graduate Director, Missouri State University, Springfield, Missouri

Deborah Krause

Professor of New Testament and Academic Dean, Eden Theological Seminary, St. Louis, Missouri

Mark D. Nanos

Soebbing Visiting Scholar, Rockhurst University, Kansas City, Missouri

Jerry L. Sumney

Professor of Biblical Studies, Lexington Theological Seminary, Lexington, Kentucky

Acknowledgments

First of all, I wish to thank the contributors to this volume. Without their dedication and cooperation, it would not have been possible. In spite of circumstances ranging from excessive teaching and administrative duties to health issues, they all came through with outstanding essays. I also wish to thank the excellent editors and staff at Hendrickson who made this project pleasurable, especially Shirley Decker-Lucke and Allan Emery. From the first time Shirley heard of this project she expressed an excitement about it that was infectious. Her editorial wisdom was invaluable. Allan oversaw the final stages of the project and also gave sage advice. Finally, although my first experience of editing a book was a very good one, I thank Victor Matthews for warning me about what I was getting myself into.

Abbreviations

Ant.	Josephus, *Jewish Antiquities*
B.C.E.	before the common era
BETL	Bibliotheca ephemeridium theologicarum louvaniensium
Bib	*Biblica*
BibInt	*Biblical Interpreter*
BJRL	*Bulletin of the John Rylands University Library of Manchester*
BZNW	Beihefte zur Zeitschrift für die neutestamentliche Wissenschaft
CBQ	*Catholic Biblical Quarterly*
C.E.	common era
CRINT	Compendia rerum iudaicarum ad Novum Testamentum
ESEC	Emory Studies in Early Christianity
ET	English translation
HB	Hebrew Bible
HTR	*Harvard Theological Review*
JBL	*Journal of Biblical Literature*
JRS	*Journal of Roman Studies*
JSJ	*Journal for the Study of Judaism in the Persian, Hellenistic, and Roman Periods*
JSNT	*Journal for the Study of the New Testament*
JSNTSup	Journal for the Study of the New Testament: Supplemental Series
JSOT	Journal for the Study of the Old Testament
JSPSup	Journal for the Study of the Pseudepigrapha: Supplement Series
NASB	New American Standard Bible

NovT	*Novum Testamentum*
NovTSup	Supplements to Novum Testamentum
NRSV	New Revised Standard Version
NT	New Testament
NTS	*New Testament Studies*
OT	Old Testament
SBL	Society of Biblical Literature
SBLDS	Society of Biblical Literature Dissertation Series
SBLSymS	Society of Biblical Literature Symposium Series
SNTSMS	Society for New Testament Studies Monograph Series
ST	*Studia theologica*
TSAJ	Texte und Studien zum antiken Judentum
TZ	*Theologische Zeitschrift*
WBC	Word Biblical Commentary
WMANT	Wissenschaftliche Untersuchungen zum Alten und Neuen Testament
WUNT	Wissenschaftliche Untersuchungen zum Neuen Testament

Introduction

Mark D. Given

This collection of essays provides the advanced undergraduate, graduate student, or interested layperson with an introduction to a wide range of fascinating approaches to Paul that are relevant to, yet go beyond, traditional theological and historical concerns. All of the contributors have previously published important work on their assigned topic. The collection grew out of a panel presentation on the topic of "Newer Perspectives on Paul" at the 2004 Central States Society of Biblical Literature meeting in St. Louis. As chair of the NT section, I did not plan the panel with the intention of producing a book, but the range of subjects covered and the quality of the presentations made it immediately apparent to the participants that we should do so. Several of us teach introductory Paul courses, and we could see how desirable it would be to have such a collection of essays available to supplement any standard textbook. It has taken some time to bring the volume to fruition, but all of the essays have been expanded and updated to include scholarship produced since 2004. Each chapter includes a bibliography that will be useful to students for further reading and research.

Mark Nanos suggested the title, *Paul Unbound*. It calls to mind the myth of Prometheus, who was bound on orders from Zeus for stealing fire and giving it, along with other gifts of knowledge, to the human race. Certainly Paul was not bound by God—at least not in this sense—but one might playfully suggest that he has often been bound by tradition and theology, and these chapters reflect some of the ways in which the study of Paul has in recent years been liberated from a variety of traditional or conventional perspectives. While contemplating Mark's suggested title, I came upon Dirck van Baburen's seventeenth-century painting, "Prometheus Bound" (see frontispiece). This painting reminded me of Caravaggio's celebrated "Conversion of St. Paul" (http://www.caravaggio-foundation .org/The-Conversion-of-St-Paul.html) and, in fact, Baburen was strongly influenced by the style of Caravaggio. Barburen's painting suggested the following allegory to me. Hermes on the right is the messenger of Zeus and thus represents theological hermeneutics. Hephaestus on the left represents the traditional historical-critical method, which has often served theology against its will. Thus, theological interpretation and traditional historical criticism have joined to constrain Paul, to keep him bound. And the contributors to this volume could be imagined like an unseen Greek chorus, which, as in Aeschylus's fifth-century B.C.E. play, *Prometheus Bound,* ultimately advocates for the liberation of Prometheus (hence, Paul).[1]

The subtitle, *Other Perspectives on the Apostle,* was my idea. It recalls such well-worn phrases in Paul scholarship as "new perspectives," which often meant new theological interpretations, and *the* New Perspective, which is important in a couple of these chapters but is not the main focus of any. This is not to say that theological issues play no role in any of these chapters—they do—but they do not command the stage.

It is thus fitting that the first chapter begins with the observation that "for a growing number of scholars, Paul's primary engagement was not with other Jesus followers or with first-century Judaism but with the Roman Empire." Warren Carter's "Paul and the Roman Empire: Recent Perspectives" surveys and evaluates the work of the Society of Biblical Literature's Paul and Politics group. Echoing Richard Horsley, he locates its origin initially in wider academic and cultural contexts, namely, the rediscovery of imperialism in other disciplines, postcolonial criticism, the influence of non-European-American scholars, and some historical Jesus work that has given attention to the Roman imperial world. The group has investigated four interrelated areas: Paul and the politics of the churches; Paul and the politics of Israel; Paul and the politics of the Roman Empire; and Paul and the politics of interpretation. Carter surveys three volumes of essays that pursue these topics: *Paul and Empire* (1997), *Paul and Politics* (2000), and *Paul and the Roman Imperial Order* (2004). He then goes on to consider other important works, especially those of Elisabeth Schüssler Fiorenza, Neil Elliot, John Dominic Crossan and Jonathan Reed, Peter Oakes, and Davina Lopez. Carter concludes with several incisive suggestions for further work.

---

[1] Aeschylus also wrote a lost play titled *Prometheus Unbound* in which Prometheus was reconciled with Zeus. Interestingly, however, in 1820 Percy Shelley published his own *Prometheus Unbound* in which Zeus was overthrown and the effects of Prometheus's actions led to a transformed humanity that was "Sceptreless, free, uncircumscribed, but man / Equal, unclassed, tribeless, and nationless" (3.4.194–195). While Shelley would have had no sympathy with the traditional Paul, the allegorical possibilities for comparing his Prometheus to the "other" Pauls of this collection abound.

Steven Friesen's "Paul and Economics: The Jerusalem Collection as an Alternative to Patronage" is an apt extension of the topics covered in Carter's chapter. Friesen argues that we need to construct a different picture of Paul the activist. Rather than describing him simply as a theologian and rhetorician, we need to examine his economic practices. For his gospel not only challenged fundamental economic ideas such as patronage but also promoted alternative economic practices of community sharing among the poor, based on Paul's understanding of the example of Christ instead of on contemporary ideas of patronage.

The next chapter is Jerry Sumney's "Paul and His Opponents: The Search." Sumney reviews the major outlines of the ways Paul's opponents have been understood from F. C. Baur's *Paul the Apostle of Jesus Christ* in 1845 down through the twentieth century. Methodological issues are the dominant concern of the chapter. These include distinguishing between those Paul opposes and those who opposed Paul; evaluating types of texts within a letter to determine their usefulness for acquiring data to identify opponents; recognizing the implications of the diverse nature of early Christianity; and the use of reconstructions of other groups within the first-century environment to supply information about Paul's opponents. Sumney concludes with an examination of two recent studies of Colossians as examples of the ways careful attention to methodology is important, and still neglected.

In "Paul and Ethnicity: A Selective History of Interpretation," Charles Cosgrove provides the first broad survey of interpretation of Paul and ethnicity, treating not only Pauline scholarship on this topic but also more popular efforts to grasp Paul's attitude toward ethnic identity. His survey of Pauline scholarship covers the subjects of "The Universal (Non-Ethnic) Human Being in Paul," "Paul and Anti-Semitism," " 'Separate but Equal' in Paul?" "Divine Impartiality in Paul," "Interpretations of Galatians 3:28," and "Paul contra Ethnocentrism." He goes on to survey other fascinating interpretations of Paul and ethnicity such those of African-American thinkers from the nineteenth and twentieth centuries; the radical nationalist translation commentary on Romans for the Zulu people by nineteenth-century missionary Bishop Colenso; Holmes Rolston's effort in 1942 to interpret Paul in an anti-racist way in and for a Southern Christian audience in America; and Daniel Boyarin's interpretation of Paul and ethnicity from a Jewish perspective. The essay also provides a discussion of post-Holocaust, dispensationalist, and recent non-Christian philosophical interpretations of Paul as they bear on the question of ethnicity.

Andrew Das's "Paul and the Law: Pressure Points in the Debate" is the first of two chapters that engage, in differing ways, the bewildering scholarly territory of Paul and the Law. Das helpfully offers the beginning student a roadmap for identifying key landmarks. He presents an introduction to the New Perspective on Paul as well as ongoing criticisms of it. Along the way, he introduces his own perspective on Paul and the Law that is not simply a middle way between the New Perspective and the traditional Lutheran one but what he argues is a *Newer* Perspective that takes seriously the strengths and weaknesses of both.

Mark Nanos's chapter is the longest in this collection and one of the most challenging for students. Its title is "Paul and Judaism: Why Not Paul's Judaism?" Nanos observes that the investigation of Paul and Judaism has traditionally proceeded as if what was written was Paul or Judaism, with the understanding that these referents represent two different religious systems. They proceed as if the two are different and something must be wrong with one or the other. Nanos believes this essentializing of difference and concomitant requirement to find fault will continue to the degree that the ethnic division that Paul's letters draw along a Jew/Gentile and Israel/other-nations line within a Christ-believing Judaism continues to be approached by his interpreters as if drawn along a Judaism/Christianity line instead. Nanos challenges prevailing interpretations of 1 Cor 9:19–23 which construe it as a "chameleon principle" that renders Paul's law observance a sham, and while appreciative of the New Perspective's improved understanding of Judaism, he finds it still inadequate in its understanding of Paul. It is still too indebted to traditional constructions of Paul and Paulinism. Nanos, however, insists that what Paul would find wrong with Paulinism is that it is not a Judaism.

The next chapter is Deborah Krause's "Paul and Women: Telling Women to Shut Up Is More Complicated Than You Might Think," which surveys recent historical-critical scholarship regarding women and the churches of Paul. The survey shows that feminist research has challenged Pauline scholars to incorporate the study of the everyday lives of women in Hellenistic Judaism and Greco-Roman culture into the study of the Pauline epistles. Such studies have moved from examining Paul's rhetoric as unique to placing it within its larger contexts of religion, economics, politics, and culture of his day. As such, women are no longer a separate subject area within Pauline studies but rather a part of the world within which Paul is understood to operate. In this sense, texts such as 1 Cor 11:1–16 or 1 Cor 14:34–36, which have traditionally been studied as evidence of Paul's attitudes toward women, are examined within their larger rhetorical contexts for what they might say about women and their activities within the church and world in general. Krause examines several Pauline texts in light of these newer approaches. In particular, the issue of women's speech provides a focus for the study of how Paul's rhetoric is engaged within a larger discourse of power. Moreover, texts from the

Pastoral Epistles (extensions of the Pauline legacy) are examined for the way in which they engage women's speech and activity within the church (e.g., 1 Tim 2:8–15; 1 Tim 5:11–13; 2 Tim 3:6–7). In sum, these texts are interpreted not as evidence for Paul's attitudes toward women but rather for how they reveal struggles of identity and power within the churches of Paul and how these struggles connect with expectations of women and their speech within the larger culture.

The final chapter is my own "Paul and Rhetoric: A *Sophos* in the Kingdom of God." After providing a brief overview of the history of the subject of Paul and rhetoric, I discuss how classical or new rhetorical criticism is applied to 1 Corinthians. Lastly, I use aspects of interpretation of 1 Cor 1–4 to contrast a classical with a more postmodern rhetorical approach. This final section broadens the subject of rhetoric and power to discuss some of the seductions of Paul's rhetoric. Why would someone want to enter the kingdom of God? Why would someone want to choose it over the empire of Rome? Intriguingly, the values and rewards of the kingdom of God turn out to have some striking similarities to those of this age. Paul's rhetorical questions, "Where is the *sophos*? Where is the scribe? Where is the debater of this age?" imply another question: Where is the *sophos,* the scribe, and the debater of the new age, the new creation? I argue that the answer is where Paul is, together with all those who will imitate him. The wisdom and knowledge he offers does not seduce with the promise of glory in the kingdom of Rome like that of the *sophos* of this age, but it does seduce with the promise a surpassing eternal weight of glory in a kingdom that is about to appear.

Not every possible other perspective on Paul is represented here. For example, while Warren Carter's essay touches on postcolonial criticism, a separate essay on this burgeoning perspective would have been desirable. Deborah Krause's essay involves gender issues, but a separate essay on Paul and sexuality would be good. Still, whatever its shortcomings, I hope this volume will prove useful and worthwhile for students and interested lay readers. If so, perhaps a future edition can include more of the present other perspectives as well as those to come. As long as there are readers of Paul, there will be always other perspectives.

Mark D. Given

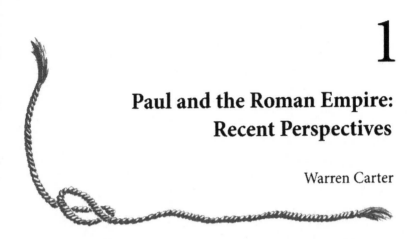

1

Paul and the Roman Empire: Recent Perspectives

Warren Carter

For a growing number of scholars, Paul's primary engagement was not with other Jesus followers nor with first-century Judaism but with the Roman Empire. How did Paul evaluate the empire? What guidance did he offer Jesus followers for negotiating it in their daily living? What similarities or differences exist between the structures of Paul's theological thinking and ecclesial communities and imperial perspectives and structures? In this chapter I will look at several significant contributions to this developing perspective on Paul, some critiques of it, and challenges for future work. Because of space limitations, the discussion and bibliography can be only illustrative, not comprehensive.

THE SBL PAUL AND POLITICS GROUP

Significant impetus for this work has come from three books edited by Richard Horsley, published between 1997[1] and 2004.[2] The three volumes contain the work of scholars associated with the Society of Biblical Literature's Paul and Politics group, of which Horsley was at the time co-chair with Cynthia Kittredge. The books, comprising some seven hundred pages and thirty-six chapters, along with various introductory pieces and responses, represent the work of about thirty scholars. Some of these scholars have written other articles and books related to Paul's

---

[1] Richard Horsley, ed., *Paul and Empire: Religion and Power in Roman Imperial Society* (Harrisburg, Pa.: Trinity Press International, 1997).

[2] Richard Horsley, ed., *Paul and Politics: Ekklesia, Israel, Imperium, Interpretation* (Harrisburg, Pa.: Trinity Press International, 2000); idem, *Paul and the Roman Imperial Order* (Harrisburg, Pa.: Trinity Press International, 2004).

engagement with the Roman Empire.[3] Collectively, the volumes offer a
significant challenge to much previous and current work on Paul and
advocate an innovative and exciting approach that cannot be ignored in
studies of Paul.

Aims and Agenda

In his introductory essay to *Paul and Empire* (1997), Horsley jus-
tifies the investigation of Paul's interaction with the Roman Empire by
observing that before it became the empire's established religion, "Christianity was a product of empire."[4] This imperial origin, though, has been
obscured from scholarly investigation by the late eighteenth century's
separation of church and state so that biblical and theological studies
concentrated on religious or spiritual matters and ignored political and
economic dimensions and imperial contexts. Horsley locates the rediscovery of the imperial world in which Paul conducts his mission in relation to
similar rediscoveries of empire in other disciplines (literary studies; HB),
the emergence of postcolonial criticism, the influence of non-European-
American scholars, and some historical Jesus work.

Horsley elaborates the agenda in his introduction to *Paul and Politics*
(2000), a volume dedicated to Krister Stendahl for his pioneering work
in "bringing greater sensitivity to concrete human relations" and thereby
preparing for this work in Pauline studies.[5] In Stendahl's significant essay,
"The Apostle Paul and the Introspective Conscience of the West,"[6] Horsley
finds five arguments that challenged the predominantly theological and
individualized interpretation of Paul:

- the Protestant focus on individual sin, salvation, and justification
  by faith missed Paul's concern with including Gentiles in the messianic community;

- the anti-Jewish bias in constructions of Paul as struggling to throw
  off law-bound first-century Judaism ignored salvation history and
  Paul's vision of Israel's salvation;

---

[3] The notes in these three volumes often signal further work.

[4] Horsley, *Paul and Empire*, 1–8.

[5] Horsley, "Introduction: Krister Stendahl's Challenge to Pauline Studies,"
Paul and Politics, 1–17, esp. 5–10; see also Elliott, "Paul and the Politics of Empire:
Problems and Prospects," 17–39.

[6] Krister Stendahl, "The Apostle Paul and the Introspective Conscience of the
West," *HTR* 56 (1963): 199–215.

- the emphasis on generalized theological issues ignored the contingent, specific, and historical, address of Paul's letters;

- the concern with theology overlooked Paul's focus on social/human relations to which theology has secondary significance;

- subsequent interpretations of Paul, especially through the lens of the socially conservative deuteropaulines, must be challenged by the original contexts of Paul's letters.

Stendahl's work opened the way for questioning conventional approaches to Paul. Participants in social movements for liberation, such as African-American, feminist, non-European and/or two-thirds world, Jewish, and dis-eased Western male interpreters, shared a common concern with the diverse and interrelated forms of domination such as race, gender, ethnicity, and social status. They examined, for instance, Paul's treatment of slavery and women and exposed the use of Paul by colonizing Western missionaries to enforce submission and by Christian scholars to perpetuate anti-Judaism.[7] The SBL Paul and Politics group emerged to investigate four interrelated areas: Paul and the politics of the churches; Paul and the politics of Israel; Paul and the politics of the Roman Empire; and Paul and the politics of interpretation.

Informed by the analyses of Elisabeth Schüssler Fiorenza and Fernando Segovia,[8] Horsley sketches further implications of "how problematic Western privatized and depoliticized interpretations of biblical texts have become."[9] He points especially to the imperialistic nature of scholarly inquiry that assumed and asserted European/American elite male interests to be universal and that silenced the interests, experiences, identities, and voices of all others; the silence of biblical scholars on major sociopolitical issues of the last fifty years; the inability of the New Perspective on Paul to move outside the traditional opposition of Paul to Judaism; and the continuing neglect of imperial and power dynamics in various other new methods developed in recent decades (social-scientific; postmodernist; cultural studies). He outlines four principles that guide the formulation of political interpretations of Paul:

---

[7] Horsley, "Introduction," *Paul and Politics*, 10–15.
[8] Elisabeth Schüssler Fiorenza, *Rhetoric and Ethic: The Politics of Biblical Studies* (Minneapolis: Fortress, 1999); Fernando Segovia, " 'And They Began to Speak in Other Tongues': Competing Forms of Discourse in Contemporary Biblical Discourse," in *Reading from This Place: Social Location and Biblical Interpretation in the United States* (ed. Fernando Segovia and Mary Ann Tolbert; Minneapolis: Fortress, 1995), 1–32.
[9] Horsley, "Introduction," *Paul and Politics*, 11.

- Texts and interpretations are sites of struggle among various voices.

- The production and interpretation of texts do not involve only ideas but also power relations, interests, values, and visions; all interpretation has an agenda.

- Both texts and interpreters occupy particular social locations and contexts requiring systemic analysis of wider political-economic-religious structures and power relations as well as of local assemblies. There is a special interest in "readings from below," in the marginalized and oppressed with demystification and liberation in mind.

- Interpreters' identity and social location are hybrid and complex, embracing multiple positions and perspectives involving various interrelationships of class, gender, race, and ethnicity.

Horsley summarizes the approach by saying: "The aims and agenda of the Paul and Politics group are, broadly, to problematize, interrogate, and re-vision Pauline texts and interpretations, to identify oppressive formulations as well as potentially liberative visions and values in order to recover their unfulfilled historical possibilities, all in critical mutual engagement among diverse participants."[10]

Content and Areas of Investigation

In order to pursue this agenda, scholars must study not only Paul but also the work of classical scholars on the structures, ideology, and practices of the Roman Empire. Thus Horsley's *Paul and Empire* (1997) begins with essays examining aspects of the Roman world with five essays being written by classical scholars. Part 1, comprising four essays by Peter Brunt, Dieter Georgi, Simon Price, and Paul Zanker, is entitled "The Gospel of Imperial Salvation." It focuses on the cluster of propaganda claims, practices, and institutions that sustains and creates the Roman imperial world, especially the imperial cult. The four articles describe what Horsley calls in the section introduction "the gospel of Imperial Salvation," the gospel of Caesar, the imperial savior, who had established "peace and security" in the cities of Paul's mission where urban elites had willingly "established shrines, temples, citywide festivals and intercity games to honor their savior."[11] The imperial cult pervaded public life, a political-religious form of power that served both rulers (the allied elite) and the ruled in estab-

---

[10] Ibid., 15.
[11] Horsley, "General Introduction," *Paul and Empire*, 3–4.

lishing and recognizing divine sanction for the prevailing order. Religion is thus not separate from or independent of the imperial order. It participates in and sanctions the political order and societal power relations. To create an alternative to this order of power, as Paul did, is to engage in a politically charged act.[12]

The second section, comprising three essays by Peter Garnsey and Richard Saller, John Chow, and Richard Gordon, is headed "Patronage, Priesthoods, and Power." This section also investigates the power relations that "held the far-flung empire of Rome together," by exploring the religio-political (Gordon) and socio-economic networks of patronage that secured the self-serving power of emperors and allied Roman and provincial elites (Garnsey and Saller, Chow) who strategically controlled the dependent lower orders, undermined bonds of solidarity among the urban poor and peasantry, and limited their access to goods and other benefits. That is, patronage, fusing the "emperor cult with the social-economic system of patronage," was a means of both social cohesion and social control.[13]

The second half of the book interprets Paul in relation to this Roman imperial context. In part 3, entitled "Paul's Counter-Imperial Gospel," Dieter Georgi discusses Paul's vocabulary in Romans (*euangelion, pistis, dikaiosynē, eirēnē*) that echoes Roman political theology and frames Paul's gospel as a "competitor of the gospel of Caesar" (ch. 8). Helmut Koester delineates Paul's evocation of and opposition to the Roman imperial boast of having established "peace and security" (1 Thess 5:3; ch. 9). Neil Elliott (ch. 10) argues that the crucified Christ is the center of Paul's anti-imperial gospel, that this crucified political insurrectionary has been enthroned as Lord and his parousia (another imperial term) is awaited. Elliott argues that Paul understands "the rulers" who crucify Jesus in 1 Cor 2:8 in the context of Jewish apocalyptic traditions as evil rulers who dominate the current order and who are "being destroyed" (1 Cor 2:6) and subjected to God's justice.[14] What then of Paul's command to "be subject to the governing authorities" in Rom 13:1–7? In chapter 11, Elliott argues that Romans addresses Gentile-Christian boasting or claims of supercessionism in a context of Jewish vulnerability to imperial violence involving agitation

---

[12]Horsley, "The Gospel of Imperial Salvation: Introduction," *Paul and Empire*, 10–24.

[13]Horsley, "Patronage, Priesthoods, and Power: Introduction," *Paul and Empire*, 88–95, esp. 95.

[14]Horsley ("Paul's Counter-Imperial Gospel: Introduction," *Paul and Empire*, 140–47) devotes much of his introduction to arguing that "Paul has in mind the concrete political rulers and authorities" (142) and that apocalyptic traditions are very much concerned with historical, political struggles (often ignored by recent approaches to Paul's "social context").

over taxes. The command for submission offers Roman Christians a temporary strategy of judicious restraint appropriate to a historical context of Jewish vulnerability and parallel to that offered in similar circumstances by Philo and Josephus.

The final section, entitled "Building an Alternative Society," focuses on ecclesial practices and structures. Horsley argues that Paul cannot be understood as converting from one religion to another or as founding a new religion.[15] Rather, Paul's Pharisaic roots connect him to movements that sought Israel's independence from Hellenistic and Roman imperial traditions. Horsley identifies Paul's communities or *ekklesia* as "comprehensive in their common purpose, exclusive over against the dominant society, and part of an intercity, international movement."[16] Paul understands the *ekklesia* ("a political term with certain religious overtones") not as cultic communities but "as the political assembly of the people 'in Christ' in pointed juxtaposition and 'competition' with the official city assembly" (also identified as *ekklesia*).[17] Forming a social alternative to *Pax Romana* and rooted in Israel's traditions, these communities (not Rome) fulfill the divine promise to Abraham to bless all the nations and enact patterns of more egalitarian socio-economic interactions that differ from hierarchical patronage systems.

Karl Donfried elaborates this interaction of an alternative society over against the Roman imperial order in his analysis of "The Imperial Cults of Thessalonica and Political Conflict in 1 Thessalonians."[18] Donfried locates the hostility and opposition to Paul's mission, gospel, and community (Acts 17:1–9) in the context of a challenge to the city's prominent imperial cult and order, rejecting claims that Paul wanted acceptance and integration.

Schüssler Fiorenza, in contrast to those who deny any political implications for the baptismal formula of Gal 3:28 ("no longer Jew or Greek . . . slave or free . . . male or female"), argues that the formula functions as "a communal Christian self-definition," shaping the social interrelationships and structures of the community marked by freedom.[19] Paul envisaged a surpassing of the central divisions in imperial society of ethnicity, societal status, and gender. "All distinctions of religion, race, class, nationality, and gender are insignificant," creating an alternative, more egalitarian community inclusive of slaves and women that denied

---

[15] Horsley, "Introduction," *Paul and Empire*, 206–14.
[16] Horsley, *Paul and Empire*, 208.
[17] Ibid., 208–9.
[18] Donfried in Horsley, *Paul and Empire*, 215–23.
[19] Schüssler Fiorenza, "The Praxis of Coequal Discipleship," in Horsley, *Paul and Empire*, 224–41.

cultural-religious male privileges and created tension with the larger, hierarchical Roman world.[20]

In the final chapter, Horsley pursues similar emphases on the formation and practices of an alternative society in "1 Corinthians: A Case Study of Paul's Assembly as an Alternative Society."[21] Paul's discussions of the crucified Christ (1 Cor 1:17–2:8) and the resurrection (1 Cor 15) frame God's definitive present and future intervention that ensures the destruction of the imperial "rulers of this age" as enemies of God's purposes (1 Cor 2:6–8; 15:24–28). The remaining discussion discloses the structure of both Paul's mission and the network of household-based assembly/ies called by Paul to "conduct (their) own affairs autonomously, in complete independence of 'the world'" (1 Cor 5–6) though with continuing mission in it. The prohibition on eating food offered to idols removes the Corinthian assemblies from fundamental societal interactions, thereby ensuring the groups' survival "as an exclusive alternative community to the dominant society" and its social and power networks (1 Cor 8–10).[22] Paul also exhorts different economic relations. His refusal of their support exemplifies "horizontal economic reciprocity" (1 Cor 9) that differed from hierarchical imperial patronage relations of benefit to the elite. And the collection of 1 Cor 16:1–4 indicates economic solidarity, horizontal reciprocity, and an "international political-economic dimension diametrically opposed to the tributary political economy of the empire."[23]

Further exploration of the Corinthian correspondence and communities is evident in other articles in *Paul and Politics* (2000). In "Rhetoric and Empire—and 1 Corinthians," Horsley identifies the conflictual communication between Paul and the assembly as comprising two competing discourses, both of which oppose the Roman imperial order, and locates them in the system of power relations constituted by elite political rhetoric (embedded in provincial alliances, advocacy of the imperial cult, and patronage) that sustained imperial and civic order, exerted control, and secured consent and harmony. Cynthia Briggs Kittredge, however, is not

---

[20] Schüssler Fiorenza (ibid., 224–41) also discusses 1 Cor 7 and the household code of Col 3 that "takes over the Greco-Roman ethic of the patriarchal household" (237). She omits any discussion of another form of the household code from about the same time as Colossians in Matt 19–20 that imitates, critiques, and provides an alternative to the dominant Greco-Roman form by insisting on mutuality and more egalitarian structures. See Warren Carter, *Households and Discipleship*, and *Matthew and the Margins* (Maryknoll, N.Y.: Orbis, 2000), 376–410.

[21] Horsley, *Paul and Empire*, 242–52.

[22] Ibid., 248.

[23] Ibid., 251.

convinced of Paul's unqualified opposition to the empire.[24] She discusses
gender relations and other voices such as the women prophets in order
to reconstruct and evaluate the various self-understandings and political
interactions within the Corinthian community. She argues that "Paul uses
imperial language to both subvert and reinscribe the imperial system,"[25] imitating its patronage, as well as its hierarchical and subordinating political
and gender relations. Sheila Briggs notes ambiguities and contradictions in
discourse about slavery in the Roman world and argues that Paul's rhetoric, originating from a free-born Christian who shared with others anxiety
about upwardly mobile slaves and about being accused of upsetting the
social order, is similarly marked (1 Cor 7:24).[26] Sze-kar Wan argues that
the collection for the poor in Jerusalem "lay at the heart of Paul's concern
with redefining Jewish group boundaries to include gentile converts" (1 Cor
16:1–4; 2 Cor 8–9).[27] Paul's metanarrative of eschatological and cosmic universalism inclusive of Jew and Gentile critiques both Jewish and Roman imperialism, including, with an emphasis on equity/mutual indebtedness, the
divine origin of prosperity and the imperial structure of patronage. Allen
Callahan identifies 1 Corinthians as "an emancipatory project"[28] in which
Paul offers ecclesial manumission (1 Cor 7, the community buys freedom
for enslaved believers), mutuality (communal interdependence in justice
[1 Cor 6:1–9]) and economics (1 Cor 16:1–4), as three communal practices
to sustain emancipation among this community comprising those without
privilege, prestige, and power, against Roman hegemony.

Other chapters investigate aspects of Paul's interactions with other
communities, especially matters concerning Israel. Pamela Eisenbaum, for
example, focuses on Paul's Abrahamic identity establishing "a new kind of
family . . . made up of Jews and Gentiles."[29] Mark Nanos rejects conventional
readings of Galatians that emphasize the struggle as "Christianity versus Judaism" or (in more recent interpretations) as an intra-Christian struggle but
styles it as an intra- and inter-Jewish debate concerned with how Gentiles

---

[24] Kittredge, "Corinthian Women Prophets and Paul's Argumentation in
1 Corinthians," in Horsley, *Paul and Politics,* 103–9, drawing on the work of Antoinette Wire, *The Corinthian Women Prophets: A Reconstruction through Paul's
Rhetoric* (Minneapolis: Fortress, 1990).

[25] Kittredge, "Corinthian Women Prophets," 105.

[26] Briggs, "Paul on Bondage and Freedom in Imperial Roman Society," in
Horsley, *Paul and Politics,* 110–23.

[27] Wan, "Collection for the Saints as Anticolonial Act: Implications of Paul's
Ethnic Reconstruction," in Horsley, *Paul and Politics,* 191–215, esp. 192.

[28] Callahan, "Paul, Ekklesia, and Emancipation in Corinth: A Coda on Liberation Theology," in Horsley, *Paul and Politics,* 216–23, esp. 216–18.

[29] Eisenbaum, "Paul as the New Abraham," in Horsley, *Paul and Politics,*
130–45, esp.132.

are to be incorporated into the people of God.[30] Alan Segal highlights Paul's inclusive focus on "Jews and Gentiles making one community."[31]

N. T. Wright locates his discussion of "Paul's Gospel and Caesar's Empire" in affirmations that religion and politics are inseparable and that Paul's gospel challenges imperial cult and ideology.[32] Under the heading "Jesus Christ Is Lord: Exegetical Studies in Paul's Counterimperial Gospel," Wright examines four points of collision between Paul's theological claims and Roman imperial theology in which Paul asserts an alternative sovereignty and loyalty: (1) the term "gospel" evokes Isaiah's hope for establishing God's reign and Jesus as "Israel's Messiah and the world's Lord"; (2) Jesus' identity as messianic "King and Lord"; (3) the revelation of God's covenant faithfulness as justice or putting right of the world that challenges in Romans the Roman goddess and claim to provide Iustitia; (4) "Paul's Coded Challenge to Empire" in a discussion of Phil 3. Wright concludes by noting that Paul's critique of empire is grounded in his Jewish heritage, that his high Christology is central to it, that this critique is maintained along with a critique of nonmessianic Judaism, that Paul's challenge cannot be confined to and by the category of "religion," and that ecclesiology, critique, and collaboration are integral to it.

The third volume, *Paul and the Roman Imperial Order*,[33] contains seven chapters along with Horsley's introduction that summarizes central emphases in this approach[34] and a response from classical scholar Simon Price. Robert Jewett reads Rom 8:18–23 in the context of and as disputing Roman imperial claims about the renewal of nature.[35] Focusing on 1 Thess

---

[30] Nanos, "The Inter- and Intra-Jewish Political Context of Paul's Letter to the Galatians," in Horsley, *Paul and Politics,* 146–59.

[31] Segal, "Response: Some Aspects of Conversion and Identity Formation," in Horsley, *Paul and Politics,* 184–90, esp. 188.

[32] Wright, "Paul's Gospel and Caesar's Empire," in Horsley, *Paul and Politics,* 160–79.

[33] Horsley, *Paul and the Roman Imperial Order.*

[34] Horsley (ibid., 1–23) discusses the conventional setting of Paul in opposition to Judaism; a spiritualized reading in which Paul is supposedly interested only in religion separated from political-economic matters; the discovery of a Jewish Paul (covenantal nomism) in mission to Gentiles (Stendahl); the discovery of the Roman imperial world as not only Paul's context but also as the order to which Paul is opposed and with which his communities of alternative identity and practices encounter conflict; features of the Roman imperial order, its impact, and its various means of maintaining control (displacement of subject peoples, slavery, patronage, imperial cult, rhetoric), as well as various means of negotiating and opposing its power.

[35] Jewett, "The Corruption and Redemption of Creation: Reading Romans 8:18–23 in the Imperial Context," in Horsley, *Paul and the Roman Imperial Order,* 25–46.

2:14–16, Abraham Smith contextualizes Paul's mission and communities in continuing conflicts among subject peoples.[36] Neil Elliott examines Paul's use of imagery from the imperial triumph to present his own anti-imperial mission.[37] Rollin Ramsaran investigates Paul's contestive rhetoric in 1 Corinthians.[38] Efrain Agosto compares elite letters of recommendation with Paul's commendatory letters to argue that Paul calls leaders to sacrificial service (not domination) in oppositional communities.[39] Erik Heen rereads Phil 2:6–11 as rejecting the elite quest for honors while God raises and exalts the crucified Jesus as a counter-emperor.[40] Jennifer Wright Knust argues that in attacking vice and immorality Paul rejects imperial claims to have restored public morality, but in advocating Christ as the master over sin, Paul reinscribes hierarchical, imperial assumptions about sex, gender, and status.[41]

Throughout the three volumes various "response" articles engage the contributions and foster further debate by affirming, restating, and contesting interpretations. Antoinette Wire, for example, affirms interest in Paul's rhetoric in the essays of Horsley, Kittredge, and Briggs,[42] criticizes Horsley for ignoring the rhetoric of others in the Corinthian assembly who might be more anti-imperial than Paul, commends Kittredge for attending to Paul's imitation of, rather than exclusive resistance to, the empire and its patronage, and agrees with Briggs's analysis that Paul's gospel might have had little social value for most slaves. Wire and Calvin Roetzel affirm Wan's attention to ethnicity and matters of power but question how the collection might subvert Roman hegemony except in the sense that Jewish hopes conflict with Roman imperialism.[43] Wire also wonders,

---

[36] Smith, "Unmasking the Powers: A Postcolonial Analysis of 1 Thessalonians," in Horsley, *Paul and the Roman Imperial Order*, 47–66.

[37] Elliott, "The Apostle Paul's Self-Presentation as Anti-Imperial Performance," in Horsley, *Paul and the Roman Imperial Order*, 67–88.

[38] Ramsaran, "Resisting Imperial Domination and Influence: Paul's Apocalyptic Rhetoric in 1 Corinthians," in Horsley, *Paul and the Roman Imperial Order*, 89–102.

[39] Agosto, "Patronage and Commendation, Imperial and Anti-Imperial," in Horsley, *Paul and the Roman Imperial Order*, 103–24.

[40] Heen, "Phil 2:6–11 and Resistance to Local Timocratic Rule: *Isa Theō* and the Cult of the Emperor in the East," in Horsley, *Paul and the Roman Imperial Order*, 125–54.

[41] Knust, "Paul and the Politics of Virtue and Vice," in Horsley, *Paul and the Roman Imperial Order*, 155–74.

[42] Wire, "Response: The Politics of the Assembly in Corinth," in Horsley, *Paul and Politics*, 124–29.

[43] Wire, "Response: Paul and Those Outside Power," and Calvin Roetzel, "How Anti-Imperial Was the Collection and How Emancipatory Was Paul's Project?" in Horsley, *Paul and Politics*, 224–30.

in response to Callahan, how Corinthians can be liberative when Paul wants slaves to remain in slavery (1 Cor 7:24; also Roetzel), women to remarry immoral husbands, and women to cover their heads and be silent in worship. Roetzel also doubts that Paul was as committed to mutualism as Callahan asserts, given Paul's sometimes threatening assertion of his apostolic authority.

The classical scholar Simon Price, whose work on the imperial cult has been significant for the "Paul and Empire" discussion, takes up two larger issues.[44] He argues that Rome itself cannot be assumed to be Paul's context, but the Roman Empire as it was encountered and negotiated in and by (Eastern) provincial cities and their local, elite-centered, structures of power. Second, concerning Paul's subversiveness, Price argues that while this is hard to assess because of limited (classical) scholarly interest, Paul "has 'political' points to make" that embrace also "local social and religious values."[45]

Price's cautions about the important distinction between Rome and Eastern cities are well taken. But his examples demonstrate that the distinction cannot be pressed too far. The provincial assembly of Asia, and Philo in mid first-century Alexandria, are demonstrably well familiar with aspects of Augustan court ideology. That Paul and his hearers in Rome or in provincial centers would be familiar with such imperial claims (comparable forms of which had existed in Hellenistic imperial claims) is not unlikely.

Price is also correct to note the general lack of classical scholarly attention to dissident and subversive voices in the empire. Its politics of interpretation has generally focused on elite interests and sources, a generally positive evaluation of Rome's empire, attention to its "successes and consent," as Price notes, and a neglect of social-scientific models of empire, resulting in relatively little attention to the diverse modes of dissent.[46] Interestingly, in cataloguing "subversive" activity in the empire (bandits; local rebel leaders; cultic activity), Price generally though not exclusively seems to equate "subversion" with violent, public attacks on imperial

---

[44] Price, "Response," in Horsley, *Paul and the Roman Imperial Order*, 175–83.
[45] Ibid.,183.
[46] Ironically Price ("Response," 176–77 n. 4) urges biblical scholars to consult volumes 10 and 11 of the *Cambridge Ancient History* (Cambridge: Cambridge University Press, 1996, 2000) as "primary points of reference" suggesting that "Biblical scholars seem hesitant to use them and instead cite less authoritative sources." While the Cambridge volumes are an invaluable resource, it is also true that they pay relatively little attention to modes of resistance and perspectives of non-elites. And the notes in these three Paul volumes hardly evidence a preference for "less authoritative sources."

interests. But James C. Scott's work on expressions of protest and dissent in peasant societies has demonstrated oppressed peasant/artisan groups rarely challenge public transcripts and their big traditions directly but prefer self-protective, calculated, strategic actions that indirectly contest public transcripts, while also maintaining little traditions that enhance dignity and envisage and sustain alternative communities and practices.[47] It is among such co-opted yet contestive, confrontational yet accommodated dynamics that we should locate Paul's "political" activity, practices, communities, and visions (as well as find comparable models).

EVALUATION

There is no doubt that these volumes presenting the work of the Paul and Politics group present a major rethinking of Paul and a reading of his letters that is both an alternative and challenge to existing work. It might be helpful to identify some significant features of this work.

This work has shown Paul's engagement with three overlapping and comprehensive societal structures and cultural traditions, namely, the assemblies of Christ believers, Israel, and the Roman Empire. It has also engaged a fourth tradition, the extensive legacy of debate and interpretation concerning Paul. To engage such areas is to wrestle with central Pauline material. To protest that the areas are not specifically theological (Christology, soteriology, eschatology) is to maintain an artificial separation of religion and politics and to miss the point that such matters cannot be isolated from the societal structures and cultural traditions of Paul's worlds.

This rereading of Paul is necessarily interdisciplinary since the worlds that Paul inhabits and constitutes are multivalent and complex. It draws on recent work on the diversity and complexity of first-century Judaisms and on classical studies. Methodologically and in terms of personnel, the work draws together African-American, feminist, non-European, and postcolonialist scholars and scholarship. Matters of power, domination, liberation, emancipation, ethnicity, gender, social status, community formation, boundaries, exclusion/inclusion, and imperialism are inevitably to the fore.

Attention to the Roman imperial world has exposed the limits and contributions of Eurocentric male scholarship, of the exclusively Jewish horizon of the New Perspective, and the cultural but not political-imperial focus of "social world" work. Especially significant is the reframing and

---

[47]James C. Scott, *Domination and the Arts of Resistance* (New Haven: Yale University Press, 1990).

promotion of the Roman imperial world from background and context to the central entity that Paul and his communities actively negotiate, imitate, and contest.

The extensive agenda and rich interdisciplinary approaches are reflected in the wide range of Pauline topics and texts engaged in the essays discussed above. Some aspects of all seven undisputed letters are discussed. Imperial negotiation, community formation, women, slavery, freedom, imperial cults, eschatology, soteriology, rhetoric, Jewish traditions (apocalyptic; Abrahamic; Gentile inclusion), Christology, and the collection for the Jerusalem church are among the prominent general categories engaged in this significant rethinking of Paul. The extensive subject matter illustrates that this inquiry is not concerned with issues peripheral to the reading of Paul.

Evident in the contributions and responses is the active debate among contributors. One debated issue concerns how to style Paul's negotiation of the Roman world. For some he is anti-imperial and builds an alternative world, communities, and practices (Horsley; Wan; Ramsaran; Heen). For others, especially women scholars, he is much more ambivalent, resisting yet imitating and reinscribing imperial structures of gender and status (Kittredge; Briggs; Wright). For Callahan, Paul is accommodationist in that while revolution is not possible, emancipatory practices and community are necessary and contestive means of negotiation "in the meantime" until the divine intervention and completion of God's purposes (also Elliott's treatment of Rom 13). Both Schüssler Fiorenza and Wire make the point that attention to Paul must not tune out the other voices, especially those of women and slaves, in the assemblies of which his is only one voice. Moreover, Wire notes that such voices and their practices (opposed by Paul) may be more anti-imperial than Paul's expressed wishes and that Paul's rhetoric can be quite imperial in asserting his will.

SELECTIVE FURTHER DISCUSSIONS

These publications reflect the work of some of the leading scholars who have engaged the question of Paul's negotiation of the Roman Empire. But it would be a mistake to suggest that this has been the only locus of engagement with this question. Various conferences[48] and periodicals[49]

---

[48] For example, Union Theological Seminary, New York, October 2004 and April 2008.

[49] For example, *Union Seminary Quarterly Review* 59 (2005); *Word and World* 25 (spring 2005).

have also explored this issue. Various books and studies have focused on aspects of this question.[50] In 2007, for example, the *Postcolonial Commentary on the New Testament* offered chapter-length discussions of each of Paul's letters in relation to Roman and contemporary imperial power.[51] In a book-length study, Neil Elliott examines Romans as the interplay between Paul's letter to the churches in Rome and Roman imperial ideology.[52] Recognizing the constraints that imperial ideology places on Paul and from which he cannot escape, Elliott focuses his discussion around aspects of Roman power, its *imperium* or rule by force, *iustitia* or justice and the justice of God, *clementia* or mercy for the subjugated, *pietas* (that of Aeneas and Abraham), and *virtus* or virtue.

Also noteworthy are contributions that have offered critique of or have developed aspects of this work summarized above. One critique has come from Schüssler Fiorenza, both in a response included in *Paul and Empire* and in several books.[53] She argues among other things that these studies of Paul, especially those by males, have tended to identify with Paul, appropriating his authority to themselves, privilege Paul "the powerful creator and unquestioned leader" at the expense of other voices in the assemblies, overemphasize the oppositional stance of Christian writings to the empire, and overlook Paul's reinscribing of structures of domination. Moreover, they have often focused on the past and neglected the present function of imperializing language for God and obedience-requiring rhetoric for readers. Such language and rhetoric need deconstructing so that contemporary readers and biblical studies, conscious of this reinscription, can engage the public task of resisting empire, "constructing a scriptural ethos of radical democracy, which provides an historical alternative to the language [and praxis] of empire."[54] In pluriform communities (*ekklesia* or *politeuma*, Phil 3:20) of difference, plurivocality, argument, persuasion, democratic participation, emancipatory struggle, and theological vision for egalitarian movements and against kyriarchal (male, imperial) leadership, a radical critique of oppressive "earthly" structures, shaped by God's justice and well-being, is possible in the present.

---

[50] For example, Warren Carter, *The Roman Empire and the New Testament: An Essential Guide* (Nashville: Abingdon, 2006).

[51] Fernando Segovia and R. S. Sugirtharajah, eds., *Postcolonial Commentary on the New Testament Writings* (London: T&T Clark, 2007).

[52] Neil Elliott, *Arrogance of Nations: Reading Romans in the Shadow of Empire* (Minneapolis: Fortress, 2008).

[53] Schüssler Fiorenza, *Rhetoric and Ethic*; idem, *The Power of the Word: Scripture and the Rhetoric of Empire* (Minneapolis: Fortress, 2007), esp. 1–33, and "Paul and the Politics of Interpretation," in Horsley, *Paul and Politics*, 40–57.

[54] Schüssler Fiorenza, *Power of the Word*, 7.

Schüssler Fiorenza's attention to the empire-inscribing function of Paul's writing and her formulation of an alternative, contemporary way of proceeding are well-placed, though the latter should not be emphasized at the expense of attention to Paul's imperial negotiation. This approach to Paul is very recent and remains either neglected or strongly contested by parts of the guild and the church. Moreover, it should not be over-looked, as much hermeneutical theory attests, that explicit attention to the inscription of empire in Paul's writings also embraces contemporary imperialism, whether that of global capitalism or nation states, given that interpreters do not leave their worlds and interests behind in interpreting texts.

Also engaging contemporary dimensions of Paul's negotiation of the Roman Empire is John Dominic Crossan and Jonathan Reed's *In Search of Paul* (2004).[55] This far-reaching and thoughtful reading of Paul takes his imperial context seriously, and a significant percentage of the book, often drawing on archaeological and classical studies, is given over to helpful delineations of imperial structures and realities. One of the book's subtitles—*How Jesus's Apostle Opposed Rome's Empire with God's Kingdom*—indicates that Crossan and Reed see Paul in essentially antithetical or oppositional relationship to the empire. They contrast in chapter 2, for example, the clash of two visions of peace—one through military victory (the empire's) and one through justice (Paul's and God's). In chapter 3, they draw a contrast between Rome's Golden Age and Paul's eschatology (1 Thessalonians). In chapter 4, they contrast the blessings of Romanization with gospel blessings (Galatians). In chapter 5, two contrasting understandings of divinity emerge (Philippians; 2 Corinthians). In chapter 6, hierarchical patronage clashes with Christian equality (1 Corinthians). In chapter 7, imperial power, with its fundamental distinction between the haves and have-nots, collides with Paul's vision of global unity under God's distributive (not retributive) justice (Romans). Throughout, they emphasize a fundamental contrast between "the normalcy of civilization itself" and Paul's communities that embody new creation in "freedom, democracy, and human rights" (xi). With this overarching theme and styling of empire as the "normalcy of civilization," Crossan and Reed take a significant step often lacking in the three volumes edited by Horsley. Their analysis of Paul not only concerns first-century Paul's opposition to the Roman Empire but also engages fundamental questions of contemporary human community and commitments. Empire is also a contemporary

---

[55] John Dominic Crossan and Jonathan Reed, *In Search of Paul: How Jesus's Apostle Opposed Rome's Empire with God's Kingdom: A New Vision of Paul's Words and World* (San Francisco: HarperOne, 2004).

phenomenon, and Paul continues to challenge and inform negotiation of it by contemporary followers of Jesus. "A subtext of *In Search of Paul* is therefore: To What Extent can America be Christian? We are now the greatest postindustrial civilization as Rome was then the greatest preindustrial one. That is precisely what makes Paul's challenge equally forceful for now as for then. . . ." (xi).

Crossan and Reed, along with many of the contributions from the Paul and Politics group, posit a fundamentally antithetical relationship between Paul and the empire. The British scholar Peter Oakes explores the relationship between Paul and empire by discussing 1 Thessalonians and Philippians.[56] In relation to terminology shared by Christians and the empire, and to possible systemic interactions in matters such as authority, Oakes posits four possible forms of interaction: Rome and Christianity follow common models from the past; Christianity follows or imitates Rome; Rome conflicts with and pressures Christianity; Christianity conflicts with Rome. Oakes concludes that 1 Thessalonians evidences the fourth option, though Paul does not seek Rome's overthrow. In Philippians, options three and four are evident. The particular conflicts center on Christology and eschatology, though in contrast to some other studies (e.g., Donfried above), Oakes does not see participation in the imperial cult as significant. Rather, he argues that Paul redraws or remaps space and time, decentering Rome's power by placing Christ at the center and strengthening suffering Christians with the assurance that they have there a safe place.

Along with his other related work,[57] Oakes's attempt to delineate accurately the nuances and complexities of interaction between Christians and the empire is helpful. Oakes's fourfold model usefully identifies some of the possible interactions, though it is not entirely satisfactory. The first category concerns the origin of common motifs. But investigating the origin of various concepts—whether in biblical traditions or in pre-Roman Hellenistic kingship ideology or elsewhere—contributes little to discerning Christian-empire relations. Whatever its origin, material can function in the present in a host of ways, as Oakes seems to recognize in his comments on κύριοι and rituals associated with officials entering Greek cities. The second category recognizes that imitation is a significant part of negotiating imperial power, yet Oakes's conclusions emphasize conflict while imitation largely disappears. A spectrum of overlapping

---

[56] Peter Oakes, "Re-mapping the Universe: Paul and the Emperor in 1 Thessalonians and Philippians," *JSNT* 27 (2005): 301–22.

[57] Peter Oakes, *Philippians: From People to Letter* (SNTSMS 110; Cambridge: Cambridge University Press, 2001).

and interconnected strategies seems to be a preferable way of engaging the matter. His conclusion in which his fourth category of conflict dominates needs more nuancing. Oakes's recognition, for instance, of Paul's use of eschatology ignores the imperially imitative quality of eschatology, and his claim that Paul does not express a desire for Rome's overthrow because Paul does not emphasize this dimension is difficult to sustain. James Scott's work emphasizes that marginalized and relatively powerless groups express opposition often in self-protective ways, avoiding explicit confrontations but relying on audiences to elaborate coded and implicit messages. A declaration from Paul that his eschatological scenarios mean the end of specific opposing realities seems rhetorically unlikely. Oakes's notion of "conflict" needs closer definition.

Work by Davina Lopez elaborates a further dimension surfaced in previous work, that of gender dimensions in both Roman imperial representations and in Paul's negotiation of the empire as "apostle to the nations/Gentiles."[58] Lopez discusses visual images—a Judea Capta coin, the cuirassed statue of Augustus from Prima Porta, and the statues from Aphrodisias—to argue that Rome commonly personified conquered "nations" subjected to Roman power as women subjected to male power. "The nations" are defeated, collective femininity, united in being subject to manly Roman power. She argues that Paul's use of the language of "the nations/Gentiles" (τὰ ἔθνη) is not adequately understood as an ethnic and/or theological division between Jews and the rest but as an imperial/political term depicting the nations subjugated by and to Rome. Paul's call as an apostle "among the nations" (Gal 1:15) means "being changed into a different *man* and even a *woman* of sorts" (her emphasis).[59] He abandons violent, masculine "power over" persecution, renouncing "his previous affirmation of the power relations made natural by Roman imperial ideology."[60] He identifies with the subjugated and vulnerable as their mother (Gal 4:19) in a new creation marked by the solidarity of Jews with other nations ("united nations" with common ancestry from Abraham) in resistance to Rome's imperially divided world of conqueror and conquered. Such an image "challenges and reconfigures [Paul's] world in gendered terms that stand in contrast to those of the dominant paradigm of his time."[61]

---

[58] Davina Lopez, "Before Your Very Eyes: Roman Imperial Ideology, Gender Constructs and Paul's Inter-Nationalism," in *Mapping Gender in Ancient Religious Discourse* (ed. Todd Penner and Caroline vander Stichele; Leiden: Brill, 2007), 115–62; idem, *Apostle to the Conquered: Reimagining Paul's Mission* (Minneapolis: Fortress, 2008).

[59] Lopez, "Before Your Very Eyes," 154.

[60] Ibid., 156.

[61] Ibid., 161.

Areas for Further Work

Further work will need to refine the central question of Paul's negotiation of the Roman Empire. The emerging complex picture indicates the unsatisfactory nature of any attempt to identify or impose a monolithic stance. Specifically, the frequent appeal to Paul's apocalyptic thinking and use of Jewish eschatological traditions needs problematizing. Such traditions are anti-imperial, as is frequently recognized, but they are also imitative of imperial strategies, including the universal imposition of power and rule and the often violent exclusion and destruction of opponents. The ambivalency of opposition and imitation is not commonly recognized. A similar examination of Paul's Christology (Lord? Savior? Son of God? Christ?) and apostolic authority in community formation is also needed. Titles such as "Lord" and "Savior," as well as claims that Jesus is a counter-emperor or victorious over the Roman order, express an equally imperial framework. That is, while Rome's imperialism must be exposed, so too must Paul's.

While the work to date draws on various disciplines such as classical and feminist studies, engagement with social science models seems minimal and may be worthwhile. The models of empire developed, for instance, by Gerhard Lenski and John Kautsky have proved significant in other NT work but get less attention in Pauline studies.[62] Likewise, while there has been much attention to rhetoric, especially in terms of elite imperial models, Elliott's call for a sustained exploration of Paul's rhetoric in relation to imperial and colonial rhetoric as evident, for instance, in the work of Scott, needs attention.[63]

The foregrounding of Paul's negotiation with the Roman imperial world is paradigm-shifting in Pauline studies. Wright's plea, though, that insights from the work of recent decades concerning Paul's Jewish identity and interaction not be lost or neglected in such a paradigm shift is well stated.[64] The challenge seems to be to not overcorrect the lengthy and sustained neglect of Paul's negotiation of the Roman imperial world at the expense of his interaction with first-century Judaism. Paul participates in both worlds. One way ahead lies in the recognition that like Paul and the believers' communities, first-century Judaisms are also participants in and negotiating Rome's world.[65]

---

[62] For a summary, see Dennis Duling, "Empire: Theories, Methods, Models," in *Gospel of Matthew in Its Roman Imperial Context* (ed. John Riches and David Sim; London: T&T Clark, 2005), 49–74.

[63] Elliott, "Paul and the Politics of Empire," in Horsley, *Paul and Politics,* 27–33.

[64] Wright, "Paul's Gospel," in Horsley, *Paul and Politics,* 163.

[65] See Warren Carter, *John and Empire: Initial Explorations* (New York: T&T Clark, 2008), ch. 2.

Discussions engage prominently three of the four interrelated areas outlined in the aims of the Paul and Politics group (Paul and the politics of the churches, the politics of Israel, and the politics of the Roman Empire). Receiving less explicit attention, apart from the work of Schüssler Fiorenza, is the fourth area, Paul and the politics of interpretation. Issues concerning women and slavery receive good attention, but there is limited discussion of the deuteropaulines, let alone of texts from the second century and later. There is much to explore in Paul's legacy and the history of interpretation. Horsley recognizes the irony of an imperial Christ as Lord in his introduction to the third volume when he writes that Paul's use of imperial christological and eschatological images "bequeathed imperial images of Christ to the church that became the established imperial religion under Constantine and remained so in Western Europe."[66] How much of this legacy should be on the agenda of Paul and Politics discussion?

While attention has focused on Paul and the politics of his churches, Israel, the Roman Empire, and the interpretive guild, much less attention has focused on Paul and the politics of contemporary churches. This neglect seems strange given Paul's significant presence in the church's canon. How might this important rereading of Paul address contemporary faith communities engaging his writings as Scripture?

FOR FURTHER READING

Carter, Warren. *Households and Discipleship: A Study of Matthew 19–20.* JSNTSup 103. Sheffield: Sheffield Academic Press, 1994.

———. *John and Empire: Initial Explorations.* New York: T&T Clark, 2008.

———. *Matthew and the Margins: A Sociopolitical and Religious Reading.* Maryknoll, N.Y.: Orbis, 2000.

———. *The Roman Empire and the New Testament: An Essential Guide.* Nashville: Abingdon, 2006.

Crossan, John Dominic, and Jonathan Reed. *In Search of Paul: How Jesus's Apostle Opposed Rome's Empire with God's Kingdom: A New Vision of Paul's Words and World.* San Francisco: HarperOne, 2004.

Duling, Dennis. "Empire: Theories, Methods, Models." Pages 49–74 in *Gospel of Matthew in Its Roman Imperial Context.* Edited by John Riches and David Sim. London: T&T Clark, 2005.

Elliott, Neil. *The Arrogance of Nations: Reading Romans in the Shadow of Empire.* Minneapolis: Fortress, 2008.

---

[66] Horsley, "Introduction," *Paul and the Roman Imperial Order,* 23.

Horsley, Richard, ed. *Paul and Empire: Religion and Power in Roman Imperial Society.* Harrisburg, Pa.: Trinity Press International, 1997.

———. *Paul and Politics: Ekklesia, Israel, Imperium, Interpretation.* Harrisburg, Pa.: Trinity Press International, 2000.

———. *Paul and the Roman Imperial Order.* Harrisburg, Pa.: Trinity Press International, 2004.

Lopez, Davina. *Apostle to the Conquered: Reimagining Paul's Mission.* Minneapolis: Fortress, 2008.

———. "Before Your Very Eyes: Roman Imperial Ideology, Gender Constructs and Paul's Inter-Nationalism." Pages 115–62 in *Mapping Gender in Ancient Religious Discourse.* Edited by Todd Penner and Caroline vander Stichele. Leiden: Brill, 2007.

Oakes, Peter. *Philippians: From People to Letter.* SNTSMS 110. Cambridge: Cambridge University Press, 2001.

———. "Re-mapping the Universe: Paul and the Emperor in 1 Thessalonians and Philippians." *JSNT* 27 (2005): 301–22.

Schüssler Fiorenza, Elisabeth. *The Power of the Word: Scripture and the Rhetoric of Empire.* Minneapolis: Fortress, 2007.

———. *Rhetoric and Ethic: The Politics of Biblical Studies.* Minneapolis: Fortress, 1999.

Scott, James C. *Domination and the Arts of Resistance: Hidden Transcripts.* New Haven, Conn.: Yale University Press, 1990.

Segovia, Fernando. "'And They Began to Speak in Other Tongues': Competing Forms of Discourse in Contemporary Biblical Discourse." Pages 1–32 in *Reading from This Place: Social Location and Biblical Interpretation in the United States.* Edited by Fernando Segovia and Mary Ann Tolbert. Minneapolis: Fortress, 1995.

Segovia, Fernando, and R. S. Sugirtharajah, eds. *Postcolonial Commentary on the New Testament Writings.* London: T&T Clark, 2007.

Stendahl, Krister. "The Apostle Paul and the Introspective Conscience of the West." *HTR* 56 (1963): 199–215.

Wire, Antoinette. *The Corinthian Women Prophets: A Reconstruction Through Paul's Rhetoric.* Minneapolis: Fortress, 1990.

2

Paul and Economics:
The Jerusalem Collection as an Alternative to Patronage

Steven J. Friesen

I t is difficult to write about recent developments in the study of Paul
and economy because, as far as I can tell, there have not been very
many.[1] No one has examined the topic of economy and Paul's assemblies in a book-length study for a long time.[2] People write a lot about Paul,
of course. A recent online search of Harvard's Hollis Library catalogue
on the subject category "Paul, the Apostle, Saint" retrieved 250 books
published since 1995. The favorite topic has clearly been Paul's theology
and thought, with Paul's biography and history running a distant second.
There has also been interest in portraits of Paul in Acts or in the disputed
letters, and in the rhetoric of Paul. But none of the 250 books had words
like "economy," "economic," "money," or "finances" in the title.

This suggests something of the interests of our discipline: we prefer
to think about Paul's ideas, his history, and—more recently—his language,
but we would rather not discuss Paul's economic practices. That is a curious state of affairs. Consider how much of your own life is intertwined
with your economic practice. Or consider how much it would cost to

---

[1] Earlier versions of this material were presented at the Midwest Regional
SBL meeting in St. Louis (2004) and at the University of Chicago Divinity School
(2006). I thank those who participated in the discussions for saving me from some
of my errors. I wish to thank especially Brandon Cline and Trevor Thompson for
their thoroughgoing critique of my poverty scale materials and for their generosity
as conversation partners.

[2] The major exception is Justin J. Meggitt, *Paul, Poverty, and Survival* (Edinburgh: T&T Clark, 1998), which has not found much acceptance in the discipline.
Meggitt's book was successful in raising critical objections and introducing new
arguments. The positive proposal—that 99% of the population in the early Roman
Empire lived in abject poverty—is difficult to sustain.

purchase those 250 books about Pauline theology, history, and rhetoric.
Paul had expenses, too, so why do we avoid these topics? After all, in the
extant letters, Paul wrote more about money than he did about the Lord's
Supper, or about baptism, or about the status of women.

So the general question of this chapter is: how would our view of
Paul's churches change if we took economic issues seriously in our research? Since that is an impossibly large topic, I will confine myself to
three aspects of the question. First I make a few comments about how NT
scholarship ignores economic inequality. Then I discuss briefly the extent
of poverty in the Roman Empire. Finally, I look at Paul's collection of
money for the Jerusalem church as an example of how our understanding
of the Pauline churches might change if we did not expunge economy and
inequality from our analysis.

Capitalist Interpretation of the Pauline Churches

You have heard it said that scholars in the early twentieth century—
following Deissmann—thought Paul's churches came from the lower
classes of society but that scholars in the late twentieth century realized
that Paul's churches were made up of a cross section of society. But I say
unto you, mainstream scholars throughout the twentieth century thought
pretty much the same thing on this issue. There was no old "lower class
consensus" nor any new "cross section consensus." Rather, there was widespread agreement throughout the century that most of the people in the
Pauline churches came from the lower classes and that a few individuals
were financially better off.

I came to this conclusion by going through more than sixty NT introductions, including at least four examples from every decade of the twentieth century.[3] The results were astonishingly homogenous: scholars either
ignored questions of social and economic status, or briefly asserted what
the so-called new consensus later claimed to have discovered; namely,
that Paul's churches were composed mostly of the lower classes but also
of some individuals from further up the social hierarchy.[4]

---

[3] I looked for a range of theological viewpoints, including major scholars and
lesser-known commentators. For a summary of the results, see Steven J. Friesen,
"The Blessings of Hegemony: The Preferential Option for the Rich in Pauline Studies," in *The Bible in the Public Square: Reading the Signs of the Times* (ed. Cynthia
Briggs Kittredge et al.; Minneapolis: Fortress, 2008), 117–28.

[4] The introductions in the second category—those that briefly mention socio-
economic factors—do so in an offhand manner without argument, indicating that
their statements are not controversial.

An examination of specialized studies from the twentieth century confirms the impression gained from the NT introductions—there was no old consensus/new consensus paradigm shift. Even Deissmann did not agree with the old consensus he is said to have promoted! Here is how two influential modern scholars described Deissmann, along with Deissmann's actual position.

> *Theissen on Deissmann*: "According to A. Deissmann, primitive Christianity was a movement within the lower strata."[5]

> *Meeks on Deissmann*: "Until recently most scholars who troubled to ask Deissmann's question at all ignored the ambiguities of the evidence that Deissmann had at least mentioned. The prevailing viewpoint has been that the constituency of early Christianity, the Pauline congregations included, came from the poor and dispossessed of the Roman provinces."[6]

> *Deissmann's words (in translation)*: "The people whose souls were moved by the mission of Paul and his faithful companions were—the overwhelming majority at least—men and women from the middle and lower classes. . . . On the other hand, Paul mentions by name certain fairly well-to-do Christians. Those who possessed rooms so large that 'house churches' could assemble there for edification . . . cannot have been poor. . . . It is noteworthy that several women whose names are honorably mentioned in connection with Paul's missionary labours, appear to have been possessed of means. . . ."[7]

This is a strange history of interpretation. Scholars held the same position but claimed to disagree, and the one thing they agreed on—that most people in Paul's churches were poor—was the one thing no one wanted to discuss. And even though nearly all scholars throughout the twentieth century agreed that most of the first-century believers were poor,[8] no one thought it was important enough to write a book about poverty in Paul's churches until 1998.[9] Scholars wrote about Pauline soteriology,

---

[5] Gerd Theissen, *The Social Setting of Pauline Christianity: Essays on Corinth* (Philadelphia: Fortress, 1982), 69.

[6] Wayne A. Meeks, *The First Urban Christians: The Social World of the Apostle Paul* (New Haven: Yale University Press, 1983), 52.

[7] Adolf Deissmann, *Paul: A Study in Social and Religious History* (2d ed.; New York: Harper & Brothers, 1957), 241–43.

[8] Theissen and Meeks are unclear on this point. Theissen dismissed the entire question of poverty with one undocumented assertion about a new level of undefined prosperity outside of Palestine (*Social Setting*, 36). Meeks claimed that the Roman imperial economy brought more prosperity than before without defining what level of prosperity had gone before or how much it improved (*Urban Christians*, 43–44), but then acknowledged that there could have been poor people in Paul's churches about whom we have no evidence (73).

[9] Meggitt, *Paul, Poverty, and Survival*.

Christology, chronology, eschatology, opponents, more soteriology, Paul's Jewishness, social status, still more soteriology, and so on. But economic inequality and deprivation deserved nothing more than a sentence or two, as if this were tangential to the real issues.

This suggests that we are not dealing simply with bad information about first-century conditions or about twentieth-century interpretation. Would that the explanation were so easy. It looks to me as though we are dealing with powerful discursive patterns, dark Foucaldian forces, if you will, that encourage us to examine a limited set of data in a limited mode of analysis. I have come to think that what we have called "mainstream inter-pretation" or "the consensus among scholars" is a misnomer. Those terms are too neutral. We seem to be dealing with an ideological orientation in our discipline that I call "capitalist criticism."[10] Let me explain what I mean by that term by describing four interrelated characteristics of this approach.

The first characteristic of capitalist criticism is that religion has no integral connection to economy. This is a theoretical assumption about the nature of religion. Capitalist critics rarely indicate where they think religion comes from, but they agree that it is not generated by economic relationships. Of course, this is not simply a theoretical question about religion but also a political issue. For with this assumption, Marxist analy-sis and godless communism are removed from the disciplinary agenda. This rejection of Marxist analysis has also taken economic analysis itself off the agenda.

The second characteristic of capitalist criticism is the assumption that Christianity was not generated by economic factors, and therefore it was not a movement of the urban proletariat in the first-century Roman Empire. The stakes are high in this denial. For if earliest Christianity was generated by the economics of poverty and dispossession, and if it was a movement of the proletariat, then the subsequent history of Christianity is perhaps not a story of miraculous growth but rather one of betrayal and cooptation by the wealthy. To illustrate what I mean, consider how many times you have seen or heard the phrase "the triumph of Christian-ity" or the "success of Christianity" in early Christian studies. Now think about the number of times you have encountered the phrase "the failure of early Christianity," or "the colonization of the church by the wealthy," or "the hijacking of the early churches by the powerful." I am not arguing for the accuracy of these dark readings of early church history. I am only suggesting that our discipline rules them out of bounds as unthinkable historical metanarratives.

---

[10]I first proposed this term in "Poverty in Pauline Studies: Beyond the So-called New Consensus," *JSNT* 26 (2004): 336.

The third characteristic of capitalist criticism is the assumption that religion operates according to market principles. The assumption seems to be that people have spiritual needs—or at least spiritual desires—and the religion that responds with the best product gets a larger market share. This market description of religion is one area where we can see a change in twentieth-century interpretation. In Deissmann's era of industrial capitalism, scholars tended to recognize the existence of economic classes in society. Then they claimed that all people, regardless of class, had the same universal spiritual need. Thus, the same gospel could save lower-class people, middle-class people, and upper-class people without changing their class location.[11]

In the 1970s and 1980s, however, a new phase of capitalist criticism took shape. The market character of religion shifted away from the framework of economic class to that of individual social status. This is seen most clearly in Wayne Meeks's landmark study, *The First Urban Christians*. According to Meeks, the Pauline believers we know about tended to be individuals who had achieved high status levels in some areas but not in others.[12] As a result, their overall status in society did not match their abilities, expectations, or achievements. So, Meeks concluded, they probably found in the church some measure of leadership, respect, and status that they were denied in the larger society.[13]

In Meeks's work, then, we see a new articulation of the relationship between economy and religion, and it looks much like a spiritual consumer's marketplace. Individuals have social needs that are not met by society, but they can find compensatory satisfaction in religion. The religion that best meets those needs is the most successful spiritual commodity. In light of the widespread (and well-deserved) acclaim for Meeks's formulation, I think we can say that the so-called new consensus marked a shift in the history of capitalist criticism from an industrial orientation—where religion was thought to transcend class barriers—to a consumer orientation where religion was thought to address the desires of individuals to move up through status barriers.

The fourth and final characteristic of capitalist criticism is that poverty is irrelevant in the interpretation of Christian origins. Part of the reason is that religion tends to be treated as a set of ideas or as beliefs and

---

[11] Ibid., 326–31.

[12] Meeks argued that the prominent members of Paul's churches—the ones we hear about in Paul's letters—show signs of status inconsistency. By that he meant that status was a complex phenomenon that included such factors as "ethnic origins, *ordo*, citizenship, personal liberty, wealth, occupation, age, sex, and public offices or honors" (*Urban Christians*, 55).

[13] Ibid., 51–73.

not as a praxis or lifestyle. But I think the problem runs deeper. I suspect that there is a larger theory of economy, society, and religion at work here, a theory so submerged in our scholarship that it is difficult to spot. Why am I suspicious? First, the so-called new consensus focused only on certain positive functions of religion and showed no appreciation for the oppressive functions of religion. This suggests a serious bias, one that distracts us from economic oppression and from poverty. As a second reason for suspicion, consider this phenomenon: any sustained discussion of the impoverished majority in Paul's churches normally brings charges of ideological bias.[14] Yet for the last thirty years NT scholars have mostly ignored widespread ancient poverty and focused instead on the small handful of people in Paul's churches who were perhaps not impoverished. But who calls those studies political or faults them for ideological bias?[15] No one even seems to notice as the poor disappear.

How shall we proceed? Criticizing the discipline is easier than making a positive contribution. I do not claim to have solved these problems. I only suggest a possible approach. It involves a more complicated definition of poverty, a definition that requires us to think both about the concrete measurement of poverty and about the reasons for the existence of poverty.

WHAT IS POVERTY AND HOW DO YOU MEASURE IT?

The question What is poverty? is much more complex than it seems at first glance. There is a long tradition of measuring poverty in terms of income, what one has or does not have, and this remains a crucial part of any consideration of poverty.[16] In recent years, however, specialists in economics and in sociology have pointed out shortcomings of measuring poverty in terms of a lack of money. One of the crucial figures to address

---

[14] For example, note John Barclay, "Poverty in Pauline Studies: A Response to Steven Friesen," *JSNT* 26 (2004): 363–66.

[15] There were a few isolated exceptions, such as Meggitt (*Paul, Poverty, and Survival*) and Robin Scroggs ("The Sociological Interpretation of the New Testament: The Present State of Research," *NTS* 26 [1980]: 164–79).

[16] For this tendency in the field of economics, see David B. Grusky and Ravi Kanbur, "Introduction: Conceptual Foundations of Poverty and Inequality Measurement," in *Poverty and Inequality* (ed. David B. Grusky and Ravi Kanbur; Stanford, Calif.: Stanford University Press, 2006), 12, 24–25. For an overview of sociological work, see David B. Grusky, "The Past, Present, and Future of Social Inequality," in *Social Stratification: Class, Race, and Gender in Sociological Perspective* (ed. David B. Grusky; 2d ed.; Boulder, Colo.: Westview, 2001), 3–51.

these problems over the last thirty years has been economist Amartya Sen. Based on work in the developing world and in other countries, Sen has argued that income is indeed an important part of assessing poverty but that we should not focus only on income. We must take a whole range of indicators into account.[17] The most significant indicators, alongside income, include mortality (both infant and adult), undernourishment, gender discrimination, health care, unemployment, and education.[18]

Sen and others also insist that these indications of poverty—mortality, nourishment, health, occupation, education, and income—are not simply the results of individual choices, as though economic inequality could be blamed on the bad decisions of poor folks. We must also look for structural reasons why people have limited resources, why people are uneducated, why people are underemployed, why some people die of treatable diseases. When we do this, we begin to see the institutions and social systems that are devoted to keeping some people poor. Some sociologists would even argue that one of the primary functions of social structure is precisely to create and sustain inequality.[19] So poverty is more than a consequence of individual choices or unfortunate accidents; it is a social location that is created and enforced by society.

What are the implications of this for studying Paul's churches? One is that we need to address income poverty as one crucial factor in overall poverty. Another implication is that we need to think about systematic deprivation. By that I mean we need to ask how the Roman Empire deprived most people of basic human needs. Then we can consider Pauline practice in relation to these institutions.

This Roman imperial system has already been outlined by Peter Garnsey and Richard Saller in *The Roman Empire: Economy, Society, and Culture*. Some two decades after publication, the text still provides an excellent framework for thinking about "the Roman system of inequality," as they put it.[20] The range of topics covered by Garnsey and Saller

---

[17] A good starting point into his work is Amartya Sen, *Development as Freedom* (New York: Knopf, 1999; repr., New York: Anchor, 2000), esp. 87–110.

[18] Natural disasters such as famine and persistent warfare can also play a significant role. Sen refuses to create a specific list of capabilities that could be used in measuring poverty (ibid., 103). Martha Nussbaum agreed in broad terms with Sen's project but argued that content is necessary. There needs to be a list of the capabilities in order to measure inequality and social justice; "Human Functioning and Social Justice: In Defense of Aristotelian Essentialism," *Political Theory* 20 (1992): 202–46. Her proposal for ten "basic human functional capabilities" can be found on 222–23.

[19] Grusky, "Past, Present, and Future," 13–15.

[20] Peter Garnsey and Richard Saller, *The Roman Empire: Economy, Society, and Culture* (Berkeley: University of California Press, 1987), 125. Because it

include imperial politics, the military, administration, city statuses, land ownership, agriculture, industry, food supply, economic class and stratification, social mobility, patriarchal family patterns, honor systems, patronage, religion, philosophy, education, and more.

If we think of these as components of the system of inequality within which Paul's churches lived, then there are ways we can explore the topic. First we must ask the income question because it is crucial: how much economic inequality was there in the Roman world and in Paul's churches? But the recent work of economists and sociologists compels us to go further. We must also inquire about the social structure of the empire that kept people poor and ask how Paul's churches acted within this system. This second task is immense and cannot be handled thoroughly in a study of this size. But we can consider one way into the problem by comparing the patronage system of dominant culture with the Jerusalem collection developed by Paul. First, however, we need to look at income poverty in the Roman Empire.

RESOURCES, OR INCOME POVERTY

In order to work on the question of economic inequality, I created a poverty scale. In the light of the preceding discussion, perhaps it would be more accurate to call it a "resource scale" or an "income poverty scale" for it does not measure the full range of poverty indicators. It deals only with the most substantial one, often called income poverty, which is one necessary facet of our considerations.[21]

The scale has seven categories, ranging from exorbitant wealth to the condition of living in perpetual crisis below the level of long-term subsistence. "Subsistence" is defined here as the resources needed to procure enough calories in food to maintain a healthy human body. The caloric needs of humans are gauged in various ways by scholars, but they usually range from 1,500 to 3,000 calories per day, depending on gender, age, physical energy required for occupation, pregnancy, lactation, and other

---

was published in 1987, when the so-called new consensus was in full bloom, the book also stands as an important contrast to developments in NT studies where systemic inequality was not a topic of conversation (at least not polite conversation).

[21] For a revision of the scale calibrated in terms of amount of income, see Walter Scheidel and Steven J. Friesen, "The Size of the Economy and the Distribution of Income in the Roman Empire," *JRS* (2009), in press. The resulting economic profile is similar to that of my poverty scale, but the new income categories are more useful for analysis.

factors. Human bodies can survive for some time at the low end of this scale, but the lives of people living below the subsistence level are usually shortened by chronic malnutrition and disease.[22]

Fig. 1: A poverty scale for analyzing early imperial populations with descriptive examples

1. Imperial elites: imperial dynasty, Roman senatorial families, a few retainers, local royalty, a few freedpersons.

2. Regional or provincial elites: equestrian families, provincial officials, some retainers, some decurial families, some freedpersons, some retired military officers.

3. Municipal elites: most decurial families, wealthy men and women who do not hold office, some freedpersons, some retainers, some veterans, some merchants.

4. Moderate surplus resources: some merchants, some traders, some freedpersons, some artisans (especially those who employ others), and military veterans.

5. Stable near subsistence level (with reasonable hope of remaining above the minimum level to sustain health): many merchants and traders, regular wage earners, artisans, large shop owners, freedpersons, some farm families.

6. At subsistence level and often below minimum level for sustaining health: small farm families, laborers (skilled and unskilled), artisans (esp. those employed by others), wage earners, most merchants and traders, small shop/tavern owners.

7. Below subsistence level: some farm families, unattached widows, orphans, beggars, disabled, unskilled day laborers, prisoners.

The amount of income needed to procure 8,000–10,000 calories of food for a hypothetical family of four on a daily basis would have varied a good deal in different areas of the early Roman Empire.[23] A tenant farm

---

[22] The best treatment of this topic for the Roman Empire is Peter Garnsey, *Food and Society in Classical Antiquity* (Cambridge: Cambridge University Press, 1999). Garnsey estimated the basic daily minimum at 1,625–2,012 calories (19). In his calculations, he was also careful to note variations in caloric need because of gender, age, class, and other factors.

[23] I use 8,000–10,000 calories rather than a specific amount (such as 2,500 calories per person) to reflect the range of estimates that different modern

family in a rural area would have produced much of their own food in normal years, which would reduce our calculation of their cash expenses, but they would still have needed money for taxes and perhaps for rent. Urban workers, however, grew little of their own food and thus would have purchased most of their food or bartered for it in addition to paying taxes (and rent?). One study used the following figures as estimates of such variations.

Fig. 2. Annual income needed by family of four[24]

Categories from the Poverty Scale (PS) are found in parentheses.

For wealth in Rome (PS3)	25,000–150,000 denarii
For modest prosperity in Rome (PS4)	5,000 denarii
For subsistence in Rome (PS5–6)	900–1,000 denarii
For subsistence in a city (PS5–6)	600–700 denarii
For subsistence in the country (PS5–6)	250–300 denarii

In order to use this resource scale for an examination of Paul's churches, we have to estimate what percentage of an urban population can be described by each category. The excruciating calculations needed in order to answer that question for the large cities of the eastern Roman Empire during the early imperial period are published elsewhere.[25] The result of those calculations is the following profile.

Fig. 3. Percentage of population in categories: Roman cities with populations over 10,000

The percentages for categories 4 and 5 are more difficult to ascertain than the others and so are listed in italics.

---

specialists employ and to take account of the fact that children in the family would usually consume fewer calories than the adults. My goal here is provide an approximate sense of the scale of the problem without creating a false sense of precision.

[24] Adapted from Ekkehard W. Stegemann and Wolfgang Stegemann, *The Jesus Movement: A Social History of Its First Century* (Minneapolis: Fortress, 1999), 81–85. Their figures are based on a daily need of 2,500 calories for an adult male. The figures also include some non-food expenses such as housing, clothing, and taxes.

[25] Friesen, "Poverty in Pauline Studies," 340–43.

Population	Poverty scale category
.04%	PS1. Imperial elites
1%	PS2. Regional elites
1.76%	PS3. Municipal elites
7%?	PS4. Moderate surplus
22%?	PS5. Stable near subsistence
40%	PS6. At subsistence
28%	PS7. Below subsistence

This profile surprises some specialists because they cannot imagine such poverty in the Roman Empire. I suggest that this is not a problem with the numbers but rather a failure of imagination. Most people in a Western setting have a more limited experience of poverty and systemic inequality. In order to illustrate this difference, I created the following chart (fig. 4). The chart moves beyond the idea of income poverty and includes other key indicators of inequality—life expectancy, infant mortality, fertility rates, and urbanization. It suggests the gap between the average exposure to poverty of people in a contemporary Western setting with the average exposure to poverty of people in other contemporary societies and people in the early Roman Empire. By this I do not mean to minimize the amount of economic inequality and suffering that exists on all continents of the contemporary world by comparison with the ancient Mediterranean world. But the Roman Empire was probably not significantly different from most pre-industrial societies before the rise of modern medicine, where life was usually shorter, more painful, and more labor-intensive than we tend to recognize in NT studies.[26]

---

[26]See Angus Maddison, *Contours of the World Economy, 1–2030 A.D.: Essays in Macro-Economic History* (New York: Oxford University Press, 2007); Gregory Clark, *A Farewell to Alms: A Brief Economic History of the World* (Princeton: Princeton University Press, 2007); Robert William Fogel, *The Escape from Hunger and Premature Death, 1700–2100: Europe, America, and the Third World* (New York: Cambridge University Press, 2004).

Fig. 4. Poverty profiles: Roman Empire compared with eight modern societies

The data for contemporary societies are for 2006. All are from UNICEF[27] except national poverty line.[28]

	Gross National Income (annual, per capita, in US$)	Urban population	Fertility rate (births/woman)[31]	Life expectancy at birth (years)	Infant mortality (deaths/1000 births)[34]	Children underweight[36] (moderate or severe)	Population below national poverty line
USA	44,970	81%	2.1	78	6	2%	12% (2004)
Japan	38,410	66%	1.3	82	3	-	11% (2001)
Germany	36,620	75%	1.4	79	4	-	-
Mexico	7,870	76%	2.3	76	29	5%	40% (2006)
Brazil	4,730	85%	2.3	72	19	6%	31% (2005)
India	820	29%	2.9	64	57	43%	25% (2007)
Pakistan	770	35%	3.6	65	78	38%	24% (2005/06)
Uganda	300	13%	6.6	50	78	20%	35% (2001)
Roman Empire	HS 240–275[29]	10–15%[30]	6–9[32]	20–30[33]	200–300[35]	-	-

27 http://www.unicef.org/statistics/index_24183.html. Accessed 20 March 2009. Similar resources are available from the World Bank http://ddp-ext.world bank.org/ext/DDPQQ/member.do?method=getMembers&userid=1&query Id=135. Tyler Watts assisted in the development of this chart.

28 https://www.cia.gov/library/publications/the-world-factbook/fields/2046 .html. Accessed 21 March 2009.

29 This range in terms of sesterces for the Roman Empire reflects the per capita GDP (not GNI), which is perhaps a better comparison because of the importance of global finance in modern economies; Scheidel and Friesen, "Size of the Economy." There is no satisfactory way to translate sesterces from the Roman imperial economy into modern currencies because the function of money is so different in the two systems. One method of indirect comparison is in terms of payment for labor: an average daily wage of an unskilled worker in the Roman Empire is thought to have been around 3–4 sesterces. The price of grain provides another indirect comparison: an annual income of HS 240–275 would have purchased about 460–570 kg of wheat, which would be approximately the amount needed for two adults to survive at a subsistence level for a year; Colin Clark and Margaret Haswell, *The Economics of Subsistence Agriculture* (4th ed.; New York: St. Martin's Press, 1970), 58–64.

30 This percentage is a rough rendering of Scheidel's estimate that perhaps one-eighth to one-ninth of the empire's population lived in urban areas; see

We can use the poverty scale to create economic profiles for Paul's assemblies. Such profiles are not precise measurements of the first-century situation. Rather, they are modern assessments that allow us to agree or disagree more accurately because they are framed in terms of discrete, defined categories. I give an example of such a profile in figure 5.[37] My rankings are based on explicit references to financial matters from the undisputed letters of Paul.[38] Here are my main three conclusions, followed by some discussion.

"Demography," in *The Cambridge Economic History of the Greco-Roman World* (ed. Walter Scheidel et al.; Cambridge: Cambridge University Press, 2007), 79. H. W. Pleket estimated that 10–15% of the imperial population lived in cities of 10,000 or more; see "Wirtschaft," in *Europäische Wirtschafts- und Sozialgeschichte in der römischen Kaiserzeit, vol. 1 of Handbuch der europäischen Wirtschafts- und Sozialgeschichte* (ed. Friedrich Vittinghoff; Stuttgart: Klett-Cotta, 1990), 145–46.

[31] More precisely, this is the estimated number of births a female will have if current rates prevail and if she survives through childbearing years.

[32] Scheidel, "Demography," 41.

[33] Ibid., 39. One reason this figure is dramatically lower than in modern societies is because infant and child mortality was so much higher in antiquity. By considering the life expectancy of a child who survives to age 10, we can factor out death at a very young age and arrive at a different comparison: for the modern U.S., life expectancy at 10 is an additional 63 years for males (i.e., to age 73) and an additional 70 years for females (to age 80); in the Roman Empire, life expectancy at 10 was about 35 years (to age 45); Bruce W. Frier, "Roman Demography," in *Life, Death, and Entertainment in the Roman Empire* (ed. D. S. Potter and D. J. Mattingly; Ann Arbor: University of Michigan Press, 1999), 87–88.

[34] More precisely, deaths in first year of life per 1,000 live births.

[35] Walter Scheidel, "Progress and Problems in Roman Demography," in *Debating Roman Demography* (ed. Walter Scheidel; Boston: Brill, 2001): 23–25; Frier, "Roman Demography," 87.

[36] For children below age 5.

[37] The creation of this profile was greatly assisted by research grants from the Society of Biblical Literature and from the Research Council of the University of Missouri, Columbia. The grants allowed me to construct a database of the members of the Pauline assemblies. I have published versions of the profile in "Poverty in Pauline Studies" and in "Prospects for a Demography of the Pauline Mission: Corinth among the Churches," in *Urban Religion in Roman Corinth: Interdisciplinary Approaches* (ed. Daniel N. Schowalter and Steven J. Friesen; Harvard Theological Studies 35; Cambridge, Mass.: Harvard University Press, 2005), 351–70.

[38] Acts is excluded from the profile because the narrative is not reliable for this kind of historical information. The deuteropauline letters and Pastoral Epistles are also excluded for similar reasons. If we did include these disputed Pauline letters it would add to the profile references to Nympha (PS4–5) from Col 4:15, Onesiphorus (PS4–6) from 2 Tim 1:16–17 and 2 Tim 4:19, and the widows (PS6–7) of 1 Tim 5:3–16.

(1) Paul's letters provide no evidence that members of the elite categories (PS1–3) participated in the assemblies.

(2) Of the individuals about whom we have economic information, at least 1 or 2 and a maximum of 7 can be classified as having moderate surplus resources.

(3) Most of the people in Paul's congregations, including Paul himself, had resources near the level of subsistence, either above it or below.

Fig. 5. Economic profile of Pauline assemblies based on undisputed Pauline letters

PS	Name	Reference	Location
(4)	(Chloe?)	1 Cor 1:11	Corinth
4	Gaius	Rom 16:23	Corinth
4–5	(Erastus)	Rom 16:23	Corinth
4–5	Philemon	Phlm 4–22	Colossae?
4–5	Phoebe	Rom 16:1–2	Cenchraea, Rome
4–5	Aquila	Rom 16:3–5	Rome (or Ephesus?)
4–5	Prisca	Rom 16:3–5	Rome (or Ephesus?)
4–5	Chloe's people	1 Cor 1:11	Ephesus
4–6	Those who have food for Lord's Supper	1 Cor 11:22	Corinth
4–7	Onesimus	Phlm 10–19	Ephesus? Rome?
5–6	Stephanas	1 Cor 16:17–18	Ephesus
5–6	The household of Stephanas	1 Cor 16:15–16	Corinth
5–6	Saints in Corinth	1 Cor 16:1–2	Corinth
5–6	Churches in Galatia	1 Cor 16:1–2	Galatia
5–7	Brothers (and sisters)	1 Thes 4:11	Thessalonica
6	Saints in Corinth	2 Cor 8:12–15	Corinth
6	The assemblies of Macedonia	2 Cor 8:1–6	Macedonia
6–7	Paul	2 Cor 11:1–22; 1 Thess 2:1–12; Phil 2:25–30; Phil 4:12–13	Corinth
6–7	Those who do not have food for the Lord's Supper	1 Cor 11:22	Corinth

(1) In the profile I have listed no one in the elite categories (PS1–3), which is in agreement with the assessment of Meeks.[39] Theissen, by contrast, argued that the majority of Paul's associates who are known to us by name were from the upper classes. He supported this conclusion by isolating four criteria that could indicate membership in the upper classes: civic office, references to households, assistance rendered to churches, and ability to travel.[40] Only the first of these criteria, however, has any relevance as a criterion of elite status, and it is the one that does not apply to anyone we know from Paul's churches.[41] A more relevant set of criteria for upper class participation can be developed from inscriptions and literature about the elite of the Roman Empire. That list of criteria would include such things as imperial office, provincial office, municipal office, high-ranking military service, major religious titles, decrees in one's honor, large benefactions, extensive landholdings, major business interests, households that included many slaves, wealthy parents or grandparents, hosting or attending lavish banquets, or elite education. None of these characterize any believers mentioned in Paul's letters.

(2) There are only two named people from Paul's letters who were clearly in the category of moderate resources (PS4)—Gaius and Chloe. There are also 4 individuals plus Chloe's people whom I would characterize as either above subsistence or with moderate resources (PS4–5); some people who could be PS4–6 (those with food at the Lord's Supper in Corinth); and Onesimus who could be anywhere from PS4–7 (from the level of his owner Philemon down to desperation).

(3) The vast majority of the people in Paul's assemblies hovered around the level of subsistence, just above or just below. The references in Paul's letters to groups are important in this regard. By my reckoning, the poor saints (defined as those living just above subsistence level, at subsistence level, or below subsistence level) included the following: Stephanas, the household of Stephanas, most saints in Corinth, most in the assemblies of Galatia, most saints in Thessalonica, most of those in the assemblies of Macedonia,

---

[39] Meeks argued that Paul's assemblies did not include the extreme upper or lower ends of the spectrum (*Urban Christians*, 73).

[40] Theissen, *Social Setting*, 73–96. Theissen's argument is hampered by an ambiguity in the definitions of key terms, such as "upper classes" and "elevated social status."

[41] The only possible exception would be the Erastus of Rom 16:23, but I would argue that the Erastus mentioned by Paul was not a participant in Paul's churches; see "The Wrong Erastus: Ideology, Archaeology, and Exegesis," in *Corinth in Context: Comparative Studies in Religion and Society* (ed. Steven J. Friesen et al.; New York: Brill, in press).

and Paul. In addition, some of the people listed in the previous paragraph as possible members of PS4 could just as easily have been at level 5 or below. In fact, we should probably assign most of them there since—given the percentages shown in figure 3—the odds are against most of them being in PS4 because it included less than 10% of the population.

It is impossible to quantify these references accurately. It is possible, however, to generate a hypothetical model using numbers consistently even though the numbers are often gross estimates. For example, we could assign all the individuals to their categories, dividing someone like Onesimus (PS4–7) evenly across four categories and someone like Prisca across two (PS5–6). Then we could assign arbitrary numbers for groups as follows: a reference to an assembly = 20 individuals; a reference to assemblies = 3 congregations; a plural reference to saints/brothers = 10 people; a household = 5 people; and Chloe's people = 3 individuals.[42] As arbitrary but consistent calculations, the numbers in figure 6 do not prove anything, nor are they intended to measure the actual size of these assemblies. They are simply another way of visualizing the profile from figure 5, a way that reminds us that references to named individuals in Paul's letters have tended to overshadow his references to unnamed groups. In our reconstructions we must compensate for the historical invisibility of the poor.

Fig. 6. Hypothetical numbers that model the references in figure 5

	People mentioned in Paul's undisputed letters
PS1. Imperial elites	0
PS2. Regional elites	0
PS3. Municipal elites	0
PS4. Moderate surplus	9.58
PS5. Stable near subsistence	50.41
PS6. At subsistence	121.91
PS7. Below subsistence	9.08

So far I have suggested that our personal and disciplinary biases have hindered us from exploring economic issues. There is, however, another reason why we have not analyzed economic inequality: we have been misled by the accounts in the Acts of the Apostles. If we construct a similar

---

[42] I have intentionally kept these arbitrary numbers low so as not to inflate the profile in a direction that would support my own conclusion.

economic profile from references in Acts and compare them with references in Paul's undisputed letters, the problem becomes clearer.

Fig. 7. Economic profile of Paul's assemblies based on Acts of the Apostles[43]

PS	Name	Reference	Location
1	[Proconsul Sergius Paulus?][44]	13:6–12	Paphos, Cyprus
2–3	Dionysios the Areopagite	17:34	Athens
2–3	Not a few of the Greek men of high standing	17:12	Beroea
2–3	Not a few of the Greek women of high standing	17:12	Beroea
2–3	Women of high standing (in the city)	17:4	Thessalonica
4	Crispus	18:8	Corinth
4?	Unnamed jailer	18:22–36	Philippi
4?	Lydia	16:13–15	Philippi
4	Titius Justus	18:7	Corinth
4–5	Jason	17:5–9	Thessalonica
5–6	Paul	18:3–8; 20:34	Corinth; Ephesus

This economic profile based on Acts is radically different from the one based on Paul's letters. According to Acts, it is possible that Paul was the only believer near the subsistence level! Everyone else about whom we are given some economic information in the narrative could be in the top 10% of the poverty scale (PS1–4). The contrast is even clearer if we place the two charts side by side as in figure 8. Note that while there are no references in Paul's undisputed letters to any members from the elite

---

[43] This profile omits references to assemblies in Judea, Samaria, and Syria, because these were not Pauline assemblies. I have also not included those from the household of Caesar because the description is too vague to be useful (anywhere from PS1–6 and maybe even 7; Phil 4:22). In addition, Crispus of 1 Cor 1:14 might be the same individual called a synagogue leader in Acts 18:8, but economic references in Acts must be treated with suspicion; see below, 43–45. Finally, Apphia and Archippus are listed close to Philemon in the second verse of that letter, but the relationship is not clear enough to give us any hints about economic status.

[44] Sergius Paulus is in square brackets because the narrative does not clearly mark him as a participant in the assemblies. The text says that he believed and was amazed at the teaching of the Lord, but it does not record a baptism, reception of the Holy Spirit, or belief by his whole house.

categories (PS1–3), in Acts there are believing members of the elites in Thessalonica, Beroea, and Athens, and perhaps on Cyprus as well.

Fig. 8. Comparison: Economic profiles from undisputed letters and from Acts

Names from undisputed letters of Paul	PS	Names from Acts
	1	(Proconsul Sergius Paulus?)
	2–3	Dionysios
	2–3	Leading men of Beroea
	2–3	Leading women of Beroea
	2–3	Leading women of Thessalonica
(Chloe)	4	Crispus
Gaius	4	Titius Justus
	4?	Unnamed jailer
	4?	Lydia
(Erastus)	4–5	Jason
Philemon	4–5	
Phoebe	4–5	
Aquila	4–5	
Prisca	4–5	
Chloe's people	4–5	
Those who have food for Lord's Supper	4–6	
Onesimus	4–7	
Stephanas	5–6	Paul
The household of Stephanas	5–6	
Saints in Corinth	5–6	
Churches in Galatia	5–6	
Brothers (and sisters)	5–7	
Saints in Corinth	6	
The assemblies of Macedonia	6	
Paul	6–7	
Those without food for Lord's Supper	6–7	

Paul appears at the bottom of the scale in both profiles. There is a great difference, however, in the way he is portrayed. In the undisputed letters Paul records no positive contact with any of the elites; rather, Paul records that the elites tortured him and threw him in prison. In Acts, Paul interacts easily with people in the top 1% of the poverty scale: proconsul Sergius Paulus, Asiarchs in Ephesus, the unnamed chiliarch who arrested Paul in Jerusalem, King Agrippa II, the procurator Felix, his wife Drusilla (sister of Agrippa II), Festus (procurator after Felix), the chiliarch Lysias, and Bernice (sister of Drusilla, sister and consort of Agrippa II, later consort of Titus until he became emperor). Whether these interactions took place is not my concern here. The important observation is that the author of Acts portrayed Paul not simply as a poor man but as a poor man who fraternized with some of the wealthiest and most powerful Roman imperialists. If we look beyond the apostle, we see that the profile generated from Acts focuses almost exclusively on the wealthiest category. So the process of diverting our attention away from poverty in Paul's churches did not begin in the 1970s with the so-called new consensus or with Deissmann and his contemporaries in the early twentieth century. The process of making the poor invisible began much earlier, at least as early as the Acts of the Apostles.[45]

Systemic Poverty and Pauline Practice: The Jerusalem Collection as an Alternative to Patronage Economics

In this final section I provide an example of how a broader focus on inequality and economic practice—one that includes but goes beyond income equality—might help us better understand Paul. My example is Paul's collection of money for the poor among the Jerusalem saints, and especially its relationship to the system of patronage.

The most helpful brief description of patronage comes from Richard Saller. Saller first quoted this broad definition from J. Boissevain.

> Patronage is founded on the reciprocal relations between patrons and clients. By patron I mean a person who uses his influence to assist and protect some other person, who becomes his 'client', and in return provides certain services

---

[45] David Downs noted that while all the undisputed Pauline letters mention funding for his work, the disputed letters do not discuss it; see "Paul's Collection and the Book of Acts Revisited," *NTS* 52 (2006): 50. So the process of obscuring Paul's economic practices may be visible in the practice of pseudepigraphy as well.

to his patron. The relationship is asymmetrical, though the nature of the services exchanged may differ considerably.[46]

Saller then went on to highlight salient features.

Three vital elements which distinguish a patronage relationship appear in this passage. First, it involves the *reciprocal* exchange of goods and services. Secondly, to distinguish it from a commercial transaction in the marketplace, the relationship must be a personal one of some duration. Thirdly, it must be asymmetrical, in the sense that the two parties are of unequal status and offer different kinds of goods and services in the exchange—a quality which sets patronage off from friendship between equals.[47]

Since Saller was dealing specifically with personal patronage, his second element needs to be understood in a specific way for the context of this study. Here I am discussing patronage as a system, not as particular personal relationships.[48] So in Saller's second element I treat "personal" not in reference to one-to-one human relationships but rather in contrast to "commercial." In other words, we are looking at a system of asymmetrical relationships among people that is regulated over long periods of time not so much by legal requirement or institutional oversight as by discursive expectations and ideology.[49] As such, it was one of the most important sys-

---

[46] J. Boissevain, "Patronage in Sicily," *Man* n.s. 1 (1966): 18, cited in Richard P. Saller, *Personal Patronage under the Early Empire* (New York: Cambridge University Press, 1982), 1.

[47] Saller, *Personal Patronage*, 1. He followed this with an important discussion (7–39) on the vocabulary and ideology of personal patronage.

[48] Terry Johnson and Chris Dandeker, "Patronage: Relation and System," in *Patronage in Ancient Society* (ed. Andrew Wallace-Hadrill; New York: Routledge, 1989), 219–45.

[49] There has been a good deal of discussion about whether and to what extent we can equate patronage with benefaction. For the early Roman imperial period the two are closely related and sometimes indistinguishable; Zeba A. Crook, *Reconceptualizing Conversion: Patronage, Loyalty, and Conversion in the Religions of the Ancient Mediterranean* (BZNW 130; New York: de Gruyter, 2004), 53–89, esp. 66; Holland Hendrix, "Benefactor/Patronage Networks in the Urban Environment: Evidence from Thessalonica," in *Social Networks in the Early Christian Environment: Issues and Methods for Social History* (Semeia 56; ed. L. Michael White; Atlanta: Scholars Press, 1992), 40. For the purposes of this study, I simply use the term "patronage" for this complex of phenomena of patronage/benefaction. With the term I reference a genus "patronage" (defined as a modern conceptual category not necessarily identical with ancient linguistic usage), within which we can distinguish several species, such as personal patronage, friendship, municipal benefaction (euergetism), imperial patronage, and so on.

tems for maintaining social control in the Roman Empire.[50] It was crucial for the maintenance of the Roman system of inequality.

Sydel Silverman provides a suitable starting point for a consideration of patronage and Paul's collection.[51] In the study of patronage, he noted, it is important to distinguish three interrelated facets of the system: the ideology or ideals of patronage (what it was said to be); what patrons and clients thought about their relationships (actual assessments by participants); and the real exchange of goods and services within this system. While the actual assessments of participants are lost to us now, my contention here is that the study of Paul's collection has focused primarily on the ideological level and needs to be complemented by attention to the real exchange of goods and services brought about by Paul's economic practice.

Three recent monographs have discussed the connection between patronage and Paul's collection for the Jerusalem saints, and all of them focus primarily on the ideological level. Stephan Joubert rightly criticized most earlier research for interpreting the collection mainly in theological terms, as though Paul was primarily a philosopher or systematic theologian.[52] Joubert focused instead on the ideology of the social relationships involved in the Jerusalem collection. He termed this an ideology of benefit exchange, which included both patronage and benefaction.[53] According to Joubert, Paul understood the collection as a benefaction by which Paul and his assemblies could assist the Jerusalem believers. But the Jerusalem church, according to Joubert, had already established itself as Paul's benefactor by recognizing his work in Antioch. So the entire complex of relationships around the Jerusalem collection worked within the framework

---

[50] Andrew Wallace-Hadrill, "Patronage in Roman Society: From Republic to Empire," in *Patronage in Ancient Society* (ed. Andrew Wallace-Hadrill; New York: Routledge, 1989); Saller, *Personal Patronage*, 37–38. L. Michael White proposed the examination of social networks as a profitable method of deepening our understanding of the mechanisms by which such control was established and maintained in the imperial period; "Finding the Ties That Bind: Issues from Social Description" and "Social Networks: Theoretical Orientation and Historical Applications," in *Social Networks in the Early Christian Environment: Issues and Methods for Social History* (Semeia 56; ed. L. Michael White; Atlanta: Scholars Press, 1992).

[51] Cited by Saller, *Personal Patronage*, 37.

[52] Stephan Joubert, *Paul as Benefactor: Reciprocity, Strategy, and Theological Reflection in Paul's Collection* (WUNT 124; Tübingen: Mohr Siebeck, 2000).

[53] For Joubert, "patronage" involved mostly Roman patron/client relationships, and "benefaction" was mostly characteristic of Hellenistic cultures in the eastern Mediterranean, and he intentionally used the latter to describe the collection; see *Paul as Benefactor*, 17–72, esp. 66–70. I disagree with the way he elaborated the distinction, but a full response is not necessary here.

of a benefit exchange in which Paul (and others) could be both benefactor
to and beneficiary of the Jerusalem church.[54]

By discussing the collection in terms of patronage/benefaction, Joubert took Paul's activism directly into the heart of the Roman system of
inequality. Joubert's conclusion that the Jerusalem collection was a form
of reciprocal benefits between Paul, Paul's churches, and the Jerusalem
church was afflicted by three important problems. One was the description of benefaction as a relationship in which the parties were benefactors
to each other; this violates the fundamental asymmetry of such arrangements. Second, Joubert described the Jerusalem collection mostly within
the expectations of patronage/benefaction, without sufficient exploration
of the ways in which the collection did not fit this model.[55] Third, Joubert
overlooked income poverty. He developed his descriptions of the practice
of patronage/benefaction from elite texts by men like Aristotle, Seneca the
Younger, and Pliny the Younger, aristocrats who discussed financial practices from the perspective of superwealthy families.[56] Because he did not
consider the widespread deprivation of most everyone else in the Roman
Empire, Joubert assumed that these elite practices would be found also in
the assemblies of Paul.[57]

James Harrison discussed Paul's collection in the context of a study
of a larger consideration of the use of Χάρις ("grace") in Paul's letters
and in the Greco-Roman world.[58] His study also worked from the axiom
that notions of reciprocity and patronage permeated social interaction.
Instead of agreeing with Joubert that patronage relationships characterized the collection for Jerusalem, Harrison argued that Paul's collection
was a complicated redefinition of patronage. Paul adopted some terms
and rhetorical strategies from the discourse of patron/client relationships
but sought to redefine the motivation. According to Harrison, Paul's collection did not rely on standard concepts of grace and their onerous burden of reciprocation. Paul drew instead on the churches' experiences of
overwhelming divine grace that required no counter-gift and no returned

---

[54] Ibid., 113–15, 150–52.

[55] Note, however, that Joubert suggests some distinctive features of patronage/
benefaction in Paul's thought; ibid., 216–18.

[56] Pliny's estimated annual income of about HS1,100,000 would have been
about 2,000 times the amount needed for subsistence for an average family.
Seneca's estimated income of HS18,000,000 would have been more than 31,000
times the level of a family's subsistence needs; Scheidel and Friesen, "Size of the
Economy."

[57] He does, however, recognize the existence of poverty that the collection was
meant to alleviate; see *Paul as Benefactor*, 111–13.

[58] James R. Harrison, *Paul's Language of Grace in Its Graeco-Roman Context*
(WUNT 172; Tübingen: Mohr Siebeck, 2003), esp. 289–332.

favor.[59] According to Harrison, this experience of divine love that subverts the dynamics of the reciprocity system was to be the basis for the collection from Paul's churches for the poor saints in Jerusalem.[60]

Harrison's analysis has the advantage of paying more attention to the way that Paul critiqued some features of traditional reciprocity and employed others. The study is hampered, however, by its focus on a cognitive concept ("grace") as the way to explain a social system. Moreover, there is a preoccupation with certain kinds of Christian theology that emphasize God's unmerited grace, for which standard ideas of reciprocity from the Roman Empire then provide the negative foil.[61] Paul's superior theology wins the day, of course.

A more profitable approach is laid out by David Downs.[62] After considering the chronology of the collection and a range of possible analogies in the gift giving of contemporary associations, Downs analyzed Paul's rhetoric related to the collection. The main conclusion of this analysis was the observation that Paul consistently framed the collection in religious language, casting the offering for the saints in Jerusalem as worship rather than as benefaction. Thus the collection was described not in terms of patronage (Joubert) or as a redefinition of patronage (Harrison), but rather as an alternative to patronage, one that "functions to subvert the values of patronage and euergetism by depicting an alternate mode of benefaction. . . ."[63]

While all three of these studies operate at the level of ideology (the ideals of what the collection was said to be), the third option is most persuasive and can be buttressed by special attention to the economic practices involved. If we examine the flow of goods and services, three factors support Downs's conclusion that Paul was promoting an alternative to patronage.

First, the contributor was communal: the money came from several groups of people rather than from an individual or family. The patronage system operated primarily on the principle of one wealthy benefactor or one wealthy family (or several families) giving a large sum that would allegedly benefit many less fortunate people. Then the subordinate beneficiaries would honor the benefactor(s) publicly by name. One needs only

---

[59] Ibid., 287–88, 314–32.

[60] Ibid., 345–49.

[61] E.g., Harrison, *Paul's Language,* 347.

[62] David J. Downs, *The Offering of the Gentiles: Paul's Collection for Jerusalem in Its Chronological, Cultural, and Cultic Contexts* (WUNT 248; Tübingen: Mohr Siebeck, 2008). I thank the author for sharing these materials with me before they were published.

[63] Ibid., 240; see also 248.

to take a stroll through an archaeological site of a Roman imperial city, town, or village to see how this focus on the benefactor worked. Public spaces were filled with inscriptions and statues that honored the big giver who was honored for his or her grace (χάρις) and goodwill (εὔνοια).

Paul, however, outlined a radically different process for the accumulation of the gift in 1 Cor 16:1–4. This accumulation process was communal and did not focus on an individual giver or family. In fact, Paul went to great lengths to distance himself or any individual from the role of benefactor. Assemblies would select representatives, and Paul would accompany them on the trip if they so desired. So the Jerusalem collection did not incorporate the patronage system's focus on the named contributor.

Second, the collection came from people with modest resources living mostly around subsistence, not from the wealthy or well-to-do. Paul envisioned a system of average saints helping the desperately poor saints. Each saint was to set aside money every week according to how he or she had prospered that week (1 Cor 16:2). The practice here is not that of benefaction, where families with huge amounts of capital or resources distribute a fraction of their surplus. It is an accumulation process geared to people with modest resources (categories 4–6 of the poverty scale). Confirmation comes from 2 Cor 8:12, where Paul reassured the Corinthian saints that the amount of their gift was not important, only their willingness to participate: "For if the eagerness is there, the gift is acceptable according to what one has—not according to what one does not have" (NRSV). Paul assumed that Corinthian believers would not be able to give much, and he indicated that, contrary to the ideology of patronage, the size of the gifts did not matter in this alternative system.

Third, Paul promoted occasional economic redistribution, not public largesse that diverted attention from the daily exploitation of the majority. The genius of the patronage system was that the benefactions of the ruling elites made it appear as though the wealthy were giving to the poor, even though it was the poor who made this possible by contributing to the wealthy on a daily basis through the normative structures of the economy. Paul's proposed collection entailed a practice different from that of patronage. In 2 Cor 8:13–15, Paul implied that in the future, the Corinthians might be in need and then the Jerusalem saints and the other assemblies would share with the Corinthian saints.[64] His rhetoric sug-

---

[64] Some commentators have maintained that Paul could not have envisioned that the Jerusalem assembly would someday contribute to the needs of others and suggest instead that Paul expected the future gift of the Jerusalem assembly to be an eschatological blessing rather than an economic contribution; Victor Paul Furnish, *II Corinthians* (2d ed.; Garden City, N.Y.: Doubleday, 1984), 419–20; Ralph Martin, *2 Corinthians* (Waco, Tex.: Word, 1986), 266–67. The arguments for

gested multidirectional, occasional, need-based redistribution, the goal of which was economic equality for everyone involved, even if that only meant resources sufficient for the day at hand.[65]

Thus the economic practice of Paul's collection confirms Downs's analysis of its ideology: the collection for the destitute among the saints in Jerusalem should not be understood as a replication of the patronage system that characterized economic relationships under Roman imperialism.[66] Rather, it was a different system, an attempt by Paul to promote financial redistribution among poor people, Gentile and Jewish, in the assemblies of the eastern Mediterranean. It contradicted the normal expectations of patronage and replaced them with an economy of voluntary redistribution among the saints.[67]

There are other topics to explore in the context of systematic deprivation and Paul's churches. We could examine the Lord's Supper as a meal shared among the poor, or Paul's manual labor as a refusal to commodify his apostolic calling. But I conclude with one final observation. All three of the Pauline economic practices just mentioned—the Jerusalem collection as a form of economic redistribution, the Lord's Supper as shared physical nourishment, and the spiritual leader who worked for a living—all three of these experiments apparently failed. While we cannot be completely certain, it looks as though the Jerusalem collection fell apart with Paul's ar-

eschatological blessing do not make good sense in the context of Paul's discussion, however, and the tide seems to be moving in favor of the economic contribution argument; Margaret E. Thrall, *A Critical Commentary on the Second Epistle to the Corinthians* (Edinburgh: T&T Clark, 1994), 2.542; F. Danker, *II Corinthians* (Minneapolis: Augsburg, 1989), 128–29; Frank Matera, *II Corinthians: A Commentary* (Louisville, Ky.: Westminster/John Knox, 2003), 193.

[65] This point is driven home by Paul's quotation of Exod 16:18 from the story of gathering manna in the wilderness: "But when they measured it with an omer, those who gathered much had nothing over, and those who gathered little had no shortage; they gathered as much as each of them needed" (NRSV). Paul cited this example of the Hebrews gathering manna in the wilderness to indicate that with God's provision and the cooperation of the saints, everyone would have enough for daily needs.

[66] Peter Lampe discussed a variety of relationships within the early Pauline churches where typically hierarchical situations were undermined in favor of egalitarian ideals: "Paul, Patrons, and Clients," in *Paul in the Greco-Roman World: A Handbook* (ed. J. Paul Sampley; New York: Trinity, 2003), 488–523. When Lampe comes to the Jerusalem collection, however, he points out that it did not fit into patronage categories at all (502–5). In light of this, the other relationships discussed in the article could also be described as moving beyond patronage expectations. Lampe calls them "ambiguous" because no one is clearly superior. Perhaps we should not describe them in patronage terms since they violate the patronage characteristic of asymmetric power.

[67] One of the few commentators to notice this was Richard A. Horsley, *1 Corinthians* (Nashville: Abingdon, 1998), 223–24.

rest at the Jerusalem temple (Acts 21–22);[68] the Lord's Supper was already a problem in Corinth before Paul wrote 1 Cor 11:20–34; and Paul's manual labor was not even practiced by his contemporary apostles. Perhaps it was necessary for Paul's boldest economic initiatives—the ones that abandoned the Roman system of inequality—to fail in order for an evolving Pauline Christianity to become over the course of time an integrated part of that system of inequality.

For Further Reading

Barclay, John. "Poverty in Pauline Studies: A Response to Steven Friesen." *JSNT* 26 (2004): 363–66.

Crook, Zeba A. *Reconceptualizing Conversion: Patronage, Loyalty, and Conversion in the Religions of the Ancient Mediterranean.* BZNW 130. New York: de Gruyter, 2004.

Downs, David J. *The Offering of the Gentiles: Paul's Collection for Jerusalem in Its Chronological, Cultural, and Cultic Contexts.* WUNT 2. Reihe, no. 248. Tübingen: Mohr Siebeck, 2008.

———. "Paul's Collection and the Book of Acts Revisited." *NTS* 52 (2006): 50–70.

Frier, Bruce W. "Roman Demography." Pages 85–109 in *Life, Death, and Entertainment in the Roman Empire.* Edited by D. S. Potter and D. J. Mattingly. Ann Arbor: University of Michigan Press, 1999.

Friesen, Steven J. "The Blessings of Hegemony: The Preferential Option for the Rich in Pauline Studies." Pages 117–28 in *The Bible in the Public Square: Reading the Signs of the Times.* Edited by Cynthia Briggs Kittredge et al. Minneapolis: Fortress, 2008.

———. "Injustice or God's Will? Explanations of Poverty in Four Proto-Christian Texts." Pages 240–60 in *The First Century.* Edited by Richard Horsley. Vol. 1 of *A People's History of Christianity.* Edited by Denis R. Janz. Minneapolis: Fortress, 2005.

———. "Poverty in Pauline Studies: Beyond the So-called New Consensus." *JSNT* 26 (2004): 323–61.

———. "Prospects for Demography of the Pauline Mission: Corinth among the Churches." Pages 351–70 in *Urban Religion in Roman Corinth: Interdisciplinary Approaches.* Edited by Daniel N. Schowalter and Steven J. Friesen. Harvard Theological Studies 35. Cambridge, Mass.: Harvard University Press, 2005.

---

[68] Downs argued that this section of Acts did not refer to the collection ("Paul's Collection," 50–70).

———. "The Wrong Erastus: Archaeology, Ideology, and Exegesis." In *Corinth in Context: Comparative Studies in Religion and Society*. Edited by Steven J. Friesen et al. New York: Brill, in press.

Garnsey, Peter. *Food and Society in Classical Antiquity*. Cambridge: Cambridge University Press, 1999.

Garnsey, Peter, and Richard Saller. *The Roman Empire: Economy, Society and Culture*. Berkeley: University of California Press, 1987.

Georgi, Dieter. *Remembering the Poor: The History of Paul's Collection for Jerusalem*. Nashville: Abingdon, 1992.

Goldsmith, Raymond W. "An Estimate of the Size and Structure of the National Product of the Early Roman Empire." *Review of Income and Wealth* 30 (1984): 263–88.

Grusky, David B. "The Past, Present, and Future of Social Inequality." Pages 1–51 in *Social Stratification: Class, Race, and Gender in Sociological Perspective*. Edited by David B. Grusky. 2d ed. Boulder, Colo.: Westview, 2001.

Grusky, David B., and Ravi Kanbur. "Introduction: Conceptual Foundations of Poverty and Inequality Measurement." Pages 1–29 in *Poverty and Inequality*. Edited by David B. Grusky and Ravi Kanbur. Stanford, Calif.: Stanford University Press, 2006.

Hendrix, Holland. "Benefactor/Patronage Networks in the Urban Environment: Evidence from Thessalonica." Pages 39–58 in *Social Networks in the Early Christian Environment: Issues and Methods for Social History*. Semeia 56. Edited by L. Michael White. Atlanta: Scholars Press, 1992.

Johnson, Terry, and Chris Dandeker. "Patronage: Relation and System." Pages 219–45 in *Patronage in Ancient Society*. Edited by Andrew Wallace-Hadrill. New York: Routledge, 1989.

Joubert, Stephan. *Paul as Benefactor: Reciprocity, Strategy, and Theological Reflection in Paul's Collection*. WUNT 2. Reihe, no. 124. Tübingen: Mohr Siebeck, 2000.

Lampe, Peter. "Paul, Patrons, and Clients." Pages 488–523 in *Paul in the Greco-Roman World: A Handbook*. Edited by J. Paul Sampley. New York: Trinity, 2003.

Meeks, Wayne A. *The First Urban Christians: The Social World of the Apostle Paul*. New Haven, Conn.: Yale University Press, 1983.

Meggitt, Justin J. *Paul, Poverty and Survival*. Edinburgh: T&T Clark, 1998.

Nussbaum, Martha C. "Human Functioning and Social Justice: In Defense of Aristotelian Essentialism." *Political Theory* 20 (1992): 202–46.

Saller, Richard P. *Personal Patronage under the Early Empire*. New York: Cambridge University Press, 1982.

Scheidel, Walter. "Demography." Pages 38–86 in *The Cambridge Economic History of the Greco-Roman World*. Edited by Walter Scheidel et al. Cambridge: Cambridge University Press, 2007.

———. "Progress and Problems in Roman Demography." Pages 1–81 in *Debating Roman Demography*. Edited by Walter Scheidel. Boston: Brill, 2001.

Scheidel, Walter, and Steven J. Friesen. "The Size of the Economy and the Distribution of Income in the Roman Empire." *JRS* (2009), in press.

Scroggs, Robin. "The Sociological Interpretation of the New Testament: The Present State of Research." *NTS* 26 (1980): 164–79.

Sen, Amartya. *Development as Freedom*. New York: Knopf, 1999. Repr., New York: Anchor, 2000.

Stegemann, Ekkehard W., and Wolfgang Stegemann. *The Jesus Movement: A Social History of Its First Century*. Minneapolis: Fortress, 1999.

Theissen, Gerd. *The Social Setting of Pauline Christianity: Essays on Corinth*. Philadelphia: Fortress, 1982.

Wallace-Hadrill, Andrew. "Introduction." Pages 1–13 in *Patronage in Ancient Society*. Edited by Andrew Wallace-Hadrill. New York: Routledge, 1989.

———. "Patronage in Roman Society: From Republic to Empire." Pages 63–87 in *Patronage in Ancient Society*. Edited by Andrew Wallace-Hadrill. New York: Routledge, 1989.

White, L. Michael. "Finding the Ties That Bind: Issues from Social Description." Pages 3–22 in *Social Networks in the Early Christian Environment: Issues and Methods for Social History*. Semeia 56. Edited by L. Michael White. Atlanta: Scholars Press, 1992.

———. "Social Networks: Theoretical Orientation and Historical Applications." Pages 23–36 in *Social Networks in the Early Christian Environment: Issues and Methods for Social History*. Semeia 56. Edited by L. Michael White. Atlanta: Scholars Press, 1992.

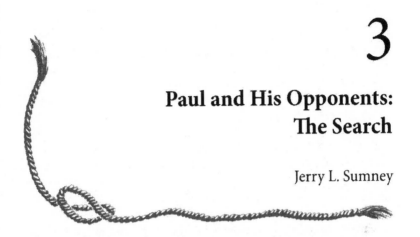

3

Paul and His Opponents: The Search

Jerry L. Sumney

Since the publication of F. C. Baur's *Paul the Apostle of Jesus Christ* in 1845, the question of the identity of those opposed in the Pauline letters has been a subject of much debate among NT scholars.[1] Since so many Pauline letters oppose other teachers or teachings, interpreters need to be as clear as possible about what or who is opposed in order to understand the settings of the letters. Given this necessity and the fact that Paul does not fully or objectively describe the people he rejects, it is not surprising to find that hypotheses about Paul's opponents have proliferated, with interpreters imposing multiple hypotheses on every letter. Proposals about opponents not only shape the interpretation of individual Pauline letters but also significantly determine one's understanding of the early church.

SIGNIFICANCE OF THE ISSUE

This question has the power to shape our reading of individual letters and our view of the early church more broadly because it tries to identify the specific beliefs and practices of various believers within individual, local churches. Paul's letters give us our earliest evidence about the early church. They are written some twenty years before the Gospels and contain inner-group communication as people in the church define themselves over against both the broader culture and members of the

---

[1] My more extensive treatment of the history of interpretations of Paul's opponents is found in "Studying Paul's Opponents: Advances and Challenges," 7–58 in *Paul and His Opponents* (ed. Stanley E. Porter; Pauline Studies; Leiden: Brill, 2005). Parts of the present chapter are drawn directly from that previous work.

synagogue who do not accept the belief that Jesus is God's Son and the savior of the world. Identifying those Paul writes against helps us see what kinds of diversity were accepted in the earliest church and what types of beliefs and practices Paul said were unacceptable.

Furthermore, Paul's choice of letters as his means of contacting and teaching his churches means that he selected a type of communication that addresses the specifics of that community's questions, issues, and problems. This very personal means of communication requires us to know as much as possible about the questions he was answering and the circumstances he was addressing if we hope to understand his message to those churches. Without properly understanding the issue at hand, we will probably misunderstand what Paul told his churches because knowing what the question is usually determines the meaning of the answer. For example, if we read "Anyone unwilling to work should not eat" (2 Thess 3:10 NRSV) as a response to a question about social policy, it sounds as though Christians should not help the chronically unemployed. If, however, we recognize that this statement responds to the claims of a group of teachers who say that because they are spiritually superior to others the rest of the church should give them money to alleviate the need for them to have a job, it sounds very different. Since context is so vital to attaining a reasonable grasp of a text's meaning, identifying Paul's opponents is one of our crucial tasks if we are to understand his letters clearly.

F. C. Baur and His Legacy

One of Baur's starting points in his search for the opponents of Paul, and so the shape of earliest Christianity, was Hegelian philosophy of history. This presupposition required Baur to identify a thesis and an antithesis that would meld into a synthesis. For Baur, the thesis was Petrine or Jewish Christianity, and the antithesis was Pauline or Gentile Christianity. Baur was so committed to this scheme that he could admit the absence of evidence that a letter opposed Petrine Christianity and still say it opposed this branch of Christianity. After all, there was no alternative!

An understanding of the early Christian movement that presupposes this sort of simple opposition of two and only two types of Christianity has remained long after the Hegelian presupposition was abandoned. For example, in the 1960s Walter Schmithals presupposed this kind of scheme when he argued that Paul's opponents everywhere and always were Gnostics. Again, a lack of evidence was no deterrent. Schmithals argued that when Paul does not argue against Gnostics, it is because he has not yet recognized that his opponents are such. When Paul understands more clearly (that is, as clearly as Schmithals), then Paul opposed the Gnostic teaching that was surely present.

Not only Baur's two-party oppositional scheme but even his identification of the two parties lives on in NT scholarship. Gerd Lüdemann argued for a modification of Baur's hypothesis in his 1980 study of Paul's opponents. As recently as 1994, Michael Goulder argued for a nearly identical view and affirmed it with respect to the Corinthian opponents in 2001.[2] Baur's scheme and hypothesis continue to have an amazingly vigorous life despite the critique of such an understanding of earliest Christianity found in Walter Bauer's 1934 work, *Orthodoxy and Heresy in Earliest Christianity,* which demonstrated (even with its own faults) a significantly wider range of diversity in the early church.[3]

While the tendency to follow Baur's two-party scheme is pronounced in studies of Paul's opponents that examine the whole Pauline corpus or a large segment of it, interpreters who work on individual letters deviate widely from such proposals. But even these works often rely unintentionally on Baur's powerful and insightful work. Minimally, most interpreters presuppose an anti-Pauline movement, with many finding its roots in Jerusalem and often in James. My reading of the Pauline letters and understanding of early Christianity finds insufficient support for this latter hypothesis. While there are anti-Pauline movements by the mid-fifties, the evidence that would link any anti-Pauline movement to the leaders of the Jerusalem church is meager indeed, and the scant materials cited as evidence are better understood in other ways.

There is insufficient space in the scope of this chapter to provide an extensive review of hypotheses about the opponents of each Pauline letter because the number of hypotheses is so large—for most letters ranging between ten and thirty. (A listing of various views taken on each letter through the mid-1970s appears in J. J. Gunther's *St. Paul's Opponents and Their Background*[4] and my recent account of the major hypotheses for each letter may be found elsewhere.[5]) Rather than attempting such a review, I

---

[2]Gerd Lüdemann, *Opposition to Paul in Jewish Christianity* (Minneapolis, Minn.: Fortress, 1989); Michael D. Goulder, *St. Paul versus St. Peter: A Tale of Two Missions* (Louisville, Ky.: Westminster/John Knox, 1994); idem, *Paul and the Competing Mission in Corinth* (Library of Pauline Studies; Peabody, Mass.: Hendrickson, 2001).

[3]Walter Bauer, *Orthodoxy and Heresy in Earliest Christianity* (ed. Robert A. Kraft and Gerhard Krodel; trans. a team from the Philadelphia Seminar on Christian Origins; Philadelphia: Fortress, 1971).

[4]J. J. Gunther, *St. Paul's Opponents and Their Background: A Study of Apocalyptic and Jewish Sectarian Teachings* (NovTSup 35; Leiden: Brill, 1973).

[5]Sumney, "Studying Paul's Opponents," 7–43.

will discuss a few important aspects of how interpreters go about the task of identifying Paul's opponents because the methods interpreters use often determine the results. I will look at two major categories of issues in which interpreters are making progress in sharpening the way they conduct this research and two in which we are making less headway.

ISSUES OF METHOD

To identify those Paul opposes more clearly and so delineate the context of Paul's letters and the shape of the early church with more precision, interpreters need more awareness of their presuppositions, more deliberateness in their methods, and more judiciousness in their use of texts. My work on Pauline opponents has attempted to make progress on these methodological issues.

Defining "Opponent" Carefully

The first methodological issue which needs more attention is that of distinguishing between those who oppose Paul and those Paul opposes. It is important to recognize that not everyone Paul writes against thought they were advocating teachings or practices Paul would reject. There are times when a Pauline letter strongly opposes a teaching or practice when its proponents may have thought they were in agreement with Paul. For example, it seems unlikely that the teachers 2 Thessalonians counters think they are opposing Paul because they draw on him as an authority (2 Thess 2:1–2). The same may be the case in Galatians, where Paul must say that he does not hold their view (Gal 5:11). And nothing in Colossians suggests that those opposed in it knew they were advocating anything Paul would reject. So while these teachers interpreted the faith in ways Paul or his successors found unacceptable, they did not intend to oppose Paul. Recognizing this distinction among those Paul opposed can significantly shape our understanding of particular situations and the contours of the early church.

Acknowledging that some people whose teaching Paul rejects do not intend to oppose him shows that a wide range of early believers recognized his authority, even as some others saw him as a renegade. It also frees us to see that Paul's teaching was understood in multiple ways within his own churches, including among those who intend to remain faithful to him. Some of this diversity was deemed acceptable; other developments Paul was compelled to reject. This indicates that diverse beliefs thrived within the Pauline churches from their earliest days. Part of the reason the debates reflected in Paul's letters arose was that the churches were still defining the range of diversity they would deem acceptable.

Distinguishing Accusation from Description

Beginning in the 1990s, many interpreters began to exercise more scrutiny about how reliably Paul's characterizations of his opponents reflect what they were really like.[6] These scholars reflect an increased awareness that polemical texts often contain statements that appear as descriptions but do not accurately describe the actual practices or teaching of the opposition. For example, when 2 Thessalonians says that the other teachers say, "The Day of the Lord has come," this is more likely an easily refutable characterization of their teaching than a direct quotation. So while the author thinks they have an overrealized eschatology (that is, they believe they enjoy more blessings of the end time than the author thinks it is possible for anyone to possess in the present), they probably do not express their view with this language. Similarly, when Paul says that the people who want Gentile believers to accept circumcision in Galatia advocate this practice only to avoid persecution (Gal 6:12), it seems unlikely that personal safety is their sole motivation. Finally, the traveling ministers Paul opposes in 2 Corinthians do not think of themselves as deceitful workers, or even as boasters, as Paul describes them (2 Cor 11:13–15).

Interpreters in recent decades more readily recognize and take account of the fact that Paul's characterizations of those he opposes are often tendentious, particularly in polemical contexts. Similarly, when Paul is defending himself, he often presents the charges others make about him in a dramatic and exaggerated form to lead his readers to dismiss those charges out of hand or to make them easier to refute. Paul's most reliable descriptions of his opponents will more likely appear in sections devoted to teaching that do not have a polemical or apologetic edge.[7] Giving careful attention to the differing purposes of various sections of a letter will keep us from accepting as straightforward descriptions the intentional caricatures Paul gives of his opponents and so will help us sketch them more accurately.

---

[6] An earlier study that signaled the importance of considering the type of context in which a statement appears and guided others to think about it was that of Nils A. Dahl, "Paul and the Church at Corinth according to 1 Corinthians 1:10–4:21," in *Christian History and Interpretation* (ed. W. R. Farmer et al.; Cambridge: Cambridge University Press, 1967), 313–35.

[7] See the detailed assessment of various kinds of statements in different contexts in Jerry L. Sumney, *Identifying Paul's Opponents; The Question of Method in 2 Corinthians* (JSNTSup 40; Sheffield: JSOT Press, 1990), 95–114.

Treating Letters Individually

It has also become more common, though by no means universal, that interpreters exercise more care in distinguishing among the historical contexts that individual letters address instead of assuming that the opponents of one letter are also the problem other letters address. Few continue to adopt a simplistic scheme that allows for a single set of opponents Paul must fight in every letter, but a number of interpreters do use the situation they perceive in one letter to determine who Paul opposes in another. This happens particularly in the case of treatments of 1 Corinthians and 2 Corinthians, documents that contain letters written to the same churches over the course of a fairly short amount of time. Given these connections, interpreters often assume that anything gleaned from 1 Corinthians can directly inform their identification of the opponents in 2 Corinthians and vice versa. While most scholars do not state this as a methodological principle, it is the practice of more than a few. But this ignores the significant change the letters manifest between internal problems Paul must deal with in 1 Corinthians and the problems generated by the arrival of rival teachers/apostles that he combats in 2 Corinthians. So even in these letters written to the same church over the course of less than five years, the circumstances Paul addresses have changed significantly.

Interpreters must, then, treat each Pauline letter individually before looking for connections with problems Paul countered in other letters. And while we may find links, the example of 1 Corinthians and 2 Corinthians indicates why many interpreters have rightly become more reticent to attribute the beliefs or practices found in one situation to the people Paul opposes in another letter. This reticence sometimes means that our sketch of those opposed remains less sharp, but it also means that our portrait is much more certain and so a firmer foundation from which to interpret the letter. At the same time, this way of proceeding leaves us open to seeing the different kinds of beliefs and practices that developed as various people thought about how to understand and live the faith in the earliest church communities. This allows us to observe the ways various leaders and teachers of the church thought about what would be acceptable and how they argued their case before the full membership.

Relating the Surrounding Culture to the Problem the Text Addresses

There has been noticeably less advance in thinking about how to relate the material and intellectual culture of the historical context to the task of clarifying the identity of the people Paul opposes. Two monographs on the opponents of Colossians, those of Troy Martin[8] and Clinton Arnold,[9] exemplify the issues involved with this point of method. These two studies make similar moves methodologically but come to very different understandings of the teaching the author of Colossians opposes. Both Martin and Arnold allow reconstructions of movements they find in the culture to determine prematurely and illegitimately their understandings of the specific teaching Colossians rejects. Both scholars make the connection between the teachers at Colossae and a particular group in the culture by means of vocabulary parallels between Colossians and the group with which they identify the opponents.

The Example of Troy Martin

Martin's study has much to commend it. Few studies of Pauline letters read the grammar and syntax of difficult passages with as open a mind as we find in Martin. Such a careful and open examination of the text demands the attention of all readers. Many of his proposals for translations of difficult passages have received too little attention, even though he provides powerful arguments for them.

Martin's basic thesis identifies the teachers Colossians opposes as non-Christian Cynic philosophers. These philosophers, he says, have visited the community and critiqued its beliefs and practices so persuasively that some are thinking about abandoning the church. Thus, the author of Colossians (who is probably not Paul) must respond at length. Martin carefully reconstructs the beliefs and practices of Cynics from their own writings and from what other ancient authors say about them. He then argues that important, in fact unique, elements of their teaching are opposed in Colossians. Particularly, he argues that their "prohibitions against perishable consumer goods and understanding of humility as severity to the body" are unique to Cynics. He then contends that since Colossians opposes both of these things, the people it opposes must be Cynic philosophers.[10] He finds some other corroborating evidence, but these are his most important pieces of evidence.

While Martin may be correct in asserting that the various ideas and practices he mentions are not combined in any other known movement in the ways they appear among Cynics, these individual elements do appear elsewhere. For example, Cynics of various kinds adopted differing

---

[8] Troy Martin, *By Philosophy and Vain Deceit: Colossians as a Response to a Cynic Critique* (JSNTSup 118; Sheffield: Sheffield Academic Press, 1996).

[9] Clinton E. Arnold, *The Colossian Syncretism: The Interface between Christianity and Folk Belief in Colossae* (Grand Rapids, Mich.: Baker, 1996).

[10] Martin, *By Philosophy and Vain Deceit*, 205.

types of moderately ascetic practices, and some attained mystical and visionary experiences. But this was true not only for Cynics; many schools of thought, both philosophies and religions, used different types of self-denying practices to attain such experiences. Indeed, some limited ascetic practice was a widely known way to attain mystical experiences.[11] So the severity to the body that Colossians associates with "humility" may have come from a number of sources.

More important methodologically, Martin allows the vocabulary parallels he finds between Colossians and some Cynic teachings to exercise too much influence on his identification of the opponents of Colossians. Because Cynics and the teachers Colossians rejects share some common terms, Martin makes the language and teaching of Cynic philosophy the lens through which he reads the whole of Colossians, and he does this at a very early stage of his interpretation of Colossians. Once the connection is assumed, he uses all kinds of purely terminological parallels to confirm the identity of these opponents. So, for example, the reference to "human tradition" becomes a reference to the Cynics' claim to be in a tradition (hardly a unique claim among philosophers) rather than a polemical accusation that denigrates the other teaching. Even if the opponents of Colossians adopted the language Cynics used to describe their self-effacing practices, that terminology alone is insufficient reason to propose that the opponents work from within Cynic thought overall.

The basic methodological problem here is that Martin's reconstruction of the Cynics determines the meaning of statements in Colossians. This is the same method Dieter Georgi used in 1964 to identify the opponents of 2 Corinthians as divine men.[12] That is, he formulated a reconstruction of a first-century movement within Judaism and then fit 2 Corinthians into that framework because he found some parallels in terminology and general outlook. Few NT scholars remain convinced by his conclusions, and most think there were significant problems in the way he made his connections with the movement he found outside the church.

Such uses of reconstructions of historical movements prematurely constrict the meaning of the primary text in its own context. The problems with such an approach become clear when we think about the broad semantic range of many words. Use of terminology parallels is

---

[11] See the examples given in Thomas J. Sappington, *Revelation and Redemption at Colossae* (JSNTSup 53; Sheffield: JSOT Press, 1991), 157–58, on the humility of angels.

[12] Dieter Georgi, *Die Gegner des Paulus im 2 Korintherbrief: Studien zur religiösen Propaganda in der Spätantike* (WMANT 11; Neukirchen: Neukirchener Verlag, 1964; ET: *The Opponents of Paul in Second Corinthians;* trans. H. Attridge et al.; Philadelphia: Fortress, 1986).

particularly problematic when we cross from the use of a word in philosophic writings to its use in the NT. There are sometimes very significant differences in the ways a Platonist uses a word and the way a NT writer uses it. Anyone who began reading Greek with the NT and then picked up the writing of the first-century Jewish philosopher Philo of Alexandria can testify to the radical differences in the meanings of words in those two contexts. The word Paul uses for "faith" is a good example. Among philosophers, the Greek word *pistis* often means a proof in an argument. It never means this in Paul but, instead, has a different range of meanings that includes faith and faithfulness.

Two examples of English words may also help us see the problem with using vocabulary parallels to say that the same ideas are present or that a group known to use the same word is causing trouble in a Pauline church. The word "problem" takes on very different meanings depending on its context. There is a big difference between talking about a math problem in a textbook and the use of the same word to refer to the difficulties that global climate change will inflict on polar bears. And of course it has yet another range of meanings when we ask someone what their problem is! The various meanings of "problem" clearly overlap, but they are obviously different. A more dramatic example is the word "set," a word that may be either a noun or a verb. If we limit ourselves to its meaning as a noun, it may refer to a segment of tennis match, a certain number of matching dishes, or a group of numbers. Hearing someone ask, "Did you win the set?" could be asking about tennis or about a lottery for a box of dishes; only context tells you which meaning is correct.[13] These examples suggest that finding similar terms in two different settings is an insufficient basis for claiming that the usage means the same thing or that there is a connection between the settings.[14]

The Example of Clinton Arnold

Arnold makes the same methodological moves as Martin but comes to a very different view of the opponents of Colossians because his reconstruction draws on a different body of material from the cultural setting

---

[13]Michael J. Gorman gives the word "fire" as another example. He notes that it means something very different when someone says it while exiting a smoking building than it does when said to a firing squad (*Elements of Biblical Exegesis; A Basic Guide for Students and Ministers* [rev. ed.; Peabody, Mass.: Hendrickson, 2009], 70).

[14]For a well-known treatment of this problem see Samuel Sandmel, "Parallelomania," *JBL* 81 (1962): 1–13. See also Sumney, *Identifying Paul's Opponents,* 89–92, and *"Servants of Satan," "False Brothers," and Other Opponents of Paul* (JSNTSup 188; Sheffield: Sheffield Academic Press, 1999), 22–23.

of the first century. Arnold holds that the teaching Colossians opposes develops from a mixing of the folk religion of western Asia Minor (today's Turkey) with Christian beliefs. He reconstructs that folk religion largely from evidence he draws from magical texts and artifacts, particularly when they appear in Jewish contexts. Arnold demonstrates well that angels were important in the religious life of both Jewish and non-Jewish residents of western Asia Minor. For example, people call upon these angels to provide protection from various kinds of evil (from the spirit world and from humans) and to grant healing from illness. Arnold infers from such widespread practices that since angel veneration was prominent in the region, Colossians' mention of "the worship of angels" (*thrēskeia tōn angelōn;* a phrase that can mean either worship that angels perform or worship that people offer to angels) must mean the opponents of Colossians also venerate angels. He makes this claim even though the Greek word used for worship in Colossians (*thrēskeia*) does not appear in the local materials he cites.

Arnold follows the same procedure when interpreting the difficult word *embateuō.* He first describes a second phase of initiation into mystery cults, particularly those known in western Asia Minor, noting that they commonly involved entering a sacred place and having ecstatic visions. He then argues that *embateuō* is a technical term for this initiatory event, thus adopting the view of the late nineteenth- and early twentieth-century scholars William Ramsay and Martin Dibelius. Arnold moves from a lengthy discussion of mystery religion initiations to assuming that because Colossians uses the term *embateuō* in association with visions, it must refer to such mystery cult rites. His supporting evidence includes materials that document a fear of evil spiritual powers among the people of western Asia Minor, a mention of the "elements" (another term that appears in Colossians) in the ancient author Apuleuis, and the known use of ascetic practices to prepare for visionary experiences in mystery initiations. Arnold uses these general and terminological similarities to argue that the opponents of Colossians had been initiated into mystery cults and were advocating that others should be. But people throughout the ancient world feared evil spiritual powers and sought protection from them. And many religions, not just the mystery cults, used some ascetic practices to induce visionary experiences.

It is certainly possible that the false teaching Colossians opposes and local mystery cults had some common features. But such similarities, even if they include using the same or similar language, do not render a direct connection probable. Additionally, Arnold draws on evidence that is as much as two hundred years later than Colossians but still assumes that geographic proximity is nearly evidence enough to posit a direct connection.

Arnold followed the same methodological procedure as Martin. Both found some parallels (mostly in terminology similarities) between an external phenomenon or movement and what is opposed in Colossians and then imposed the chosen external frame of thought on the letter. This way of developing a hypothesis involves the interpreter in too much circular reasoning. If we establish a connection between a system of thought outside a Pauline letter and the problem Paul addresses with a few words or phrases they have in common and then confirm that identification of the opponents by reading the letter in light of the presupposition that they are the problem, we have offered little proof.[15] As the history of scholarship has shown, interpreters can attach all kinds of contradictory hypotheses to the same letter using this procedure.

Both Martin and Arnold bring important and interesting data to our attention. Furthermore, there is no doubt that the surrounding culture and even the subcultures of various regions influenced the various ways the early church expressed its newfound faith. But this does not mean that they imported whole systems of thought or all elements of those other practices when they adopted and adapted parts of them. Interpreters must marshal more evidence than a few common words or ideas to demonstrate that such connections are valid.

Like Georgi's earlier treatment of 2 Corinthians, Martin and Arnold begin with the text of Colossians, identify a few key ideas or phrases, and then turn to reconstruct an external school of thought or expression of religion: for Martin, Cynic philosophers; for Arnold, practitioners of regional popular religions. When Martin and Arnold return to the text of Colossians, they each interpret its texts according to the scheme of the reconstruction rather than first in the context of the letter itself. Thus the reconstruction dominates the exegesis.

The Methodological Principle

At least part of the problem with such a method is evident in the radically different proposals that Martin and Arnold advocate. Each can find vocabulary similarities or apparent conceptual contacts with parts of the movement they identify as the trouble. Each then reads everything else through the lens of that outside movement. With such a procedure, one can identify the problem Colossians addresses with a vast number of movements. Methodologically, a reconstruction of a movement external

---

[15] All interpretation involves some circularity, as interpreters read the whole in light of a new understanding of a particular passage and then reread the same passage through their new understanding gained of the whole. But the circularity in Martin and Arnold is both too tight and of a bit different sort.

to the letter in question should not be allowed to determine the meaning of particular texts, especially when the text is being used to identify the opponents. Again, that sort of circularity provides no real basis for identifying the opponents of a letter.

A more certain identification of the opponents of Colossians must rely on the text of Colossians without imposing an outside movement on that reading. Reading in this mode, I conclude that Colossians opposes teachers who urge others to adopt practices designed to induce visions in which they see angels worship God and participate in that angelic worship. These teachers assert that anyone without this experience is still in sin and so does not have the relationship with God they need for forgiveness and salvation. In this reading, the other teachers do not advocate the practice of venerating angels. The better reading of the evidence, including the language of seeing and entering used in connection with the mystery religions, is that the other teachers attain visions through moderately ascetic practices. It is in these visions that they see angelic worship. I have argued this view in detail elsewhere, and the readings of Martin and Arnold do not dissuade me from it.[16]

Colossians does not oppose these teachers because they attain visions; that was a common experience for early Christians, and Paul was among those with such experiences. Colossians opposes them because they make the acquisition of visions a condition for forgiveness of sin and so for a relationship with God. The writer indicates that this is the central problem by framing the extensive liturgical material he quotes in Col 1:15–20 with assurances of forgiveness through Christ and by his emphasis on baptism as the place one receives forgiveness.

CONCLUSION

The studies of Martin and Arnold are two recent examples of the need evident in studies of opponents for most Pauline letters, including other studies of Colossians, to give more careful attention to the ways we draw on the surrounding culture to inform our understanding of the problems Paul's letters address. When we do not allow reconstructions of other movements or detailed reconstructions of the early church (e.g., those such as Baur's that posit just two or any specific number of types of early believers) to dominate our identifications of opponents, we will gain more clarity about Paul's opponents and the shape of early Christianity. We will be able to recognize a breadth of diversity among

---

[16]See Sumney, "Servants of Satan," 188–213.

early believers that disallows simplistic and false frameworks such as the
"orthodox church" and the "heretics" for the first-century church. We will
see more clearly the multiplicity within the range of beliefs that individuals and groups thought were acceptable, and perhaps something of why
they drew the lines where they did. Even the long-held simple categories
of Jewish Christianity and Gentile Christianity fail to pass the test of
accuracy when we do not start with them as presuppositions. As we pay
better attention to the distinctiveness of the settings of various letters
and especially to how reconstructions of other movements should (and
should not) influence our readings of Pauline letters, we may gain more
precision about the people, practices, and teachings those letters oppose.
In turn, we will understand both the early church and the Pauline letters
more clearly. This is the promise of improving our work of identifying
Paul's opponents.

For Further Reading

Arnold, Clinton E. *The Colossian Syncretism: The Interface between Chris-
tianity and Folk Belief in Colossae.* Grand Rapids, Mich.: Baker, 1996.
———. "Returning to the Domain of the Powers: *Stoicheia* as Evil Spirits
in Galatians 4:3, 9." *NovT* 38 (1996): 55–76.
Aune, David E. *The Cultic Setting of Realized Eschatology in Early Christi-
anity.* NovTSup 28. Leiden: Brill, 1972.
Barclay, John M. G. "Mirror-Reading a Polemical Letter: Galatians as a
Test Case." *JSNT* 31 (1987): 73–93.
Barrett, C. K. "Cephas and Corinth." Pages 1–12 in *Abraham unser Vater;
Juden und Christen im Gespräch über die Bibel.* Edited by O. Betz et
al. Arbeiten zur Geschichte des Späatjudentums und Urchristentums.
Leiden: Brill, 1963.
———. "Christianity at Corinth." *BJRL* 46 (1964): 269–97.
———. "Paul's Opponents in 2 Corinthians." *NTS* 17 (1971): 233–54.
Baur, F. C. "Die Christuspartei in der korinthischen Gemeinde, der Ge-
gensatz des petrinschen und paulinischen Christentum in der äl-
testen Kirche, der Apostel Petrus in Rom." *Tübingen Zeitschrift für
Theologie* 4 (1831): 61–206.
———. *Paul, the Apostle of Jesus Christ—His Life and Work, His Epistles
and Doctrine.* Translated by Eduard Zeller. 2d ed. 2 vols. London: Wil-
liams and Norgate, 1876. Repr., Peabody, Mass.: Hendrickson, 2003.
Bieder, Werner. *Die kolossische Irrlehre und die Kirche von heute.* Theologische Studien 33. Zürich: Evangelischer Verlag, 1952.
———. "Paulus und Seine Gegner in Korinth." *TZ* 17 (1961): 319–33.

Brown, Raymond E. "Not Jewish Christianity and Gentile Christianity but Types of Jewish/Gentile Christianity." *CBQ* 45 (1983): 74–79.

Dahl, Nils A. "Paul and the Church at Corinth according to 1 Corinthians 1:10–4:21." Pages 313–35 in *Christian History and Interpretation*. Edited by W. R. Farmer et al. Cambridge: Cambridge University Press, 1967.

DeMaris, Richard E. *The Colossian Controversy: Wisdom in Dispute at Colossae*. JSNTSup 96. Sheffield: Sheffield Academic Press, 1994.

Dibelius, Martin. "The Isis Initiation in Apuleius and Related Initiatory Rites." Pages 61–122 in *Conflict at Colossae: A Problem in the Interpretation of Early Christianity Illustrated by Selected Modern Studies*. Edited by Wayne A. Meeks and Fred O. Francis. Sources for Biblical Study 4. Missoula, Mont.: SBL, 1973.

Donfried, Karl P. "The Cults of Thessalonica and the Thessalonian Correspondence." *NTS* 31 (1985): 336–56.

Dunn, James D. G. "The Colossian Philosophy: A Confident Jewish Apologia." *Bib* 76 (1995): 153–81.

Ellis, E. Earle. "Paul and His Opponents: Trends in the Research." Pages 264–98 in *Christianity, Judaism, and Other Greco-Roman Cults; Part 1*. Edited by J. Neusner. Leiden: Brill, 1975.

Forbes, Christopher. "Comparison, Self-Praise and Irony: Paul's Boasting and the Conventions of Hellenistic Rhetoric." *NTS* 32 (1986): 1–30.

———. "Paul's Opponents in Corinth." *Buried History* 19 (1983): 19–23.

Francis, Fred O. "The Christological Argument of Colossians." Pages 192–208 in *God's Christ and His People*. Edited by J. Jervell and Wayne A. Meeks. Oslo: Universitetsforlaget, 1977.

———. "Humility and Angelic Worship in Col 2:18." Pages 163–96 in *Conflict at Colossae: A Problem in the Interpretation of Early Christianity Illustrated by Selected Modern Studies*. Edited by Wayne A. Meeks and Fred O. Francis. Sources for Biblical Study 4. Missoula, Mont.: SBL, 1973.

———. "Humility and Angelic Worship in Col 2:18." *ST* 16 (1962): 109–34.

———. "Visionary Discipline and Scriptural Tradition at Colossae." *Lexington Theological Quarterly* 2 (1967): 71–78.

Francis, Fred O., and W. A. Meeks, eds. *Conflict at Colossae: A Problem in the Interpretation of Early Christianity Illustrated by Selected Modern Studies*. Sources for Biblical Study 4. Missoula, Mont.: SBL, 1973.

Freyne, Sean. "Vilifying the Other and Defining the Self: Matthew's and John's Anti-Jewish Polemic in Focus." Pages 117–43 in *"To See Ourselves As Others See Us": Christians, Jews, "Others" in Late Antiq-*

uity. Edited by Jacob Neusner and Ernest S. Frerichs. Studies in the Humanities. Chico, Calif.: Scholars Press, 1985.

Gager, John G. "Jews, Christians and the Dangerous Ones in Between." Pages 249–57 in *Interpretation in Religion.* Edited by S. Biderman and B. A. Scharfstein. Leiden: Brill, 1992.

Georgi, Dieter. *Die Gegner des Paulus im 2 Korintherbrief: Studien zur religiösen Propaganda in der Spätantike.* WMANT 11. Neukirchen: Neukirchener Verlag, 1964. ET: *The Opponents of Paul in Second Corinthians.* Translated by Harold Attridge et al. Philadelphia: Fortress, 1986.

Goulder, Michael D. *St. Paul Versus St. Peter: A Tale of Two Missions.* Louisville, Ky.: Westminster/John Knox, 1994.

Grant, Robert M. "Charges of 'Immorality' against Various Religious Groups in Antiquity." Pages 161–70 in *Studies in Gnosticism and Hellenistic Religions.* Edited by R. van den Broek and M. J. Vermaseren. Leiden: Brill, 1981.

Gunther, J. J. *St. Paul's Opponents and Their Background: A Study of Apocalyptic and Jewish Sectarian Teachings.* NovTSup 35. Leiden: Brill, 1973.

Hooker, Morna D. "Philippians: Phantom *Opponents* and the Real Source of Conflict." Pages 377–95 in *Fair Play: Diversity and Conflicts in Early Christianity: Essays in Honor of Heikki Räisänen.* Edited by Ismo Dunderberg et al. Leiden: Brill, 2002.

———. "Were the False Teachers in Colossae?" Pages 315–31 in *Christ and the Spirit in the New Testament.* Edited by B. Lindars and S. S. Smalley. Cambridge: Cambridge University Press, 1973.

Howard, George. *Crisis in Galatia.* SNTSMS 35. 2d ed. Cambridge: Cambridge University Press, 1990.

Jewett, Robert. "The Agitators and the Galatian Congregation." *NTS* 17 (1971): 198–212.

———. "Conflicting Movements in the Early Church as Reflected in Philippians." *NovT* 12 (1970): 362–90.

Johnson, Luke Timothy. "2 Timothy and the Polemic against False Teachers: A Re-examination." *JRS* 6–7 (1978–79): 1–26.

Lyons, George. *Pauline Autobiography: Toward a New Understanding.* SBLDS 73. Atlanta: Scholars Press, 1985.

Marshall, Peter. "Hybrists Not Gnostics in Corinth." SBL Seminar Papers 23 (1984): 275–87.

———. "Invective: Paul and His Enemies in Corinth." Pages 359–73 in *Perspectives on Language and Text.* Edited by E. W. Conrad and E. G. Newing. Winona Lake, Ind.: Eisenbrauns, 1987.

Martin, Troy. *By Philosophy and Vain Deceit: Colossians as a Response to a Cynic Critique.* JSNTSup 118. Sheffield: Sheffield Academic Press, 1996.

Martyn, J. Louis. "Apocalyptic Antinomies in Paul's Letter to the Galatians." *NTS* 31 (1985): 410–24.

———. "Events in Galatia; Modified Covenantal Nomism versus God's Invasion of the Cosmos in the Singular Gospel: A Response to J. D. G. Dunn and B. R. Gaventa." Pages 160–80 in *Pauline Theology*. Vol. 1: *Thessalonians, Philippians, Galatians, Philemon*. Edited by J. M. Bassler. Minneapolis: Fortress, 1991.

———. "A Law-Observant Mission to Gentiles: The Background of Galatians." *Scottish Journal of Theology* 38 (1985): 307–24.

Nanos, Mark. *The Irony of Galatians: Paul's Letter in First-Century Context*. Minneapolis: Fortress, 2002.

Porter, Stanley E., ed. *Paul and His Opponents*. Pauline Studies. Leiden: Brill, 2005.

Sappington, Thomas J. *Revelation and Redemption at Colossae*. JSNTSup 53. Sheffield: JSOT Press, 1991.

Schmithals, Walter. *Gnosticism in Corinth*. Translated by John E. Steely. Nashville: Abingdon, 1971.

———. *Paul and the Gnostics*. Translated by John E. Steely. Nashville: Abingdon, 1972.

Schweizer, Eduard. "Christianity of the Circumcised and Judaism of the Uncircumcised: The Background of Matthew and Colossians." Pages 245–60 in *Jews, Greeks, and Christians: Religious Cultures in Late Antiquity*. Edited by R. Hamerton-Kelly and R. Scroggs. Leiden: Brill, 1976.

———. "Die 'Elemente der Welt' Gal 4,3. 9; Kol 2,8. 20." Pages 245–59 in *Verborum Veritas*. Edited by O. Böcher and K. Haacker. Wuppertal: Theologischer Verlag Rolf Brockhaus, 1970.

Smith, Jonathan Z. "What a Difference a Difference Makes." Pages 3–48 in *"To See Ourselves as Others See Us": Christians, Jews, "Others" in Late Antiquity*. Edited by Jacob Neusner and Ernest S. Frerichs. Studies in the Humanities. Chico, Calif.: Scholars Press, 1985.

Sumney, Jerry L. *Identifying Paul's Opponents; The Question of Method in 2 Corinthians*. JSNTSup 40. Sheffield: JSOT Press, 1990.

———. *"Servants of Satan," "False Brothers," and Other Opponents of Paul*. JSNTSup 188. Sheffield: Sheffield Academic Press, 1999.

———. "Studying Paul's Opponents: Advances and Challenges." Pages 7–58 in *Paul and His Opponents*. Edited by Stanley E. Porter. Pauline Studies. Leiden: Brill, 2005.

4

Paul and Ethnicity: A Selective History of Interpretation

Charles H. Cosgrove

The question of ethnicity, its nature and value, has become particularly acute in theological circles in recent years. Although not identical with the concept of "race," the idea of ethnicity incorporates elements of older notions of race without taking over the scientifically flawed biological ideas that have historically been part of the modern concept of race. Ethnicity is also related to but not identical with national identity, a form of communal self-understanding which, in its modern forms, is sometimes but not always rooted in ethnic identity.

Over the past two centuries, Paul has been invoked from time to time by those seeking to stake out a Christian position on race or ethnicity. Scholarship has also weighed in, directly and indirectly. Some have interpreted Paul as the advocate of a universal conception of humanity that accords no value to ethnicity. Others have found affirmations of ethnic particularity in Paul.

What follows is a selective and illustrative history of inquiry into Paul's assumptions and teaching about ethnicity that draws on diverse traditions of interpretation: a variety of contributions from Pauline scholarship, a sampling of nineteenth- and twentieth-century African-American perspectives, a nineteenth-century missionary commentary on Romans, a selection of dispensationalist and post-Holocaust perspectives in comparison, a recent Jewish interpretation of Paul, and two new philosophical engagements with Romans.

THE UNIVERSAL (NON-ETHNIC) HUMAN BEING IN PAUL

I will not repeat here the long history[1] of the idea that Christians constitute a *genus tertium* or "third race."[2] Suffice it to say that the concept has
exerted a lasting attractiveness in the West. Nineteenth-century historical
scholarship did not subject it to doubt and critical interrogation but em-
braced it. The influential F. C. Baur, for example, interpreted the Pauline
notion of the new humanity as a universalism beyond ethnic differentiation.[3] No one, least of all Baur himself, considered that his descriptions
of Paul's theology might reflect his particular ethnocultural location and
ethnocentrism. One did not ask such questions of interpretations in Baur's
day, and the intellectual tools for a critical analysis of ideology in interpretation were just being invented.

The view that transethnic universalism is a Pauline ideal persisted
into the twentieth century. Any evidence in Paul tending to undermine
this interpretation was chalked up to Paul's momentary failures to live
up to his ideal. In a brief comment on Rom 11:26, C. H. Dodd charged
Paul with giving in to his own Jewish patriotism when he prophesied the
salvation of "all Israel" according to the elective promises of God.[4] This
prophecy, Dodd maintained, conflicts with the larger, universalistic vision
of Romans. According to Dodd, "the arguments by which Paul asserts
the final salvation of Israel are equally valid (in fact are valid only) if they
are applied to mankind at large."[5] If we understand that Paul's ideal is a
universal humanity, then we should take the thought of 11:26 as expressing the "high destiny" promised to humanity (not just Israel) in "all the

---

[1] In addition to the following interpretations from the history of Pauline
scholarship, a number of other interpretations presented below under other
headings belong equally to the category of Pauline scholarship: the work of Brad
Braxton and Demetrius Williams (under the African-American section), that
of Daniel Boyarin (under recent Jewish interpretation), and some of the contributions discussed under dispensationalist and post-Holocaust interpretation
of Paul.

[2] The relevant patristic texts can be found in Adolf von Harnack, *The Mission and Expansion of Christianity in the First Three Centuries* (vol. 1; trans. James
Moffatt; London: Williams & Norgate, 1904; repr., New York: G. Putnam's Sons,
1904), 300–314, 336–52.

[3] See, for example, F. C. Baur, *The Church History of the First Three Centuries*
(vol. 1; 3d ed.; trans. Allan Menzies; London and Edinburgh: Williams & Norgate,
1878), 47, 59, 73.

[4] C. H. Dodd, *The Epistle of Paul to the Romans* (London: Hodder & Stoughton, 1932), 183–84. See also F. W. Beare, *Paul and His Letters* (London: A&C Black,
1962), 103–4.

[5] Dodd, *Epistle to the Romans,* 184.

great religions."[6] Paul sees Jewish ethnicity as a form of particularism or "patriotism." That patriotism and, *mutatis mutandis,* any other similar particularism or patriotism, is replaced by the gospel's vision of a universal humanity. This is a liberal political reading of Romans, consistent with mid-twentieth-century liberal views about equality and race.

More recently, James Dunn has argued that Paul abandoned the high ethnic self-consciousness characteristic of Jews in his day and did not think of himself as a Jew, except in an inner, spiritual sense.[7] This take on Paul continues a tradition of interpretation represented by Willem van Unnik, for example, in his summarizing comments on Paul and nationalism in a 1955 essay: "we may conclude that while Paul is familiar with national distinctions they are for him totally unimportant; there is no place for nationalistic activity. The centre lies not on earth but in heaven. . . ."[8]

Paul and Anti-Semitism

The story of the use of the NT and the letters of Paul in the ideology of anti-Semitism in the West is well known. In the wake of the Nazi campaign against Jews, Christian theologians began to examine critically not only cultural attitudes of anti-Semitism but also aspects of Christian theology conducive to those attitudes. In the process, they challenged traditional interpretations of what the NT has to say about Jews and marshaled NT evidence to their side in combating anti-Semitism and opening up lines of Jewish-Christian dialogue. Increasing numbers of NT scholars participated in various aspects of this effort, from interfaith conferences to individual scholarship. This work produced a general consensus that Paul's teaching is opposed to any form of anti-Jewish sentiment. Proponents of this consensus worked out a number of exegetical positions in support of it, including variations of the following: that Paul's teaching accommodates distinctive Jewish-Christian self-expression (the right of Jewish Christians to maintain their Jewish identity and not be absorbed into Gentile Christianity)[9] and

---

[6] Ibid., 183.

[7] James D. G. Dunn, "Who Did Paul Think He Was? A Study of Jewish-Christian Identity," *NTS* 45 (1999): 180–82, 192.

[8] W. C. van Unnik, "Christianity and Nationalism in the First Centuries of the Christian Church," in *Sparsa Collecta: The Collected Essays of W. C. van Unnik* (part 3; NovTSup 31; Leiden: Brill, 1983), 85.

[9] William Campbell has argued that Paul's universalism rules out anti-Semitism but makes room for valuing Jewish distinctiveness. See William S. Campbell, "Religious Identity and Ethnic Origin in the Earliest Christian Communities," in *Paul's Gospel in an Intercultural Context: Jew and Gentile in the Letter to the Romans* (Frankfurt: Peter Lang, 1991), 98–121.

that Paul affirms both the Torah for Jews and a new way without the Torah for the Gentiles as two valid ways of salvation.[10]

In recent years, Pauline scholarship has wrestled with how to interpret as a unity (rather than a contradiction) Paul's teaching that the Jewish people have a unique call as Israel, which distinguishes them from the Gentiles, and his equally firm affirmation that God is impartial toward all. Some have spoken of a paradox;[11] others have argued that the two are not in contradiction because they are about different issues and hence do not really compete.[12] In a study of "Israel" in Romans, I have suggested that one possible way to interpret the Jewish people's special election in the light of divine impartiality is to understand that Gentiles as distinct peoples also enjoy a status in God's eyes similar to what Paul affirms for Jews as a people.[13] This never becomes an explicit theme or point in Paul's letters but may be an implication that we can draw to resolve the logical tension between divine impartiality and the special status of Israel in Paul. In that case, there is a basis in Paul for the idea of ethnic diversity in equality, which is something more than saying simply that Gentiles (an ethnically undifferentiated category) are equal to Jews in God's eyes.

Early on, the effort to purge Pauline interpretation of anti-Semitism by means of better exegesis met up with a serious challenge. In a controversial

---

[10] See Lloyd Gaston, *Paul and the Torah* (Vancouver: University of British Columbia Press, 1987), 147–49; John Gager, *Reinventing Paul* (New York: Oxford University Press, 2000), 147. The earliest proponent of this view was apparently Krister Stendahl, who found a basis in Paul for rejecting Christian "religious imperialism" against Judaism and other religions. See Krister Stendahl, *Paul among Jews and Gentiles and Other Essays* (Philadelphia: Fortress, 1976), 132; idem, *Meanings: The Bible as Document and Guide* (Philadelphia: Fortress, 1984), 215.

[11] According to Elizabeth Johnson, Paul maintains a "balanced tension" between God's faithfulness to ethnic Israel and God's impartiality toward all peoples. See E. Elizabeth Johnson, "Romans 9–11: The Faithfulness and Impartiality of God," in *Pauline Theology* (ed. David M. Hay and E. Elizabeth Johnson; vol. 3, *Romans;* Minneapolis: Fortress, 1995), 22.

[12] This is how I interpret Campbell's treatment of these themes in Romans: Paul's affirmation of Israel's unique call is about divine faithfulness; Paul's stress on impartiality is about the equality of Gentiles with Jews; the two themes are also related in that the teaching about the destiny of Israel also counters Gentile prejudice against Jews and is thus functionally similar to the impartiality theme, although it flows from a different theological source. See Campbell, "A Theme for Romans?" in *Paul's Gospel in an Intercultural Context,* 161–99. To my mind, the main difficulty with this and similar views is that they do not ask the prior question, which Paul's emphasis on divine impartiality must have (or logically should have) caused him to ask: how is God's impartiality expressed in relation to the original act of choosing Israel out of all the nations of the earth?

[13] See Charles H. Cosgrove, *Elusive Israel: The Puzzle of Election in Romans* (Louisville, Ky.: Westminster/John Knox, 1997), 65–90.

book, *Faith and Fratricide,* Rosemary Ruether, a Christian theologian and a staunch opponent of anti-Semitism, argued that the roots of Christian anti-Semitism nevertheless *do* go back to earliest Christianity and *are* found in Paul, as well as in other NT writers.[14] Ruether's work has either been ignored or rejected by most Pauline scholars, but her observations stand as a reminder that some of Paul's statements about the Jewish people lend themselves to anti-Jewish uses (whether fairly or unfairly). Paul's own views about Israel and the Jewish people are complicated enough and at points what he writes is obscure enough (at least for us) to resist clear exegetical solutions to many of the questions we ask. Historical-critical rigor requires honesty about the multiple ways in which Paul's statements can be reasonably construed.[15]

"Separate but Equal" in Paul?

In a series of lectures delivered at Union Seminary in Virginia in 1942 and subsequently published in a little-known book on social ethics in Paul, Holmes Rolston examined Paul's teaching about Jews and Gentiles from the standpoint of "the order of race."[16] Speaking as a conservative white Southerner and operating on the assumption that a faithful portrait of Paul must rely on all the NT letters attributed to him and also on the portrait of Paul in Acts, Rolston reached the following conclusions:

(1) The racial feeling of the Jews was religious and messianic, the conviction of having a national mission in history as bearers of God's revelation. This racial feeling, expressed in exclusivism, at times became "narrow and selfish."[17] But the ancient Jewish heritage also displays universal concern for all people.

(2) The racial exclusivism of the Jews has a positive side. "The world owes far more to the Jews who refused to be absorbed in the Gentile world than it does to the ten tribes who became lost in the life of Assyria."[18] Although racial feeling often leads to excesses that should be condemned, "[a] people which intermarries will in time become a people absorbed."[19]

(3) Paul, in his words to King Agrippa in Acts 26:26–27 and in his remarks in Rom 3:1–2, shows that he affirms Israel's messianic destiny, which can be ful-

---

[14]Rosemary Ruether, *Faith and Fratricide: The Theological Roots of Anti-Semitism* (New York: Seabury, 1974), 95–107.

[15]See Cosgrove, *Elusive Israel,* 97–100.

[16]Holmes Rolston, *The Social Message of the Apostle Paul: The James Sprunt Lectures, 1942* (Richmond: John Knox, 1942), 124–54.

[17]Ibid., 125.

[18]Ibid.

[19]Ibid.

filled in and for the world only if Israel maintains a strong racial consciousness. A "strong racial consciousness and a narrow racial exclusivism" are typically found in a people that believes itself to be the bearer of something important to the world. Not only Jews but also Greeks, the Romans, the Anglo-Saxons, the Russians, the Germans, and the Japanese have exhibited such a racial consciousness, conceiving themselves as bearers of some ideal in history.[20]

(4) Paul preached a universal faith that came in "conflict with Jewish nationalism and Jewish racial exclusiveness."[21] Through Paul, Christianity became more than a "movement within Judaism"[22] and "passed to the Gentile world."[23] "Paul built in the Roman empire a fellowship in which the divisions of race were transcended."[24]

5) In his speech on Mars Hill, Paul looks at humanity as a biological unity. But he also recognizes human variety when he says that "God has determined 'their appointed seasons, and the bounds of their habitation.'"[25] This suggests that "Paul would not object to certain races occupying definite portions of the surface of the earth or discharging a peculiar function in history."[26]

(6) The refusal of whites in the American South and in other parts of the world to be absorbed through intermarriage and cultural assimilation into other races and cultures has not been based only on racial prejudice. It has also "usually represented on the part of the white man the feeling that only by this method could his civilization and his culture be preserved."[27] "It may be that in the end the Anglo-Saxon races in various parts of the globe will have best served the undeveloped races of the earth through their decision to preserve their culture by remaining white."[28] "No Christian white man could defend the racial injustice that goes on within the South today, but we must recognize that underlying this injustice there is a decision of a portion of the white race to remain white."[29]

(7) Paul calls believers to remain in the state in which they were called, a principle that applies to racial identity on the individual level because the individual cannot change society and also "cannot at once break from his whole racial inheritance."[30] Nevertheless, "*Christianity has utterly no inner*

---

[20] Ibid., 126–27.
[21] Ibid., 130.
[22] Ibid., 129.
[23] Ibid., 130.
[24] Ibid., 135.
[25] Ibid., 136.
[26] Ibid.
[27] Ibid., 146.
[28] Ibid., 147.
[29] Ibid.
[30] Ibid., 149–50.

interest in the preservation for one race of a privileged position as over against another race. . . . *The inner drive of Christianity is always toward the building of a society in which the brotherhood of all mankind is realized.*"[31]

(8) "Paul was quite willing to leave the outer form of the orders of society untouched if he was permitted to build within the fellowship of the church a new society in which the unity of all mankind in Christ was realized."[32] "The basic criticism of the church in the South is not that she has failed to make a frontal attack on the whole of the racial situation. The church would misunderstand the nature of her task in society if she identified herself with this principle of violent revolution."[33] The true task of the church in society "is to realize in her own inner life the unity of all men in Christ."[34]

From the preceding it is evident that Rolston wants Southern churches to become racially integrated, Southern society to remain segregated to preserve white culture, and Southern blacks to have equal rights with whites. Mixed into his attacks on American racism are views that most of us today regard as racist. He appears to operate with no feeling for African Americans as a people with a distinctive culture worth preserving but sees blacks as a threat to white culture. He expresses racist fears of miscegenation, as if preserving culture requires racial purity. In this he apparently assumes that race is a viable biological concept, which it is not. He also seems to imply that blacks are culturally inferior to whites, and he operates with some version of white people's manifest destiny.

Divine Impartiality in Paul

In a 1964 essay, "The Doctrine of Justification: Its Social Function and Implications," Nils Dahl commented on the question of racial prejudice from the perspective of Paul.[35] Dahl stressed that Paul's teaching about justification by faith expresses his view that there is no distinction between Jews and Gentiles.[36] This conviction about God's impartiality is the basis for Paul's attacks on any behaviors in the church that involve the elevation of one group over another. Hence, Paul opposes favoritism, the treatment

---

[31] Ibid., 151 (emphasis original).

[32] Ibid., 152.

[33] Ibid., 153.

[34] Ibid.

[35] Nils A. Dahl, "The Doctrine of Justification: Its Social Function and Implications," in *Studies in Paul: Theology for the Early Christian Mission* (Minneapolis: Augsburg, 1977), 95–120 (originally published in *Norsk teologisk tidsskrift* in 1964).

[36] Ibid., 108 (# 4). Dahl emphasized the theme of divine impartiality in his comments about racial discrimination.

of some as second-class Christians, the superior attitudes of the so-called strong in despising the so-called weak, and so forth.[37]

By understanding justification by faith as based in something even more fundamental in Paul's thinking—his conviction that the gospel expresses God's impartiality—Dahl aimed to show that racial equality is not secondary to the evangelical ministry of the church. Overcoming racial discrimination belongs within the preaching of the gospel itself as a central part of the church's mission.[38]

According to Dahl, Paul does not ask Jews or Gentiles to give up their ethnic identities. "As Christians, Gentiles should remain part of the ethnic group from which they came, Greek, Galatian, or whatever."[39] But the church must embody the principle of impartiality. If it had done so faithfully in the United States and elsewhere, this "would have meant far more than countless pious appeals for tolerance, far more than demonstrations; it would also have made it easier to find political solutions to racial problems."[40] Perhaps with racial problems still in view but thinking as well of class distinctions, Dahl suggested that the principle of impartiality is contradicted by the church when "full acceptance into a suburban congregation presuppose[s] a certain social standard and certain patterns of behavior."[41] These and other such social and cultural requirements are the "ceremonial and ritual law of our time."[42]

Interpretations of Gal 3:28

The baptismal formula of Gal 3:28 has figured prominently in discussions of Paul and ethnicity. In an essay dealing with this passage and its significance for gender distinctions, Judith Gundry-Volf also touched on the question of ethnicity.[43] For Paul, she opined, religio-ethnic and gender distinctions are *adiaphora* (matters of indifference) in Christ. The gospel

---

[37] These are highlights of Dahl's discussion of the social implications of justification in "The Doctrine of Justification," 108–13.

[38] Ibid., 119.

[39] Although Dahl did not reassert this Pauline principle in his discussion of racial discrimination, I quote it here because it has relevance for how one thinks about Pauline solutions to racial conflict. The statement occurs at the beginning of Dahl's discussion of the social implications of justification ("The Doctrine of Justification," 108).

[40] Ibid., 119–20.

[41] Ibid., 120.

[42] Ibid., 120 (see also 119).

[43] Judith Gundry-Volf, "Christ and Gender: A Study of Difference and Equality in Gal. 3:28," in *Jesus Christus als die Mitte der Schrift* (ed. Christof Landmesser et al.; Berlin: Walter de Gruyter, 1997), 439–77.

does not erase but preserves them; in preserving them, however, the gospel also relativizes them. Hence, the expression "no longer Jew or Greek" means both Jew and Greek on equal terms in their distinctive identities. It is important to Paul that Gentiles remain Gentiles and not become Jews; likewise Jews should not become Gentiles (1 Cor 7:18–19). Paul calls not for the obliteration of differences but for a revalorization of them: being a Jew or Gentile does not matter for the new creation in Christ. Preserving distinctions under this new value system is important not because the distinctions count in themselves but because to do otherwise would suggest that one ethnic-religious or gender identity counts more than others. If Gentiles become Jews or Jews become Gentiles in an effort to express the end of distinctions, they would simply be reinstating the valorization of these differences.

Another treatment of Gal 3:28, which comes to similar conclusions, is William Campbell's argument that Gal 3:28 abrogates inequality, not distinctions. According to Campbell, Paul's understanding of "male and female" in Christ does not entail a present obliteration of differences but only some kind of equality. *Mutatis mutandis*, the end of "Jew or Gentile" does not spell the end of ethnic distinctions.[44] Campbell's interpretation differs from Gundry-Volf's in that he sees differences relativized but not turned into *adiaphora*. They remain important in the gospel, and Paul makes room for them in the interest of diversity. Brad Braxton has recently made the same point about Gal 3:28. I describe his position below in the section on African-American interpretations of Paul.

Another NT scholar who has discussed the bearing of Gal 3:28 on our question is J. Louis Martyn. In a 1982 essay, Martyn recalled a faculty meeting at Union Theological Seminary in New York when the question of the "make-up" of the faculty was discussed with "an accent on what was phrased as 'the imperative of appointing more blacks and women.'"[45] Reconstructing the tenor of the ensuing discussion, Martyn remembered that one faculty member invoked Gal 3:28 as support for the proposition that faculty appointments should not be based on considerations of gender or race.[46] But another colleague observed that "[i]n order to perceive that this Seminary Faculty is not in Christ [as Gal 3:28 defines it], all one

---

[44] Campbell, "Religious Identity and Ethnic Origins in the Earliest Christian Communities," 110. Campbell also suggests that even if Gal 3:28 is open to competing interpretations, the analogy to Paul's discussion of male/female relations in the Corinthian correspondence provides a valuable guide to his views about Jews and Gentiles.

[45] J. Louis Martyn, "Galatians 3:28, Faculty Appointments, and Overcoming Christological Amnesia," *Katallagete* 8/1 (1982): 40–44.

[46] Ibid., 40.

needs to do is to glance around this room! The discrepancy between the text you have cited [Gal 3:28] and the present 'make-up' of the faculty shows that the text is, in fact, a summons to justice."[47] Pondering Paul's baptismal formula in the light of this exchange, Martyn came to the following conclusions:

> (1) Gal 3:28 does not sanction the status quo; it is a "counter-culture text."[48]
>
> (2) Gal 3:28 "is not a summons to what Caesar calls justice,"[49] even the justice of liberal Caesars.[50]
>
> (3) Gal 3:28 is a "thoroughly apocalyptic text about God's victorious call to life in the real world," but it does not express this call in the imperative mood of command but speaks rather in the indicative mood of God's new creation.[51]

Martyn called for the church to adopt a "bifocal" reading of the world, in which one sees the world as it is in Christ (Gal 3:28) and also as it is under the continuing influence of the old age. Paul expresses this kind of bifocal vision in his apocalyptic ὡς μή ("as if not") in 1 Cor 7. Paul is "a person *who noticed as though not noticing* that some of his colleagues in the Theological Faculty at Ephesus were women, while others were men."[52] Applying this to the question of ethnicity, we might say that Martyn's Paul cares about ethnicity as though not caring and does so in a way that has disruptive apocalyptic significance.

Paul contra Ethnocentrism

In the traditional Protestant picture of ancient Judaism, the Jewish religion is a legalistic program for earning one's own salvation; in Pauline language it is works righteousness. This view was perpetuated in Pauline scholarship until sometime in the early 1980s, when the field as a whole began to embrace E. P. Sanders's arguments against it in *Paul and Palestinian Judaism*, published in 1977.[53] Since the 1980s, alternative interpreta-

---

[47] Ibid.

[48] Ibid., 41.

[49] Ibid.

[50] Martyn offered as an illustration of Caesar's justice an assertion by Supreme Court Justice Harry Blackmun that in order to overcome racism it is sometimes necessary to take account of race. Martyn commented: "Before rushing to apply that remark to the making of Faculty appointments in a *theological* seminary, we do well to realize that it is the sort of thing an enlightened Caesar may say, but it is all that Caesar *can* say" ("Galatians 3:28," 44).

[51] Ibid.

[52] Ibid., 43 (emphasis original).

[53] E. P. Sanders, *Paul and Palestinian Judaism: A Study of Patterns of Religion* (Philadelphia: Fortress, 1977). For an insightful survey of the debate since the

tions of Paul, the law, and Jewish piety have been proposed. One of these is the so-called New Perspective, a term introduced by Krister Stendahl and adopted by James Dunn as a programmatic descriptor in his influential lecture, "The New Perspective on Paul."[54]

The New Perspective has become closely associated with Dunn's interpretation of "works of the law" in Paul as badges of ethnic identity. According to this view, Paul did not claim that Jews use works to justify themselves and thus win salvation through their own merits; he opposes "works of the law" as expressions of ethnic distinctiveness. Paul is challenging the "racial" and "ethnic" boasting[55] of Jews, their "ethnic pride" and "nationalistic zeal,"[56] which were based in the law and expressed by fidelity to those commandments that marked Jews off from Gentiles (circumcision, Sabbath observance, and dietary laws).

Some have suggested that Dunn's way of interpreting "works of the law" in Paul risks becoming a new form of anti-Jewish interpretation.[57] If Paul attacks ethnocentrism, is this a specifically Jewish trait? Or is it characteristic of many if not most ancient peoples (and non-ancient peoples)? It is important to stress that Dunn has no intention of repeating in a new form the kind of anti-Jewish interpretation characteristic of the past. Dunn, although he thinks that Jewish nationalism was pervasive in Paul's day, also stresses that this holds for Paul's time, not all times, and that it was a matter of overemphasis on Jewish distinctiveness by some but not all first-century Jews.[58]

---

publication of Sanders's book, see Stephen Westerholm, *Perspectives Old and New on Paul: The "Lutheran" Paul and His Critics* (Grand Rapids, Mich.: Eerdmans, 2003).

[54] See Stendahl, *Paul among Jews and Gentiles,* 95; James D. G. Dunn, "The New Perspective on Paul," in *Jesus, Paul, and the Law: Studies in Mark and Galatians* (London: SPCK, 1990), 183–206 (originally presented as the Manson Memorial Lecture at the University of Manchester, 4 November 1982).

[55] N. T. Wright, "Romans and the Theology of Paul," in *Pauline Theology* (ed. David M. Hay and E. Elizabeth Johnson; vol. 3, *Romans;* Minneapolis: Fortress, 1995), 141; idem, *The Climax of the Covenant: Christ and the Law in Pauline Thought* (Edinburgh: T&T Clark, 1991), 240–42; idem, *What Saint Paul Really Said* (Oxford: Lion, 1997), 129.

[56] James D. G. Dunn, *Romans 1–8* (WBC 38A; Dallas: Word, 1988), lxxii. On the New Perspective and the question of ethnicity, see John M. G. Barclay, "Neither Jew Nor Greek: Multiculturalism and the New Perspective on Paul," in *Ethnicity and the Bible* (ed. Mark G. Brett; Leiden: Brill, 1996), 197–214.

[57] Neil Elliott raises this question in *Liberating Paul: The Justice of God and the Politics of the Apostle* (Maryknoll, N.Y.: Orbis, 1994), 70–71.

[58] This is how I interpret the careful language in, for example, James D. G. Dunn, *The Epistle to the Galatians* (London: A&C Black, 1993), 172; idem, *Jesus, Paul, and the Law,* 249–50. Stendahl (*Paul among Jews and Gentiles,* 132), who in

Robert Jewett's interpretation of Paul shares certain features with
Dunn's, particularly a social framing of the question of "works of the law"
in Romans. According to Jewett, Paul's understanding of the cross "reveals
a fundamental distortion of honor-shame relations in which a universal
desire for superior status ends up in a hostile assault on God."[59] Paul regards his past self as an example of this. His desire for superior status led
him to persecute the church out of misguided loyalty to the Mosaic law. As
a believer in Christ, Paul now sees this loyalty as an expression of sin and
a typical way in which sin operates as a blinding and enslaving power in a
Jewish cultural context, where sin (or "the flesh") turns the Mosaic law into
"a system of status acquisition."[60] Thus, at the social level the law becomes a
vehicle for national zealotry and religious bigotry against non-Jews, who
are regarded as inferior.[61] At the personal level, the individual shares in
the pleasure of group honor and is encouraged to seek individual honor
through the law and other means. But these are not just Jewish tendencies.
The whole Greco-Roman society manifests impulses to zealotry, bigotry,
and status seeking.[62] Hence, the Jewish way of using the Mosaic law (and
divine election) as a ground of social superiority is simply an example of
a pervasive aspect of Greco-Roman culture; everyone is engaged in status
seeking, in one way or other, within the competitive system of an honor/
shame-based society. Paul sees all of this as a basic perversion of God's
intention for human community. In response, Paul teaches the "revolutionary equality of all nations";[63] his gospel excludes "boasting of either
ethnic or theological superiority."[64]

William Herzog, building on the work of Stendahl, found an attack
on Jewish-Christian ethnocentrism in Galatians and an attack on both
Jewish-Christian and Gentile-Christian ethnocentrism in Romans.[65] Following Melville Herskovits, Herzog distinguished between a mild form of
ethnocentrism that involves no more than a healthy affirmation of one's
own culture and stronger types of ethnocentrism that absolutize their own

---

important ways has been an inspiration to the New Perspective, expressly aims to
overcome interpretations of Paul in which Judaism becomes "a code word for all
wrong attitudes toward God."

[59] Robert Jewett, *Romans: A Commentary* (assisted by Roy D. Kotansky; ed.
Eldon J. Epp; Hermeneia; Minneapolis: Fortress, 2007), 158.

[60] Ibid., 467, 468.

[61] Ibid., 469–70.

[62] Ibid., 46–59. See also 296 and 466, where Jewett stresses that Jews are not
exceptional in their tendencies to cultural boasting, zealotry, or bigotry.

[63] Ibid., 299.

[64] Ibid., 301.

[65] William R. Herzog II, "The New Testament and the Question of Racial
Justice," *American Baptist Quarterly* 5 (1986): 25–26 (12–32).

culture, becoming intolerant of others.[66] Although Herzog did not stress the value of ethnicity (his focus being on resources in the NT against racism), the implication of his use of Herskovits's model seems to be that Paul attacks the strong, absolutizing form of ethnocentrism, not the mild form.[67]

According to John Barclay, Paul does not deny all positive significance to cultural specificities but relativizes them in such a way that "Jews and Gentiles are simultaneously *affirmed* as Jews and Gentiles and *humbled* in their cultural pretensions."[68] Thus, in Rom 14, Paul shows himself to be tolerant of cultural differences but not in a way that supports cultural distinctives as a core identity. Hence, the so-called weak at Rome are not likely to be happy with Paul's position because his "relativization" of the significance of cultural differences "somehow threatens the very seriousness with which they are taken by their practitioners."[69] Barclay affirmed Daniel Boyarin's call for a dialectical synthesis that combines shared values in human solidarity with the preservation of differences that make for distinctive cultural identities (on Boyarin see further below) and concluded that Paul may be a positive resource in contemporary efforts at this kind of multiculturalism.[70] Nevertheless, he cautioned, an impediment to embracing Paul as such a resource is his christological exclusivism, which seems to set up a new religious particularism in place of the cultural particularism he rejects. This impediment can be overcome, Barclay proposed, if we recognize that Paul's radical teaching about the grace of God at least "partially deconstructs his . . . Christological exclusivism."[71] It is hard to imagine that Paul himself would have recognized this as a valid inference, but Barclay was suggesting that interpreters today can draw this inference.[72]

---

[66]Ibid., 13–14.

[67]In describing Paul's relativization of culture/ethnicity, Herzog wrote of Paul's rejection of "zealous" or "malignant" ethnocentrism ("The New Testament and the Question of Racial Justice," 24, 29) which I take to be the strong, "distorted" type (see 14) but sometimes simply wrote without a qualifier of Paul's rejection of ethnocentrism (25, 30). So it is not altogether clear whether Herzog meant that Paul's relativization of ethnicity preserved the value of what Herzog earlier in his essay (in his introduction) called "wholesome" ethnocentrism (14).

[68]Barclay, "Neither Jew Nor Greek," 211 (emphasis original).

[69]Ibid., 212.

[70]Ibid., 212–13.

[71]Ibid., 213.

[72]I understand Barclay's use of the postmodern term "deconstructs" to have the loose (not technical philosophical) sense that a writing entails internal contradictions of which the author was unaware and hence invites readers to draw inferences beyond those of the author and perhaps even against the author's own convictions.

Paul and Ethnicity in African-American Perspective

Already in the eighteenth century but especially in the years leading up to the Civil War, popular interpretations of the Bible engaged the
question of ethnic identity in terms of the concept of race and the question of slavery.[73] Passages from Paul's letters were sometimes discussed in
these debates but usually in a kind of proof-texting way that did not pay
attention to context or to Paul's own way of framing the questions in his
historical and ecclesial situation. Nevertheless, uses of Paul and allusions
to Paul could be insightful and provocative. Consider the following words
from an 1853 address entitled "Our Rights as Man," by black abolitionist
William Watkins. He was speaking to white America:

> You are the Jews, the chosen people of the Lord, and we are the poor rejected
> Gentiles. But the times of refreshing are still coming from the presence of the
> Lord, and we wait, with anxious expectation, the arrival of the auspicious era;
> for then, we trust, the fullness of the Gentiles will be brought in.[74]

Here we meet allusions to Acts 3:19 ("times of refreshing") and Rom 11:25
("the fullness of the Gentiles"). The allusions suggest a typology in which
white America is cast as a type of Israel and black America is "the Gentiles."
The "times of refreshing" in Acts 3 are coming for the people of Israel on
the condition that they repent. But Watkins is not talking about Peter's
Jewish audience in the first century; he has in mind white America in the
nineteenth century. His implication is that times of refreshing for white
America will come only if white America repents its racist attitudes and
practices. Likewise, if the fullness of the Gentiles stands for blacks, then
it is the inclusion—the emancipation—of blacks that must precede any
hope for white America, which is imagined (via Rom 11) as blind Israel,
opposed to God's messianic purposes. All of this is ironic rhetorical play,
telegraphed in a few carefully chosen biblical phrases to make the point,
"Why should *you* be a chosen people more than *we*?"[75] Of special interest for us is that Watkins interprets the Pauline gospel to the Gentiles in
nationalistic, not individualistic, terms.

A more developed black nationalist interpretation of Paul, also focusing on Rom 11:25, was offered by Theophilus Steward in an 1888 book,

---

[73] The following is based on Charles H. Cosgrove, "Paul in African American
Perspective," in *Cross-Cultural Paul: Journeys to Others, Journeys to Ourselves* (ed.
Charles H. Cosgrove et al.; Grand Rapids, Mich.: Eerdmans, 2006).

[74] William Watkins, "Our Rights as Man," in *The Voice of Black America: Major
Speeches by Negroes in the United States* (ed. Philip S. Foner; New York: Simon &
Schuster, 1972), 135.

[75] Ibid., 139 (emphasis original).

The End of the World; or, Clearing the Way for the Fullness of the Gentiles.[76]
In this study and in two subsequent responses to critics, Steward presented a historicizing interpretation of biblical eschatology, arguing that the "end of the world" spoken of in biblical prophecy refers to the end of the present age but not to the end of history. Steward interpreted Rom 11:25 (together with other eschatological passages) within the framework of a then-popular Christian philosophy of history, according to which God guides history and nations toward the earthly kingdom of God. Steward's version of this process has four great epochs: the patriarchal age, the Jewish age, the present age (which he calls the "Roman" age), and the future millennial age, which he expects to appear soon. Steward, reacting to the white racist ideology of Josiah Strong's popular book, *Our Country,*[77] held that the Anglo-Saxon race, far from being the pinnacle and destiny of the civilizing kingdom of God in the world, is in fact the last great impediment to that kingdom. The kingdom will truly dawn only when the fullness of the Gentiles comes in, that is, when the Afro-Asiatic peoples embrace the gospel and establish justice and peace. As Steward put it, after "[t]he westward wave of civilization will have reached the ultimate shore and have dissipated itself upon the obstructing beach,"[78] God's promise to bless many nations through Abraham will finally touch the remaining two-thirds of the world. Then, "a new era of righteousness shall prevail, and the peaceful, loving spirit of the Lord Jesus Christ shall reign over all the earth."[79] Again, of special interest for us is Steward's nationalistic way of reading references to the Gentiles in Paul. Gentiles are not non-Jewish "individuals" devoid of ethnic identity; they are peoples. But we also note the reverse racism of Steward's vision and especially the ominous expression "clearing the way" with its connotations of a divine ethnic cleansing.

Since the rise of Black Power and multiculturalism, an increasing number of African Americans have come to read Paul out of a dialectic of integrationism *and* black nationalism,[80] non-discrimination *and* ethnic self-affirmation. For example, many of my African-American students

---

[76] Theophilus Gould Steward, *The End of the World; or, Clearing the Way for the Fullness of the Gentiles,* with an Exposition of Psalm 68:31 by James A. Handy (Philadelphia: A.M.E. Church Books, 1888).

[77] Josiah Strong, *Our Country: Its Possible Future and Its Present Crisis* (New York: Baker & Taylor, 1885).

[78] Steward, *The End of the World,* 62.

[79] Ibid., 69–71.

[80] These are James Cone's terms for two dominant impulses present in the thinking of virtually every influential African-American figure. See James H. Cone, *Martin and Malcolm and America: A Dream or a Nightmare* (Maryknoll, N.Y.: Orbis, 1991), 4 and passim.

interpret Gal 3:28 as supporting the concept "black is beautiful" and as not only providing a basis for individual equality but also for valuing diverse cultural and ethnic identities in Christ. (But they also report that the churches they come from typically interpret Gal 3:28 as a basis for racial equality but not racial self-affirmation, black pride, and so on.)

Demetrius Williams has noted an ambivalence in African-American scholarship toward any programmatic use of Gal 3:28 in Christian theology and community formation.[81] The passage strikes some as a positive principle in its affirmation of equality but a liability in its implication that cultural distinctions no longer hold. "Some African Americans fear that the phrase 'no longer . . . but all are one' will lead to the loss of cultural/ethnic identity and uniqueness" in an America, where reclaiming and developing African-American cultural heritage is still a vital agenda for blacks.[82] Against this reservation, Williams has urged recognition that the use of Gal 3:28 by African Americans in generations past served egalitarian claims without undermining ethnic identity and pride.[83]

In recent decades black evangelist Tom Skinner[84] has insisted in his preaching that Paul's gospel does not eliminate ethnic difference, as if it were an irrelevant category, but includes and affirms it. Skinner criticized those who use Gal 3:28 to ask others to give up their culture while the dominant culture remains in place and regulative. According to Skinner, Gal 3:28 means the end of the worldly, discriminatory connotations that get attached to ethnic and other differences but not the end of those differences themselves. Skinner described Paul as an example of someone who, far from forsaking his cultural identity, was so passionately Jewish that he was willing to be cursed for the sake of his own people. The allusion here is to Rom 9:1–5, where Paul calls on the Holy Spirit as witness to his love for his people according to the flesh. In Skinner's view, Paul's celebration of Jewish identity is not an instance of ethnocentrism but an ethnic self-affirmation that God approves, so long as it is not discriminatory.

In a thoughtful book work directed toward the black church, Braxton also treated Gal 3:28 as a warrant for both diversity and equality. Diversity

---

[81] Demetrius K. Williams, "The Bible and Models of Liberation in the African-American Experience," in *Yet with a Steady Beat: Contemporary U.S. Afrocentric Biblical Interpretation* (ed. Randall C. Bailey; Semeia Studies 42; Atlanta: SBL, 2003), 33–59 (see 57–58).

[82] Ibid., 57.

[83] Ibid., 57–58.

[84] The following description of Skinner's interpretations of Gal 3:28 and Rom 9:2–3 is based on *Tom Skinner: The New Community* (video; Tracy's Landing, Md.: Tom Skinner Associates, n.d.), which presents a group of speeches by Skinner dating probably to the 1980s or 1990s.

means freedom from the "tyranny of sameness," as he puts it.[85] We should not take Gal 3:28 as a basis for abolishing social distinctions, since Gal 3:28 proclaims "not the obliteration of distinctions but rather the obliteration of *dominance*."[86] Hence, oneness in Christ does not mean "an amalgamated or undifferentiated identity" but rather practices of equality and mutuality "in the midst of our many differences."[87] The miracle of unity becomes evident only when "the social distinctions that define us are present and even accentuated."[88] Differences are therefore not *adiaphora*. Hence, Gal 3:28 expresses God's gift of freedom in Christ "to say 'Yes' to blackness."[89]

Braxton qualified this interpretation of Paul by noting that when Paul defends Gentile equality with Jews he "does not appear to be encouraging the Galatians to say 'yes' to Gentile culture *per se*."[90] Hence, "Paul's assessment of cultural distinction," Braxton suggested, "could be described as a 'negative' understanding, namely one that defined Gentile identity by what it was not."[91] In other words, as a Jew, who thinks of ethnic identity in Jewish categories, Paul aims to preserve non-Jewish identity and, in this qualified sense, "Paul preached a law-free gospel among the Gentiles in order to ensure ethnic diversity in the church."[92]

Zulu Nationalism in Bishop Colenso's Commentary on Romans

An interesting foray into the interpretation of Romans by an outsider to the guild of NT scholarship is Bishop John William Colenso's commentary on Romans. Colenso, an Anglican missionary to the Zulu people of Natal in Africa during the latter half of the nineteenth century, published his Romans commentary in 1861.[93] Written for English-speaking

---

[85]Brad Braxton, *No Longer Slaves: Galatians and African-American Experience* (Collegeville, Minn.: Liturgical Press, 2002), 94.

[86]Ibid., 94 (emphasis original).

[87]Ibid., 94–95.

[88]Ibid., 95.

[89]Ibid.

[90]Ibid., 70.

[91]Ibid.

[92]Ibid., 94.

[93]J. W. Colenso, *St. Paul's Epistle to the Romans: Newly Translated, and Explained from a Missionary Point of View* (Ekuhanyeni, South Africa, 1861; repr., Bishop John William Colenso, *Commentary on Romans* [ed. with an introduction by Jonathan A. Draper; Pietermaritzburg, South Africa: Cluster Publications, 2003]). In what follows, I rely heavily on Jonathan A. Draper, "Colenso's

readers (above all the Church of England) from a missionary perspective, the commentary anticipated the twentieth-century emphasis in Pauline scholarship on the significance of justification by faith for ethnic ("racial," "national") identities and relations. Colenso's commentary was a focus of a Society of Biblical Literature seminar in Nashville in 2000 (Romans through History and Culture),[94] and Robert Jewett's recent commentary on Romans is dedicated to the memory of Colenso.[95]

Although Colenso wrote of the Zulu people in patronizing ways at points, perhaps with an eye to his European audience, his commentary was in many respects an attack on European imperialism and a defense of Zulu cultural identity. Colenso argued that no church existed in Rome when Paul wrote his letter to the Romans. It was not to a church that Paul wrote but to Jews and Gentile proselytes to Judaism who had come to a basic belief in Jesus as the Messiah but remained attached to the synagogue. The Jewish believers were imbued with racial pride based on their election and their adherence to the law. Paul countered this religio-ethnic prejudice with the doctrine of justification by faith, which expresses God's impartiality toward all peoples. This may sound like F. C. Baur, a nineteenth-century scholar who cast Pauline Christianity as the overcoming of parochial Jewish ex-clusivism for the sake of universal humanity, a take on Paul that, wittingly or not, fed upon and encouraged European anti-Semitism. The difference in Colenso is that he expressly aimed his interpretation of justification by faith at European prejudice against Jews, arguing that contemporary Jews are not deserving of the negative caricatures applied to them by Christians and that their resistance to the Christian gospel is understandable given Christians' abominable treatment of them.[96]

References to Colenso's own time are rare in the commentary, but by attending to the social setting of the commentary, the controversies surrounding it, and evidence elsewhere of Colenso's attitudes and aims, Jonathan Draper has discovered an anti-imperialist message between the

---

Commentary on Romans: An Exegetical Assessment," in *The Eye of the Storm: Bishop John William Colenso and the Crisis of Biblical Inspiration* (ed. Jonathan A. Draper; London: T&T Clark, 2003), 104–25.

[94] The papers and responses from this seminar can be found in K. K. Yeo, ed., *Navigating Romans through Cultures: Challenging Readings by Charting a New Course* (Reading Romans through History and Cultures Series 3; London: T&T Clark [Continuum]), 2004. The paper on Colenso is Jonathan Draper, "A 'Frontier' Reading of Romans: The Case of John William Colenso (1814–1883)."

[95] Jewett, *Romans*, dedication page. There are also quotations from Colenso here and there.

[96] Colenso made a clear distinction between ancient Jews and modern Jews and argued that it is no longer Jews but Christians (and missionaries) who practice bigotry and cruelty toward other peoples (*Commentary on Romans*, 51).

lines.[97] In this reading, Colenso developed an implicit typological application of Paul's teaching about Jews and Gentiles. The imperialist European colonists correspond to the arrogant and hidebound Jews of Romans, and contemporary Jews and the Zulu people are the Gentiles against whom Paul's Jews assert their "boast." Hence, Colenso's typological application of Romans to his own time was in effect a rejection of all forms of ethnocentrism in any time and place.[98] In working out the logic of Romans along these lines, Colenso did not argue for a notion of universal humanity against national/cultural distinctions. More specifically, he did not fall into the missionary error of assuming that his own culture was universal and, on that basis, invite others to conform to his culture as if Europeanization were God's plan for a universal humanity. Rather, his interpretation of Paul was an important part of Colenso's overall theology, which "encouraged the emergence of a Zulu national identity and cultural revival."[99]

Paul and Ethnicity in Recent Jewish Interpretation

Over the years, a number of Jewish thinkers—including theologians, philosophers, and specialists in Jewish antiquity—have applied themselves to Paul. Some have touched indirectly or by implication on the question of ethnicity in Paul. In *Two Types of Faith,* Jewish philosopher Martin Buber argued that while Paul speaks of Jews and Greeks, he never does so "in connexion with the reality of their nationalities."[100] Paul is "only concerned with the newly-established community, which by nature is not a nation."[101] By contrast, talmudic scholar Daniel Boyarin has proposed that Paul's theology is fundamentally about human identity and in ways that clearly implicate ethnic identity.

---

[97] In addition to Draper's article, "Colenso's Commentary on Romans," see also his introduction to Colenso's *Commentary on Romans,* ix–xxxix.

[98] Draper, "Colenso's Commentary on Romans," 116.

[99] Ibid., 125. Draper argued that Colenso's affirmation of Zulu national identity and cultural revival was connected to Colenso's interpretation of revelation and justification by faith in Romans. Colenso understood justification by faith as entailing the equality of all peoples, and he affirmed a concept of natural religion as true knowledge of God accessible to all humanity through conscience. These two interpretations contributed to Colenso's conviction that Zulu culture could express divine revelation in the same way that Europeans thought of their own culture as founded on divine revelation (in Scripture). See Draper, "Colenso's Commentary on Romans," 121–24.

[100] Martin Buber, *Two Types of Faith* (trans. Norman P. Goldhawk; London: Routledge & Kegan Paul, 1951), 172.

[101] Ibid., 172–73.

In *A Radical Jew: Paul and the Politics of Identity*,[102] Boyarin described
Paul as a seminal thinker in the history of the West whose influential
voice helped set in motion the intellectual and cultural forces that produced the ideal of universal human equality in the West. For Boyarin, this
Pauline legacy has been a positive force for good in the world but also has
its shadow side. When universality means the devaluation of ethnic and
cultural difference, typically in a setting where the social arrangements
already favor the preservation of a dominant ethnicity and culture at the
expense of other groups, the ideal of an equality of universal humanity
becomes all too often a justification for the dominance of a single cultural
tradition, which is treated as if it were universal. A rabbinic alternative
to Paul, Boyarin suggested, is the affirmation of fleshly Israel in its ethnic
difference and particular cultural identity. While rabbinic particularism
harbors the danger of degenerating into a racist social system, it offers
an important corrective to Paul—the preservation of the particularities
of ethnicity against oblivion in the universal of Pauline humanity. Hence,
the rabbinic and Pauline visions are equally valuable, equally partial, and
mutually corrective.

One of Boyarin's most compelling statements of this thesis appeared
in an essay he co-authored with his brother, cultural anthropologist Jonathan Boyarin.[103] Speaking of Pauline universalism and rabbinic particularism as heritages of the West, the Boyarins wrote:

> When Christianity is the hegemonic power in Europe and the United States,
> the resistance of Jews to being universalized can be a critical force and model
> for the resistance of all peoples to being Europeanized out of particular bodily
> existence. When, however, an ethnocentric Judaism becomes a temporal hege-
> monic political force, it becomes absolutely, vitally necessary to accept Paul's
> critical challenge—although not his universalizing, disembodying solution—
> and to develop an equally passionate concern for all human beings.[104]

PAUL AND ETHNICITY IN DISPENSATIONALISM AND
POST-HOLOCAUST CHRISTIAN SCHOLARSHIP

Paul's regard for Jewish ethno-religious identity is one way in which
he expresses his valuation of ethnicity. Christian affirmations of Jewish

---

[102] Daniel Boyarin, *A Radical Jew: Paul and the Politics of Identity* (Berkeley:
University of California Press, 1994).

[103] Daniel Boyarin and Jonathan Boyarin, "Diaspora: Generation and the
Ground of Jewish Identity," *Critical Inquiry* 19 (1993): 693–725.

[104] Ibid., 720.

ethno-religious identity, based on fresh interpretations of Paul, have been especially important in dispensationalism and in post-Holocaust scholarship.[105]

For dispensationalists, ethnicity has no value theologically except in one instance or form: that of the Jewish people as Israel. Two central tenets of dispensationalism closely linked to a certain way of reading Paul (and particularly Rom 11) are that God's covenant with Israel is irrevocable and that the Israel of this irrevocable covenant (we might say "true Israel") is not the church but the Jewish people—in the past and throughout history. This central core of dispensationalism has made the fortunes of the Jewish people in history of vital interest for dispensationalist theology. Dispensationalists think of Israel as a nation and have therefore been keenly interested in the "restoration" of Israel to "the land" (Palestine) and have been committed to Israel's continuing security and flourishing in the land (which for post-World War II dispensationalists has meant celebration of and political commitment to the state of Israel).

According to dispensationalism, Jews are not to be absorbed into other nations but are to maintain their religio-ethnic identity in order to fulfill their divine calling in history.[106] In the millennium, when Christ establishes the kingdom on earth, the nation of Israel as a whole will be saved and enjoy the blessings of earthly peace, justice, and prosperity. This theological privileging of the Jewish people and the state of Israel continues in dispensationalist circles today and has left a lasting imprint on many evangelical Christians who in other respects no longer think in dispensationalist terms.

I have used the term "ethnicity" in describing dispensationalism. It is not a dispensationalist term, but it is at least an implicit concept in the way dispensationalists have traditionally understood Israel in God's economy: as a people with a cultural identity defined by the Mosaic law, a religious identity that necessarily assumes socio-ethnic and, in the view of many dispensationalists, national form. In the late nineteenth century, two influential dispensationalist theologians in the United States had a disagreement over whether the Christian mission to Jews should require that Jewish converts to Christian faith give up the Mosaic law (specifically the Jewish practices of Sabbath observance and dietary laws). Ernst Ströter took the view that it pleases God for Jews to remain Jews

---

[105] In what follows, I summarize parts of my larger treatment of dispensationalism and post-Holocaust theology in "The Church *with* and *for* Israel: History of a Theological *Novum* before and after Barth," *Perspectives in Religious Studies* 22 (1995): 259–78.

[106] For most dispensationalists, there is a place for a Christian mission to the Jews, but in God's providence the majority of Jews will not become Christians.

in religio-ethnic identity and practice whether they become Christians or not. Arno Gaebelein, who originally held the same position, changed his mind and concluded that the giving up of the Mosaic law is a necessary prerequisite for entering the church. Gaebelein and Ströter parted ways amicably. Ströter left their joint venture, the magazine *Our Hope*, and returned to his native Germany. Both continued to believe that in God's overall plan, Jews were to remain faithful to the Mosaic law as God's people under the Mosaic covenant alongside the church as God's people in Christ.[107]

Long after the advent of dispensationalism, the claim that, in Paul's thinking, the Jewish people are irrevocably true Israel, not to be supplanted by the church, was taken up by Karl Barth.[108] A surprising and little-known fact of this history is that Barth's exegetical thinking on this subject was significantly shaped by a German commentary on Rom 9–11 by Ernst Ströter (the dispensationalist scholar mentioned above), a story I have narrated in detail elsewhere.[109] Barth's students, above all Paul van Buren, developed Barth's new theology of Israel,[110] and the idea that the Jewish people have an irrevocable divine election became a central claim of Pauline scholars engaged in post-Holocaust Jewish-Christian dialogue and of others who shared their concerns.[111] If the most virulent Christian anti-Semitism cast Jews as monstrous Christ killers and a milder form regarded them as merely spiritually blind and legalistic, both

---

[107] See Cosgrove, "The Church *with* and *for* Israel," 267–68.

[108] See Karl Barth, *Church Dogmatics,* vol. 2, part 2, sec. 34, 4 (ed. G. W. Bromiley and T. F. Torrance; Edinburgh: T&T Clark, 1936–1969). For scholarship on Barth's view of Israel, see, for example, Friedrich-Wilhelm Marquardt, *Die Entdeckung des Judentums für die christliche Theologie: Israel im Denken Karl Barths* (Munich: Christian Kaiser, 1967); Michael Wyschogrod, "Why Is the Theology of Karl Barth of Interest to a Jewish Theologian?" in *Footnotes to a Theology: The Karl Barth Colloquium of 1972* (ed. H. Martin Rumscheidt; Waterloo, Ont.: Corporation for the Publication of Academic Studies of Religion in Canada, 1974); Katherine Sonderegger, *That Jesus Christ Was Born a Jew* (University Park: Pennsylvania State University, 1992).

[109] Cosgrove, "The Church *with* and *for* Israel," 268–69.

[110] Paul M. van Buren, *A Theology of the Jewish-Christian Reality:* part 1, *Discerning the Way;* part 2, *A Christian Theology of the People Israel;* part 3, *A Theology of the Jewish-Christian Reality* (San Francisco: Harper & Row, 1980, 1983, 1988).

[111] See, for example, Bernhard Mayer, *Unter Gottes Heilsratschluß: Prädestinationsaussagen bei Paulus* (Würzburg: Echter, 1974), 290; Franz Mussner, *Traktat über die Juden* (Munich: Kösel, 1979), 59–60; Ottfried Hofius, "Das Evangelium und Israel: Erwägungen zu Römer 9–11," *Zeitschrift für Theologie und Kirche* 83 (1986): 297–324; Martin Rese, "Die Rettung der Juden nach Römer 11," in *L'Apôtre Paul: Personalité, Style et Conception du Ministère* (ed. A. Vanhoye; Leuven: Leuven University Press, 1986), 429–30.

dispensationalism[112] and post-Holocaust Christian scholarship sought to undo these traditional caricatures.

ETHNICITY IN RECENT PHILOSOPHICAL INTERPRETATION OF PAUL

Recently, two philosophers, one French and the other Italian, have taken an interest in Paul.[113] In *Saint Paul: La Fondation de l'universalisme,* Marxist philosopher Alain Badiou interpreted Paul as "the founder of the universal subject."[114] Badiou focused on the intersection of two morally crippling paths: the path of relativism (pluralism) and the path of revolutionary disillusionment (the death in our time of all motivating utopias). We live in an era in which universal truths no longer have any claim. Instead each particularity—religious ethnic, national, sexual—has an unimpeachable right to its own truth. As a result, there is no moral or intellectual standpoint from which to critique global capitalism in its march to shape the world in its own image (as it homogenizes culture and depersonalizes human beings).[115] Badiou sketched a philosophical program for dealing with this situation in which he claimed Paul as an ally.

According to Badiou, Paul engages the two master discourses of his day: the discourse of Jewish particularism and the discourse of Greek universalism (a false universalism, according to Badiou). Rejecting both, Paul founds a new discourse: the equality of sons, the true universalism in which human beings become co-workers with God.[116] Badiou extended

---

[112] David Rausch has been a tireless defender of dispensationalism as a voice against anti-Semitism. He has probably overstated his case, and other historians have assessed dispensationalism more negatively on this point. But it is clear that certain leaders within early dispensationalism managed to rise well above the surrounding cultural prejudice against Jews. For bibliography on the question, see Cosgrove, "The Church *with* and *for* Israel," 267, n. 28.

[113] The following discussion is indebted to Alain Gignac, "Taubes, Badiou, Agamben: Reception of Paul by Non-Christian Philosophers," a paper presented to the Romans through History and Cultures Seminar of the Society of Biblical Literature (annual meeting, Toronto, 2002).

[114] Alain Badiou, *Saint Paul: La Fondation de l'universalisme* (Les Essais du Collège International de Philosophie; Paris: Presses universitaires de France, 1997); ET: *Saint Paul: The Foundation of Universalism* (trans. Ray Brassier; Stanford, Calif.: Stanford University Press, 2003); idem, "Saint Paul, fondateur du sujet universel," *Etudes Théologiques et Religieuses* 75 (2000): 323–33.

[115] Badiou, *Saint Paul,* 7–14 (ET: 6–13); "Saint Paul, fondateur du sujet universel," 323–24.

[116] Badiou, *Saint Paul,* 63 (ET: 59–60).

this interpretive framework to all the major topics in Paul: Jew and Greek, law and grace, Spirit and flesh, the crucifixion and resurrection of Christ, first and second Adam, and so forth. Paul affirms a universalism in which the subject is confronted ever anew by the resurrection event, which expresses the "youthfulness" of the truth (youthful signified by the resurrected one being a "son"), a superabundance that opens up the process of a truth procedure.[117] The universal is not a static reality, not a particular expression of the truth; it rejects "closed particularities" (*particularités fermés*) signified by the law.[118] The universal is rather an endless youthful new creation process in which no individual particularity ultimately matters.[119] Nevertheless, Paul does not negate differences but rather takes them for granted and seeks to bring the process of truth into an ever-widening frontier of differences.[120] In this mission, Paul cultivates "an indifference tolerant to differences."[121]

Giorgio Agamben took up Paul's letter to the Romans in *Il tempo che resta: un commento alla Lettera ai Romani*.[122] According to Agamben, Paul's messianic faith erases identity by suspending all identities in the "as if" (ὡς μή) of 1 Cor 7:25–31. Yet Paul does not establish an undifferentiated universal humanity. Instead of eliminating the division between Jews and Gentiles, Paul multiplies identities by dividing them further. The paradigm for this is Paul himself. "Being a Jew" divides in Paul as both Paul the Pharisee and Paul the apostle, which expresses in a microcosm the larger division of "Israel" and "Israel," a distinction that Agamben detected in Paul's assertion that "not all from Israel are Israel" (Rom 9:6). In working out the logic of Paul's use of the name Israel in different senses, Agamben inferred a kind of "rest" (peace) between these two identities of Israel, a rest that replicates itself for all identities.[123] There are no monolithic identities; instead the messianic cut or fracture creates a rest between the divisions of all identities. In this messianic rest one lives "as if" (ὡς μή).

Badiou's and Agamben's readings of Paul are serious; they show acquaintance with Pauline scholarship and the historical context of the letter to the Romans. But they are not exegetical in any conventional sense. Instead they are philosophical meditations in which Paul's language—and

---

[117] Ibid.

[118] Ibid., 67–68 (ET: 64).

[119] Ibid., 68 (ET: 64).

[120] Ibid., 105–6 (ET: 98–99).

[121] Ibid., 106 (ET: 99) (the original is in italics).

[122] (Torino: Bollati Boringhieri, 2000).

[123] There exists "a kind of rest between each people and itself and between each identity and itself" (*Il tempo che resto*, 54).

to a certain extent the historical Paul's thought—provides grist for philosophical discourse. Agamben, for example, presented his interpretation as a commentary on the first ten words of Romans. He ventured into other parts of Paul's letters, but his aim was philosophical reflection through philological analysis in a way reminiscent of Martin Heidegger. Of interest for our topic is the fact that both Badiou and Agamben, despite their differences of method and result, have attempted to work out a dialectic in which Paul both affirms and transcends difference, including ethnic difference.

DID PAUL VALUE ETHNICITY?

In a study devoted to the question whether Paul valued ethnicity,[124] I have observed that when we pose this question to Paul's letters we likely have in mind one or more of the following ways of thinking about one's own and others' identities:

(1) regarding one's own identity as superior to that of others (ethnocentrism) and sometimes as entailing a special mission or service to the world (messianic ethnocentrism);

(2) valuing one's own ethnicity as the people and traditions one loves, but not in a way that becomes ethnocentric (although this may still involve some sort of messianism);

(3) valuing ethnicity in the interests of fairness by recognizing that every people's ethnicity has a special and unique value for them and deserves to be protected;

(4) valuing ethnicity in the interests of diversity, the greater human richness that comes from the interaction and contributions of different ethnic groups.[125]

Without rehearsing all the evidence from Paul's letters for how he understood ethnic identity, I will bring my survey of Paul and ethnicity to a close by summarizing a number of my conclusions with respect to these different senses of valuing ethnicity.

As for regarding one's ethnicity as superior to that of others (ethnocentrism), Paul does not regard Jews as morally superior to Gentiles because of Jewish possession and practice of the law. But if some Jews accused Paul of disaffection from his people, Paul insists that his mission to the Gentiles has not dampened his ardor for Israel (Rom 9:1–5). There is

---

[124]Charles H. Cosgrove, "Did Paul Value Ethnicity?" *CBQ* 68 (2006): 268–90.
[125]Ibid., 271.

96 Charles H. Cosgrove

nothing inherently ethnocentric about this affirmation. It assumes some form of what people called ἔρως πατρίδος—love of one's own people. When Philo and Josephus use this expression, it carries no ethnocentric overtones but describes an affection implanted by God in each person.[126] Paul appeals to the Holy Spirit as witness to his anguish over Israel and his willingness to give himself up and be "cut off from Christ" for the sake of "my brothers, my kinfolk according to the flesh" (Rom 9:1–3, author's translation).

Yet one thing that most Jews prized as central to their cultural identity—specifically, the way of life specified by the law—is no longer a defining mark of Paul's own identity. For proof, one has only to look at Phil 3:2–11, where he says that he now counts his former Jewish identity in the law as "garbage" because of the superior value of knowing Christ. In 1 Cor 9:19–23, Paul describes his missionary strategy of becoming "all things to all people." This does not mean that Paul no longer values the law. He does, insisting that the law is a revelation of the good (Rom 7:12; 13:8–10; Gal 5:14) and a witness to his gospel (Rom 3:21). Perhaps we could say that he no longer values the law as an ethnic identity marker, but even that would be misleading. Paul appears to assume that the Jewish people have a continuing election as Israel.[127] If he also assumes that the law is what makes Israel Israel (a basic Jewish assumption), then the law is a condition of the existence of Israel as God's elect people. In this way the law as an identity marker is logically entailed in Paul's conception of the irrevocable election of Israel (see Rom 11:29). Nevertheless, Paul is not worrying about how Jews will continue to maintain their ethnic identity through history. He expects the near end of the age when the "hardening" of the present generation of Israel will be lifted (Rom 11:25–26). When this world ends, the fullness of the new creation will be established, and Jewish identity based in the law will be surpassed.

As for valuing ethnicity in the interests of fairness by recognizing that every people's ethnicity has a special and unique value for them that deserves to be protected, Paul may have assumed that love for one's own people naturally entails cherishing those ways in which one's own group is special and unique. But we see no evidence in his letters that Paul was concerned to honor and protect specific ethnic identities of "Gentiles," whom he typically lumps together under that generic name or under "Greek" as a term for non-Jews. Moreover, the idea that ethnicities, as cultural heritages, deserve social protection is a modern idea, off the intellectual

---

[126] Philo, *On the Embassy to Gaius* 277; Josephus, *Ant.* 1.317.

[127] Today, most interpreters hold that Rom 11 (especially vv. 17–29) teaches the irrevocable election of the Jewish people as God's people Israel.

map of ancient Mediterraneans, including Paul. Nothing in Paul opposes it; nothing implies it.

Similarly, when it comes to valuing ethnicity in the interests of diversity (the greater human richness that comes from the interaction and contributions of different ethnic groups), this is also a modern value. Although Paul values forms of diversity (such as the diversity of the body of Christ with different gifts contributing to the unity and health of the whole—1 Cor 12), he does not explicitly interpret the mission to Jews and Gentiles in terms of diversity. He nowhere states in so many words that the goal of the Gentile mission is to bring different Gentile ethnicities into the church in order to achieve a whole made up of different ethnic parts. Moreover, to the extent that the modern way of valuing diversity is utopian (a projection of an ultimate ideal), it clashes with Paul's own utopian vision, the ultimate eschatological future when all this-worldly difference will come to an end in the full realization of the new creation (Gal 3:28; 6:15; 1 Cor 7:31). It is nevertheless important that Gentiles remain Gentiles (until the end). And if "the fullness of the Gentiles" toward which Paul's mission aims (Rom 11:25) is not simply a numerical quantity but a geo-ethnic diversity representing the peoples of the world, then in this sense, too, the ethnicity of the non-Jew is a value for the time before the end. In other words, representational ethnic diversity, emblematic of the reconciliation of diverse peoples in Christ, is an aim of the Pauline mission. This goal impels Paul to move from one city to the next and even to plan a difficult mission to Spain, the western edge of the earth for an ancient Mediterranean.

For Further Reading

Barclay, John M. G. "Neither Jew Nor Greek: Multiculturalism and the New Perspective on Paul." Pages 197–214 in *Ethnicity and the Bible.* Edited by Mark G. Brett. Leiden: Brill, 1996.

Boyarin, Daniel. *A Radical Jew: Paul and the Politics of Identity.* Berkeley: University of California Press, 1994.

Braxton, Brad. *No Longer Slaves: Galatians and African-American Experience.* Collegeville, Minn.: Liturgical Press, 2002.

Campbell, William S. "Religious Identity and Ethnic Origin in the Earliest Christian Communities." Pages 98–121 in *Paul's Gospel in an Intercultural Context: Jew and Gentile in the Letter to the Romans.* Frankfurt: Peter Lang, 1991.

Cosgrove, Charles H. "Did Paul Value Ethnicity?" *CBQ* 68 (2006): 268–90.

Cosgrove, Charles H. et al., eds. *Cross-Cultural Paul: Journeys to Others, Journeys to Ourselves*. Grand Rapids, Mich.: Eerdmans, 2006.

Dahl, Nils A. "The Doctrine of Justification: Its Social Function and Implications." Pages 95–120 in *Studies in Paul: Theology for the Early Christian Mission*. Minneapolis: Augsburg, 1977.

Dunn, James D. G. "Who Did Paul Think He Was? A Study of Jewish-Christian Identity." *NTS* 45 (1999): 174–93.

Stendahl, Krister. *Paul among Jews and Gentiles and Other Essays*. Philadelphia: Fortress, 1976.

van Unnik, W. C. "Christianity and Nationalism in the First Centuries of the Christian Church." Pages 77–94 in *Sparsa Collecta: The Collected Essays of W. C. van Unnik*. Part 3. NovTSup 31. Leiden: Brill, 1983.

5

Paul and the Law:
Pressure Points in the Debate

A. Andrew Das

Not a year goes by without a spate of monographs and essays appearing on Paul and the Law,[1] and the controversy shows no sign of abating. In 2004, Stephen Westerholm published *Perspectives Old and New on Paul*.[2] Westerholm intended his lengthy work to serve as an introduction. He began with an overview of some twenty-five different theorists on Paul and the Law over the last hundred years. The array of options represented by these theorists would be dizzying for the beginning student. Even James D. G. Dunn's recent eighty-eight-page introductory essay represents a nuanced reflection stemming from a lifetime of work.[3] The nuances may be difficult for those not already immersed in this discussion. What the introductory student needs is a roadmap that outlines the key landmarks along the way. Where are the pressure points in this scholarly tussle?

---

[1] In view of the position taken in this essay that Paul uses νόμος exclusively for the Mosaic Torah throughout Romans and Galatians, the word "Law" is ordinarily capitalized. The meaning of νόμος will be discussed later in this essay, but see also my *Paul and the Jews* (Library of Pauline Studies; Peabody, Mass.: Hendrickson, 2003), 155–73. Since the term "gentile" does not refer to a specific ethnic group but is a general term used by Jews for non-Jews, the word is not capitalized here; see the further discussion in my *Solving the Romans Debate* (Minneapolis: Fortress, 2007), 1n3.

[2] Stephen Westerholm, *Perspectives Old and New on Paul: The "Lutheran" Paul and His Critics* (Grand Rapids, Mich.: Eerdmans, 2004).

[3] James D. G. Dunn, "The New Perspective: Whence, What, and Whither," in *The New Perspective on Paul: Collected Essays* (Tübingen: Mohr Siebeck, 2005), 1–88.

Paul's Jewish Milieu

The catalyst for the modern discussion of Paul and the Law was E. P. Sanders's *Paul and Palestinian Judaism* (1977), but the story really begins before Sanders. New Testament specialists had thought that Paul's fundamental problem with the Jewish Law was that people are unable to satisfy its demand for an obedience commensurate with God's own holiness. In the footsteps of Martin Luther, NT scholars thought that in Paul's day the Jews were wrongly trying to earn their way into heaven by their good works. Paul responded that justification must be through God's unmerited grace and mercy in Jesus Christ. Several Jewish and English-speaking scholars in the early and mid-twentieth century recognized serious problems in the reigning paradigm's approach to first-century Judaism, not the least of which was an inadequate attention to the primary sources, but they were unable to shake the confidence of NT specialists.[4] Sanders succeeded where others had failed in large measure because his voice came from within the halls of NT scholarship.

Sanders's watershed work described a "pattern of religion" in which the demands of God's Law were embedded within the gracious framework of God's election and covenant relationship with the Jewish people. God had provided repentance and atoning sacrifice for restoring that relationship in the wake of human failure and sin. The earnest striving to obey God's Law was a response to God's love rather than some legalistic means of earning it. Within this gracious framework with its provision for sin, no Jew would have had to obey God's Law perfectly. Sanders labeled this pattern of religion "covenantal nomism." One of the major pressure points in the current discussion of Paul and the Law remains whether Sanders was correct in his contention that a gracious framework enveloped the demands of the Law in Second Temple Judaism (515 B.C.E.–70 C.E.). Sanders's work, while widely hailed, has nevertheless had its detractors. Jacob Neusner, a leading rabbinic specialist, conceded the broad strokes of Sanders's grace-oriented Judaism but faulted Sanders's methodology.[5]

---

[4] For reviews of that history, see E. P. Sanders, *Paul and Palestinian Judaism* (Minneapolis: Fortress, 1977), 33–59; A. Andrew Das, *Paul and the Jews* (Library of Pauline Studies: Peabody, Mass.: Hendrickson, 2003), 4–9.

[5] In his initial review, Neusner wrote: "So far as Sanders proposes to demonstrate the importance to all the kinds of ancient Judaism of covenantal nomism, election, atonement, and the like, his work must be pronounced a complete success" ("Comparing Judaisms," *History of Religions* 18 [1978]: 180; see also 177–78). As late as 1993: "I find myself in substantial agreement with both the classificatory language he uses ["covenantal nomism"] and the main points of his characterization of that common piety of ancient Israel in the first century"

Sanders had not demonstrated that the sayings or actions ascribed to first-century rabbis were authentic. Neusner also questioned the value of the common pattern Sanders had discerned in Second Temple literature. Sanders had minimized too many crucial differences: "For what each Judaic system had in common with others proves, as we shall see, systematically inert, hardly active, let alone definitive, in setting forth what to any given Judaism proved its critical point . . . what was a given to all systems gave life and power to none of them."[6] John Collins maintained that covenantal nomism was only one of several patterns of religion for diaspora Jews. In apocalyptic literature, for instance, the demands of God's Law were grounded not in the covenant relationship but rather in revelation. In wisdom literature, a universal human nature grounded the demands of the Law. Entry into the community of the wise did not necessarily entail becoming a member of the Jewish covenant community, even if such membership were the ideal.[7] The Second Temple specialists contributing to volume 1 of *Justification and Variegated Nomism* agreed that covenantal nomism, as a descriptive category, is too reductionistic to be of descriptive value. The authors affirmed Sanders's key contention that the variety of Second Temple Judaism defied description as a strictly merit-based system of quid pro quo.[8] Sanders's language of an overarching "framework" of grace enveloping the demands of the Law should probably be dropped in favor of viewing God's mercy and grace as at one end of a continuum with the demand for obedience at the other end. Jewish literature may be positioned somewhere between these two poles of mercy and demand with the exact formulation varying from author to author and genre to genre.[9]

(Jacob Neusner, *Judaic Law from Jesus to the Mishnah: A Systematic Reply to Professor E. P. Sanders* [South Florida Studies in the History of Judaism 84; Atlanta: Scholars Press, 1993], x).

[6] Neusner, *Judaic Law*, 53. For instance, the Mishnah may or may not assume covenant and election. It is simply silent on the matter as its concerns lie elsewhere. Sanders should have let the materials themselves present their own categories. Neusner also faulted Sanders for ignoring the OT origin of these underlying motifs.

[7] John J. Collins, *Between Athens and Jerusalem: Jewish Identity in the Hellenistic Diaspora* (2d ed.; Grand Rapids, Mich.: Eerdmans, 2000), 21–23, 35, 79, 189–90, 192, 260, 273–75.

[8] D. A. Carson et al., eds., *The Complexities of Second Temple Judaism*, vol. 1 of *Justification and Variegated Nomism* (Grand Rapids, Mich.: Baker, 2001).

[9] Chris VanLandingham, a student of George W. E. Nickelsburg, has argued in a wide-ranging challenge to Sanders that Second Temple Judaism was indeed a thoroughly merit-driven religion, especially in its emphasis on a judgment according to works even for the elect (*Judgment and Justification in Early Judaism and the Apostle Paul* [Peabody, Mass.: Hendrickson, 2006]). Rather than return to the pre-Sanders contrast between the grace-oriented Paul and the merit-driven Judaism of his day, VanLandingham contended that Paul is just as merit-driven as

Legalism

Sanders's work on Judaism forced scholars to grapple afresh with what Paul found problematic about Moses' Law. Some specialists have continued to maintain that Paul was combating Jewish attempts to earn God's favor by a legalistic observance of the Law.[10] A second major pressure point is whether Jewish legalism is an object of Paul's critique. Sanders distinguished "getting in" to Judaism from "staying in." While one got into the Jewish people by God's unmerited grace, staying in required obedience to the Law. Several scholars have observed that the ultimate or eschatological salvation of an individual in Second Temple Judaism would also depend on that individual's works. Within the Reformation tradition, such "synergism" would compromise the *sola gratia* principle that God saves by grace alone. Westerholm, while granting divine grace and mercy in Second Temple Judaism, distinguished "hard legalism"—a salvation purely by one's own works—from a synergistic "soft legalism"—salvation by one's own works along with God's grace.[11] The problem with Westerholm's reasoning is that a simple contrast between Paul and his Jewish peers on this point is not possible. Paul likewise affirms human works as the basis for God's judgment at the last day (e.g., Rom 2:6–11; cf. Phil 2:13).[12] Simon Gathercole joined Charles H. Talbert and Timo Eskola in qualifying the comparison of Paul's "Christian" with the synergistic Jew: "Paul has an understanding of obedience that is radically different from that of his Jewish contemporaries. We saw above that, for Paul, divine action is both the source and the continuous cause of obedience for the Christian."[13] This contrast is likewise

his Second Temple peers. Regardless of whether one agrees with VanLandingham's approach to Paul, his work demonstrates how a reconstruction of Second Temple Judaism may radically influence Pauline interpretation.

[10] E.g., Thomas R. Schreiner, *Paul, Apostle of God's Glory in Christ: A Pauline Theology* (Downers Grove, Ill.: InterVarsity Press, 2001), 118–23.

[11] Westerholm, *Perspectives Old and New on Paul*, 332–33. Westerholm described Second Temple Judaism in terms of soft legalism (350–51).

[12] See the comments in A. Andrew Das, review of Stephen Westerholm, *Perspectives Old and New on Paul: The "Lutheran" Paul and His Critics*, *Journal of the Evangelical Theological Society* 48 (2005): 164–67, esp. 166. The recognition of a judgment according to deeds is a strength of Gathercole's study.

[13] Simon J. Gathercole, *Where Is Boasting? Early Jewish Soteriology and Paul's Response in Romans 1–5* (Grand Rapids, Mich.: Eerdmans, 2002), 102, 135, 214–15, here 264. For a similar contrast of synergistic Jew with divinely empowered, Pauline Christian, see Charles H. Talbert, "Paul, Judaism, and the Revisionists," *CBQ* 63 (2001): 1–22, esp. 20–22, relying on the work of Timo Eskola (*Theology and Predestination in Pauline Soteriology* [WUNT 2.100; Tübingen: Mohr Siebeck, 1998]; idem, "Paul, Predestination and 'Covenantal Nomism'—Re-Assessing Paul

problematic: Second Temple Jews *did* frequently state that their obedience was a result of God's empowerment.[14]

On the contrary, Paul claims in Gal 3:15–17 that the Law simply came 430 years after God's saving promises to Abraham. Paul does not hint of a problem with legalistic striving. In Rom 2, Paul criticizes an imaginary Jewish interlocutor for thinking that Jewish ethnic identity suffices in mediating a place in the world to come. Paul does not seem to be targeting Jewish legalism or perfectionism in his critique of the Law. The Law is simply unable to save (e.g., Gal 2:21; 3:21). Paul's conclusions with respect to the Law do not stem from a reaction to synergism but rather are a reflex of his christological reasoning. The primary difference between Paul and his peers is that he understands God's grace to be located exclusively "in Christ" and not in Judaism's Law.[15] If saving grace is operative in Christ and apart from the Law, then the Law cannot mediate access to the world to come for the Jewish people. Paul would certainly condemn legalism, but that condemnation would be a by-product of his reasoning rather than its primary thrust.

"Works of the Law"

Dunn has proposed a new and very different object of Paul's critique of the Jewish Law since legalism does not appear to be the target.[16] Dunn noted the recurrent, ethnic dimension of the apostle's reasoning as Paul juxtaposes Jew and non-Jew in the passages where he is discussing Moses'

---

and Palestinian Judaism," *JSJ* 29 [1997]: 390–412), who contrasted the Second Temple's "synergistic nomism" with Paul's position.

[14] See the overview of Second Temple evidence in A. Andrew Das, "Paul and Works of Obedience in Second Temple Judaism: Romans 4:4–5 as a 'New Perspective' Case Study," *CBQ* (forthcoming).

[15] Westerholm (*Perspective Old and New on Paul*) classified my position in the "Lutheran" camp alongside Schreiner, but Schreiner and I fundamentally differ on this crucial matter of legalism. Since I do not think that Paul is combating Jewish legalism or synergism, my position departs from the defining "Lutheran" premise regarding first-century Judaism. Westerholm (213n22) recognized my difference from Schreiner but underestimated its significance.

[16] Advocates or variations of Dunn's "new perspective" include N. T. Wright, *Climax of the Covenant: Christ and the Law in Pauline Theology* (Minneapolis: Fortress, 1991); Francis Watson, *Paul, Judaism and the Gentiles: A Sociological Approach* (SNTSMS 56; Cambridge: Cambridge University Press, 1986); Michael Cranford, "Abraham in Romans 4: The Father of All Who Believe," *NTS* 41 (1995): 71–88; idem, "The Possibility of Perfect Obedience: Paul and an Implied Premise in Galatians 3:10 and 5:3," *NovT* 36 (1994): 242–58.

Law and the issues the Law raised for his missionary work among gentiles. The Jews had treated the Law as a boundary marker and had not recognized that the Scriptures had anticipated the inclusion of the gentiles. The Jewish Christians were wrongly requiring the gentiles to live like Jews. Paul responds that the boundary marking God's people is not circumcision, Sabbath, or any of the other "works of the Law" (ἔργα νόμου), but rather an existence "in Christ." Whenever Paul speaks positively of the Law, it is the Law understood apart from Jewish ethnic identity. Whenever Paul speaks negatively of the Law, his purpose is to identify these ethnic boundary markers or "works of the Law." In other words, the fundamental problem Paul has with the Law does not stem from a pessimistic anthropology in which humans are unable to accomplish the demands of the Law. Paul is opposing Jewish ethnic particularism and presumption as at odds with the universal and inclusive grace of God in Christ.[17] A third major pressure point in the debate over Paul's view of the Law, then, is the contention that the phrase "works of the Law" (ἔργα νόμου), refers primarily to those aspects of the Law that serve as boundary markers of separation.[18]

---

[17] Dunn's Christ therefore died to free humanity from the curse of a wrong understanding of the Law:

> The curse which was removed by Christ's death therefore was the curse which had previously prevented that blessing from reaching the Gentiles, the curse of a wrong understanding of the law. It was a curse which fell primarily on the Jew (3.10; 4.5), but Gentiles were affected by it so long as that misunderstanding of the covenant and the law remained dominant. It was that curse which Jesus had brought deliverance from by his death. (*Jesus, Paul, and the Law: Studies in Mark and Galatians* [Louisville, Ky.: Westminster/John Knox, 1990], 229)

This particular articulation of the significance of Christ's death within Dunn's "new perspective" understandably remains troubling for many. Dunn (*Jesus, Paul, and the Law,* 237) tried to resolve this problem by suggesting that in Christ God's covenant love "now" (eschatologically) reaches beyond the old boundaries to include those previously outside the covenant. If that were the case, Paul could hardly be criticizing a misunderstanding on the part of the Jews, since God's historic relationship with Israel had indeed placed the gentiles outside the covenant, at least until the dawn of the Christ. On what basis would there be a curse upon the Jews prior to Christ? Dunn's Christ, it appears, has brought a curse rather than blessing upon the Jews because of their subsequent failure to recognize his significance for the gentiles.

[18] Despite Dunn's emphasis against his critics that he does not limit "works of the Law" to the boundary-markers of circumcision, Sabbath, and food laws and that the phrase refers to obedience of the Law in its entirety, he nevertheless maintained in his most recent work: "In speaking of 'works of the law' Paul had in mind this boundary-marking, separating function of the law" (James D. G. Dunn, "The New Perspective: Whence, What and Whither," in *The New Perspective on Paul: Collected Essays* [WUNT 185; Tübingen: Mohr Siebeck, 2005], 8; cf. also 22–26,

Many specialists have expressed doubt whether Paul uses the phrase "works of the Law" with the specialized sense that Dunn proposed. Many scholars have not seen boundary-marking features at issue in every context where Paul employs the phrase.[19] Taking "works of the Law" in a broader sense of the entirety of the Law, apart from a necessary notion of separation, neatly avoids these issues. The claim that the boundary-marking features of the Law are primarily in view in *every* instance Paul employs "works of the Law" is perhaps analogous to what James Barr cautioned against years ago (but in this case a phrase rather than an individual word): "The value of the context comes to be seen as something contributed by the word, and then it is read into the word as its contribution where the context is in fact different. Thus the word becomes overloaded with interpretive suggestion."[20]

In contending that Paul's phrase "works of the Law" (ἔργα νόμου), necessarily includes the notion of boundaries, Dunn has placed great emphasis on the use of the corresponding phrase (מעשי תורה) in the Qumran writings, especially in 4QMMT, a document that lists various sectarian legal rulings that serve to distinguish the Qumran community. Dunn flagged 4QMMT C 27 with the full phrase "works of the Law" (מעשי תורה) in support of his position that "works of the Law," or the shortened "works" always referred to those aspects of the Law that distinguished the sectarian community. Within the same paragraph, however, 4QMMT C 23 employs "works" (מעשיהם) in relation to the actions of the kings of Israel, including David as "a man of good deeds" (איש חסדים), When 4QMMT C 26 mentions the forgiveness of David, his adulterous affair would have immediately come to mind for the Second Temple Jew (CD 5.5b–6a; 2 Sam

---

43). The boundary-markers remain *primarily* in view since they are those aspects of the entire Law that are in particular situations "contentious" (Dunn, "The New Perspective," 26, also 24). Likewise Kent L. Yinger (*Paul, Judaism, and Judgment According to Deeds* [SNTSMS 105; Cambridge: Cambridge University Press, 1999], 171): "Though the meaning of ἔργα νόμου ['works of the Law'] is broader than a few selected identity markers, the focus of Paul's usage is on circumcision and food laws because it was precisely this subset of religious activity which both Jews and non-Jews recognized as *the distinguishing identifiers* of Jewishness and which Paul understood to be relativized through faith in Christ." As Jewish sectarian groups (e.g., the Qumran community) define themselves over against other Jews, the distinguishing "works of the Law" will be different.

[19] Dunn has argued a boundary-marking sense for "works of the Law" throughout Paul's letters. Not all have judged his efforts successful with respect to individual passages; e.g., Andrew Das, *Paul, the Law, and the Covenant* (Peabody, Mass.: Hendrickson, 2001), 234–67.

[20] James Barr, *The Semantics of Biblical Language* (Oxford: Oxford University Press, 1961), 233–34; see also 218, 222.

12:13; 1 Kgs 15:5—note also the proximity to C 27 of C 23–26). These references in the immediate context to the general behavior or "works" of the kings is decisive for the interpretation of the full phrase "works of the Law" (מעשי תורה) in C 27.[21] Taking "works of the Law" in the broader sense of the entirety of the Law, apart from a *necessary* notion of separation, neatly avoids the problems that 4QMMT C 23 poses.

THE GENERATIVE CORE: ETHNIC EXCLUSIVITY?

Dunn is certainly correct that scholarship prior to Sanders had largely neglected the intensely ethnic aspect of Paul's reasoning.[22] No account of Paul and the Law can now ignore that ethnic dimension. A fourth pressure point on Paul and the Law is whether Paul's ethnic concerns are the fundamental basis for his critique of the Law or whether they are a consequence of other considerations. Sanders is known for the phrase "solution-to-plight." Several specialists have made the case that Paul the Pharisaic Jew had viewed Christ and the Law as mutually exclusive approaches to enjoying a right relationship with God.[23] After Paul's encounter with the risen Christ, the apostle came to the conclusion that salvation must be in Christ and not the Law. Further, if the Law is not God's instrument to save, then surely the Law's boundary markers do not identify a people enjoying salvation on the basis of their ethnic identity. Sanders granted that Paul could be inconsistent in his thinking on the Law because the apostle's position was a direct consequence of his experience of the risen Christ. Dunn's dissatisfaction with the unnecessary inconsistencies in Sanders's Paul led, in part, to his "new perspective." If Sanders is right that Paul begins with

---

[21] Dunn ("4QMMT and Galatians," in *The New Perspective on Paul: Collected Essays* [WUNT 185; Tübingen: Mohr Siebeck, 2005], 333–39, here 336–37) thought that C 27's use of the phrase "some of the works of the Torah" should be interpreted alongside B 2, but this connection is not rendered explicit by 4QMMT. Too much of the original context of B 2 has been lost to be sure of Dunn's reasoning. Dunn and others have assumed that "works" in B 2 is a noun. It may just as well be a qal active masculine plural participle. B 2 could be reconstructed in a parallel fashion to C 23's "Contemplate their deeds": התבנן ב[מעשים שא א[נ]] [ח]נועשינו: "Contemplate the deeds which we have performed" (cf. Gen 20:9; 1 Sam 8:8; 2 Kgs 23:19; Jer 7:13; Eccl 1:14); see Jacqueline C. R. de Roo, *"Works of the Law" at Qumran and in Paul* (Sheffield: Sheffield Phoenix, 2007), 91.

[22] George Howard was an earlier proponent of what would become Dunn's position. See Howard's "Christ the End of the Law," *JBL* 88 (1969): 331–37; idem, "Romans 3:21–31 and the Inclusion of the Gentiles," *HTR* 63 (1970): 23–33.

[23] Thus Terence L. Donaldson, *Paul and the Gentiles: Remapping the Apostle's Convictional World* (Minneapolis: Fortress, 1997).

Christ as the solution, then the inclusion of the gentiles is not the starting point of Paul's thought but a consequence.[24] In that case, a christological starting point could have other implications as well, especially for the law's demands.

PERFECT OBEDIENCE AS A FACTOR

In denying the traditional, pessimistic "Lutheran" anthropology in Paul, "new perspective" interpreters, like Dunn, have emphasized that perfect obedience of the Law is never a factor in Paul and that Sanders had proven perfect obedience not to be a factor in Second Temple Judaism.[25] A fifth pressure point, then, is whether perfect obedience of the Law factors into Paul's thinking or Second Temple Judaism. New perspective interpreters have perennially confused the gracious framework of "covenantal nomism" with its embedded demand. Sanders maintained that the Law demands strict obedience, even if the practical result of God's merciful provision is that less-than-perfect individuals

---

[24]This does not exclude a "solution-to-plight" thought pattern in Paul's writings as he articulated faith in Christ *after* his initial exposure to the solution; see Frank Thielman, *From Plight to Solution: A Jewish Framework for Understanding Paul's View of the Law in Galatians and Romans* (NovTSup 61; Leiden: Brill, 1989). In his descriptions of his pre-Christian past as a Jew, Paul never identifies a plight. He views his observance of the Law as "blameless" in Phil 3:6. He had excelled in Judaism beyond his peers in Gal 1:14. The failures he cites in Rom 7:7–25 pertain not to his pre-Christian past but rather to *gentiles'* seeking control over their sinful passions and desires in Moses' Law. On Rom 7:7–25, see A. Andrew Das, *Solving the Romans Debate* (Minneapolis: Fortress, 2007), 203–35. "In Christ" Paul came to recognize the genuine problem of sin (e.g., Rom 3:10–18, 23).

[25]James D. G. Dunn (*The Epistle to the Galatians* [Black's New Testament Commentary; Peabody, Mass.: Hendrickson, 1993], 171) wrote:

> The mistake, once again, has been to read into the argument the idea that at this time the law would be satisfied with nothing less than sinlessness, unblemished obedience, that the law was understood as a means to achieving righteousness from scratch. But in Jewish thought to 'abide within all that was written in the law and do it' meant living within the provisions of the law, including all its provisions for sin, through repentance and atonement (see particularly Sanders, *Paul*). That was why Paul was able to describe himself as 'blameless' before his conversion (Phil. Iii.6; see also on i.14); *not* because he committed no sin, *not* because he fulfilled every law without exception, but because the righteousness of the law included use of the sacrificial cult and benefit of the Day of Atonement. That the Judaism, against which Paul here reacts, called for an impossible perfection is not part of the context of the argument at this point and should not be read into it.

could enjoy a "blameless" or righteous status.[26] One Second Temple text that Sanders analyzed categorically stated: "All of [God's] commands and his ordinances and all of his law" are to be carefully observed "without turning aside to the right or left" (*Jub.* 23:16).[27] The author praised the patriarchs and matriarchs of Israel for their "perfect" conduct in "all" their actions.[28] The author looked forward to the day when Israel would be perfectly obedient (*Jub.* 1:22–24; 5:12; 50:5).[29] Sanders conceded: "Perfect obedience is specified. . . ."[30] He added: "As we have now come to expect, the emphasis on God's mercy is coupled with a strict demand to be obedient."[31] While God would grant mercy to the elect, the requirement of right conduct "in all things" (*Jub.* 21:23) was upheld and admonished through these exemplary models. Strict and perfect obedience remained the ideal (*Jub.* 1:23–24; 20:7). Greater care must be exercised before making categoric statements ruling out perfect obedience in Second Temple Judaism.

---

[26] For a more thorough review of the motif of perfect obedience in *Jubilees*, Philo, the Dead Sea Scrolls, apocalyptic literature, and the Tannaim, see Das, *Paul, the Law, and the Covenant*, 12–69. I selected these documents for analysis since they were Sanders's exemplars in *Paul and Palestinian Judaism* and in his article "The Covenant As a Soteriological Category and the Nature of Salvation in Palestinian and Hellenistic Judaism," in *Jews, Greeks and Christians* (ed. Robert Hamerton-Kelly and Robin Scroggs; Leiden: Brill, 1976), 11–44. Independently, Friedrich Avemarie took a similar approach to rabbinic literature in *Tora und Leben: Untersuchungen zur Heilsbedeutung der Tora in der frühen rabbinischen Literatur* (TSAJ 55; Tübingen: Mohr Siebeck, 1996; see especially his conclusions on 575–84).

[27] Translation from James H. Charlesworth, *Old Testament Pseudepigrapha* (2 vols.; New York: Doubleday, 1985), 2:35–142.

[28] E.g., Noah, Abraham, Leah, Jacob, Joseph. In *Jub.* 5:19: "[God] did not show partiality, except Noah alone . . . because his heart was righteous in all of his ways just as it was commanded concerning him. And he did not transgress anything which was ordained for him." Noah, while the recipient of God's mercy (10:3), did "just as it was commanded" and was "righteous in all of his ways." "He did not transgress." Jacob was also "a perfect man" (27:17). Leah "was perfect and upright in all her ways," and Joseph "walked uprightly" (36:23; 40:8). God told Abraham in 15:3 to "be pleasing before me and be perfect." Abraham was then praised in 23:10 since he "was perfect in all of his actions with the Lord and was pleasing through righteousness all of the days of his life."

[29] Frank Thielman (*From Plight to Solution*, 28–45) has demonstrated that sorrow over human inability and failure prompted many Jews in the Second Temple period to look to the future age when God would enable an obedience that had not been possible in this age. Thielman demonstrated the same motif within the pages of the Hebrew Bible.

[30] Sanders, *Paul and Palestinian Judaism*, 381.

[31] Ibid., 383.

Jouette Bassler, in a recent essay, highlighted Gal 3:10 and Rom 4:4–5 as passages that do not conform well to the "new perspective" approach.[32] In Rom 4:4–5 Paul appears to draw a contrast between "works" as a matter of human striving and God's unmerited grace.[33] Paul articulates this contrast without any reference to ethnic boundary markers. Galatians 3:10, the other problematic passage, leaves one of the premises of a logical enthymeme unstated: no one perfectly does all that the Law requires. Bassler has recognized that these passages "yield more naturally to the old perspective."[34] Nevertheless, she faulted recent critics of the new perspective for lapsing into a legalistic view of Second Temple Judaism: "All of these explanations . . . fail to account for the central role of divine mercy, forgiveness, and atonement in first-century Judaism."[35] Apparently unaware of any other alternative in the debate, Bassler concluded:

> We are left, then, with an apparent stalemate. Legalistic (soft or hard) interpretations of Paul's criticism of "works of the law" fail to do justice to the realities of Second Temple Judaism or to the thrust of Paul's argument in several crucial passages. The new perspective, on the other hand, requires strained exegesis of some other crucial passages [Rom 4:1–5; Gal 3:10–14].[36]

A solution to the impasse was readily available at the time of Bassler's essay.[37] Bassler, Dunn, and others have been wrong in assuming that Paul viewed the "divine mercy, forgiveness, and atonement in first-century Judaism" as effective for the salvation of an individual. Paul never grants that an animal sacrifice, as prescribed by the Law, can offer the forgiveness of sins, which comes solely in Christ's death (Gal 1:4; 3:13).[38] Reconciliation to God has taken place in Christ.[39] Paul never grants to Israel an election that avails to salvation apart from Christ (e.g., Gal 3:27–29: "Jew or

---

[32] Jouette M. Bassler, *Navigating Paul: An Introduction to Key Theological Concepts* (Louisville, Ky.: Westminster John Knox, 2007), 15–16.

[33] See the discussion of these two verses and the problem they pose for the new perspective in Das, "Paul and Works of Obedience in Second Temple Judaism."

[34] Bassler, *Navigating Paul,* 15.

[35] Ibid., 16.

[36] Ibid., 17.

[37] Das, *Paul, the Law, and the Covenant.*

[38] Many Second Temple texts suggest a shift away from sacrifice as a means of atonement. See Tob 12:9; Sir 3:3, 30; 45:23; 4 Macc 17:22; *Pss. Sol.* 3:8. The Qumran community likewise viewed its good works as a substitute means of atonement in the place of the Temple (e.g., 1QS 3:6–12; 8:3, 6, 10; 9:4–7); see Mark A. Seifrid, *Justification by Faith: The Origin and Development of a Central Pauline Theme* (NovTSup 68; Leiden: Brill, 1992), 93–108. On the lack of atoning sacrifice in Paul, see ch. 5 of Das, *Paul, the Law, and the Covenant.*

[39] On reconciliation taking place "in Christ," see A. Andrew Das, "Reconciliation," *New Interpreters Dictionary of the Bible* (forthcoming).

Greek"; Gal 6:14–16: "Israel of God"; Rom 10:9–13: "all"). If the Law could save by means of its provisions for failure, then Christ's death would have been unnecessary (Gal 2:21; 3:21).[40]

Paul is not making the claim that Judaism is legalistic. He has simply reconceptualized God's grace in terms of Christ and thereby left the Law's commands without their corresponding provisions for failure and sin. Obedience to the Law is a genuine problem for the Law-observant, since forgiveness and salvation are located solely in Christ.[41] Paul can therefore describe the "wretched" plight of the "I" under the Law who is incapable of obeying the commands (Rom 7:7–25).[42] To follow the Law apart from Christ is to engage in a merely human endeavor, an exercise in empty "works." This "newer perspective" neatly resolves Bassler's stalemate by recognizing not only the elements of grace and mercy in Judaism but also the implications for the Law of Paul's christological priorities. A more positive appraisal of Second Temple Judaism and a recognition of Paul's intense concern with the inclusion of the gentiles in God's salvation are perfectly compatible with a reading of Gal 3:10 and Rom 4:4–5 in the manner Bassler saw as most natural.

THE MEANING OF "NOMOS"

Heikki Räisänen has demonstrated a wide range of usage for νόμος ("law") in the first-century world.[43] Not all the Pauline passages that employ the word "law" (νόμος) may necessarily refer to the Mosaic Law. The meaning of νόμος ("law"?) is a sixth pressure point. Three passages—Rom 3:27–31, Rom 7:7–8:4, and Gal 6:2—have proven particularly contentious. Some scholars have thought that Paul is using νόμος consistently to refer to Moses' Torah.[44] Others concluded that Paul

---

[40] I belabored Sanders's key categories of grace of covenant, election, and atoning sacrifice in chs. 3–5 of *Paul, the Law, and the Covenant*. None of these categories avails for salvation.

[41] See the critique of the two-covenant or *Sonderweg* approach with its special path to God for the Jews apart from Christ in Das, *Paul and the Jews*, 96–106.

[42] This is underscored by the variation of terms: κατεργάζομαι, ποιέω, πράσσω. While the "I" wants to do what is good, sin and the flesh prevent the "I" from being able to "do" the good. Ethnic boundaries figure nowhere in the plight of the "I" under the Law.

[43] Heikki Räisänen, *Jesus, Paul, and Torah: Collected Essays* (trans. David E. Orton; JSNTSup 43; Sheffield: Sheffield Academic Press, 1992), 69–88.

[44] Paul W. Meyer, "The Worm at the Core of the Apple: Exegetical Reflections on Romans 7," in *The Conversation Continues: Studies in Paul and John in Honor of J. Louis Martyn* (ed. Robert T. Fortna and Beverly R. Gaventa; Nashville: Abingdon,

is playing on the broad range of meanings νόμος ("law") could have in the ancient world.[45]

Should the phrase νόμος πίστεως in Rom 3:27 be translated as the "principle of faith" or as "the Torah (in its witness to) faith"? In Romans 4, which immediately follows, Paul stresses the faith of the Torah's Abraham; this context favors taking νόμος as "Torah" in 3:27. The Abrahamic "promise" of Rom 4 would be the equivalent of "the Law of faith" in Rom 3:27.[46] Stephen Westerholm has disagreed: "But are we really to assume that Paul thought his readers would identify 'promise' and 'law of faith' with the Mosaic law when he explicitly contrasts the 'promise' with the 'law' in 4:13-14?"[47] On the other hand, taking Rom 3:27's disputed phrase as "the Law in its witness to faith" would agree with Paul's affirmation in 3:21 that the Law and the prophets both bore witness to the promised righteousness of God in Christ. Paul contrasts the Law from the point of view of its works with the Law as a witness to faith in 3:27.[48] In Rom 4 Paul contrasts the Law and the Abrahamic promise. An explanation is readily available for why Paul does not maintain the same terminology in Romans 4 as at the end of Romans 3. The apostle distinguishes the eras of Abraham and Moses in Gal 3:15-18: the promise of a Seed came in the time of Abraham and the patriarchs long before Moses' legislation. Although Moses' Law as Scripture bears witness to the promise, the legislation comes from a later era. Since Paul's topic in Rom 4 is Abraham, he switches to a more appropriate terminology to express the contrast.[49]

1990), 78-80; John M. G. Barclay, *Obeying the Truth: Paul's Ethics in Galatians* (Minneapolis: Fortress, 1988), 125-42; Paul J. Achtemeier, "Unsearchable Judgments and Inscrutable Ways: Reflections on the Discussion of Romans," in vol. 4 of *Pauline Theology* (ed. E. Elizabeth Johnson and David M. Hay; SBLSymS 4; Atlanta: Scholars Press, 1997), 18-20; J. Louis Martyn, "The Crucial Event in the History of the Law (Gal 5:14)," *Theology and Ethics in Paul and His Modern Interpreters: Essays in Honor of Victor Paul Furnish* (ed. E. H. Lovering Jr. and J. L. Sumney; Nashville: Abingdon, 1996), 48-61. See also the discussions in Das, *Paul, the Law, and the Covenant*, 192-200, 228-32, 242-47; idem, *Paul and the Jews*, 155-73.

[45] Räisänen, *Jesus, Paul, and Torah*, 48-68, 89-94; Westerholm, *Perspectives Old and New on Paul*, 321-30; Michael Winger, *By What Law? The Meaning of* Νόμος *in the Letters of Paul* (SBLDS 128; Atlanta: Scholars Press, 1992).

[46] Gerhard Friedrich, "Das Gesetz des Glaubens Röm. 3,27," *TZ* 10 (1954): 401-17, esp. 416.

[47] Westerholm, *Perspectives Old and New on Paul*, 324.

[48] The Law, when considered from the point of view of its testimony to faith in/of Jesus Christ, would indeed preclude boasting in one's own works; contra Westerholm's claim (*Perspectives New and Old on Paul*, 324) of a "decisive" argument.

[49] For a more comprehensive treatment of this approach to Rom 3:27-31, see Das, *Paul, the Law, and the Covenant*, 192-200.

Romans 7:21–25 is frequently cited as proof that νόμος should not always be translated as the Mosaic Law. In Romans 7:21: "So I find it to be *a principle* (νόμος) that when I want to do what is good, evil lies close at hand"? On the other hand, the verse may also be translated: "So I find *with respect to* the Law (νόμος), when I want to do good, evil lies close at hand"? Westerholm discounted the second translation of 7:21 with little discussion and concluded instead that in 7:21–25 Paul is playing on the different meanings for νόμος in the Greco-Roman world.[50] Michael Winger, upon whom Westerholm depended, at one point conceded (tellingly) of this play on the meaning of νόμος: "there are so many νόμοι that they can scarcely be kept straight. . . ."[51] Such confusion is unnecessary. Klyne Snodgrass has made a strong case that the Law functions within spheres of apocalyptic power, the very forces at work throughout Rom 5–8.[52] Sin, as one of these powerful cosmic forces, has taken hold of the Law and distorted the Law for its own purpose to work death (Rom 7:7–11). Paul therefore employs the summarizing phrase in 8:2 "the Law in the hands of Sin and death" (νόμος τῆς ἁμαρτίας καὶ θανάτου). The Law has no power of itself. God's Spirit can take hold of the Law and work a very different result (8:3). "Law" (νόμος) is best taken as referring to the Torah throughout Rom 7–8.

Paul vigorously contrasts Christ and the Law throughout Galatians: a person is not justified by the works of the Law but rather by faith in Christ (2:16). Christ and the Law represent opposing approaches to justification. Toward the end of the letter in Gal 6:2, Paul unexpectedly coins the rather jarring phrase "the law of Christ" (νόμος τοῦ Χριστοῦ). Perhaps Paul is playing on the word "law" (νόμος) in 6:2 and means the "principle" (of love) that Christ exemplifies. On the other hand, Christ's teachings, to which the apostle refers, may explicate *how* the Mosaic Law applies to the Christian life. In that case, Gal 6:2 would be referring to the Mosaic Law as interpreted by Christ: "the Law in the hands of Christ."

The context offers strong considerations in favor of the translation "the Law in the hands of Christ." In the preceding verse (Gal 6:1), Paul admonishes the Christian community to help restore those guilty of "transgression" (παράπτωμα). "Transgression" regularly refers in Jewish literature to violations of the Mosaic Law (cf. Rom 5:20). Furthermore, the language of Gal 6:2 explicates the reference to the Mosaic Law in Gal 5:14. Paul uses in Gal 6:2 a Greek word for "fulfill" (ἀναπληρόω) alongside "Law" (νόμος); "fulfill" in 6:2 is a cognate of 5:14's "fulfill" (πληρόω), which

---

[50] At the same time, Westerholm overlooked the key studies on this verse by Meyer, Snodgrass, and Achtemeier.

[51] Winger, *By What Law?* 186.

[52] Klyne R. Snodgrass, "Spheres of Influence: A Possible Solution to the Problem of Paul and the Law," *JSNT* 32 (1988): 93–113.

is likewise used alongside "Law" (νόμος). Paul's admonition to mutual Christian service in 6:2's "bear one another's burdens" echoes 5:13's "become slaves to one another." Galatians 5:14, for its part, is clearly discussing Moses' Law. Paul's reference to fulfilling "the whole Law" (ὁ πᾶς νόμος) by love in 5:14 answers the obligation to obey the entire Law in Gal 5:3 (ὅλος ὁ νόμος). Paul cites in Gal 5:14 the words of Lev 19:18: "You shall love your neighbor as yourself" (NRSV). Jewish literature employed Lev 19:18 as a means of summarizing all the commands of the Law.[53] Christians are therefore obliged to fulfill the stipulations of the Mosaic Law by loving their neighbors. Paul's fulfilling the "Law of Christ" (6:2) therefore advances his discussion of the Torah in 5:14.

Scholars have been gravitating in recent years toward a more consistent translation of νόμος as Torah in Galatians and Romans. Richard Hays initially dismissed a reference to the Mosaic Law in Gal 6:2 but subsequently joined those who contend that νόμος refers to the Torah throughout Galatians and Romans.[54] Thomas Schreiner experienced a similar change of mind on the meaning of νόμος in Rom 3:27–31.[55] Hays's and Schreiner's "conversions" likely presage the future of this discussion. Harm Hollander's study has made a strong case that νόμος in 1 Corinthians does not, in each instance, refer to the Torah. Paul's use of νόμος may be specific to a letter.[56] The debate over the meaning of νόμος leads to a seventh pressure point: does Paul view the Mosaic Law as a continuing norm for the Christian life?

The Law as Norm

Throughout Gal 3 Paul is adamant that the Law was temporary and ceased with the coming of faith and Christ's saving work. Temporal

---

[53] Sanders, *Paul and Palestinian Judaism*, 112–14; Barclay, *Obeying the Truth*, 132–33, 135–36. In *b. Shabbat* 31a, Jesus' contemporary, the great teacher of the law Hillel, reportedly told an aspiring convert: "What is hateful to you, do not do to your neighbor: that is the whole Torah, while the rest is commentary thereof; go and learn it." Paul's Letter to the Romans offers confirmation of this point. After listing several of the Ten Commandments, Paul adds in Rom 13:9–10 (NRSV): "[these] and any other commandment, are summed up in this word, 'Love your neighbor as yourself.' Love does no wrong to a neighbor; therefore love is the fulfilling of the law."

[54] Compare Richard B. Hays's earlier work in "Christology and Ethics in Galatians" (*CBQ* 49 [1987]: 268–90) with his later essay, "Three Dramatic Roles: The Law in Romans 3–4" in *Paul and the Mosaic Law* (ed. James D. G. Dunn; WUNT 89; Tübingen: Mohr Siebeck, 1996), 151–64.

[55] Schreiner, *Romans*, 202n3.

[56] Harm W. Hollander, "The Meaning of the Term 'Law' (NOMOS) in 1 Corinthians," *NovT* 40 (1998): 117–35.

markers dominate this section of Paul's letter.[57] Westerholm therefore
concluded that the Law has come to an end for the Christian.[58] Dunn
came to a different conclusion: what has ceased is the wrongful emphasis
on the Law's ethnic identity markers.[59] One may also argue that the Law
no longer functions as an enslaving demand which leads to curse.[60] If passages such as Gal 6:2 ("Law in the hands of Christ") and Rom 8:4 ("the Law
in the hands of the Spirit of life") refer to the Torah, then the Law may be
grabbed hold of by the Spirit (Rom 8:4) to produce a Christ-like behavior
that fulfills the commands (Gal 5:14; 6:2).[61] Although the debate over the
Law's continuing role has historically centered on Romans and Galatians,
Peter Tomson and Brian Rosner have demonstrated that Paul frequently
draws upon the Torah as a warrant in admonishing Christian behavior
in 1 Corinthians.[62] The exact shape of Law's role in the Christian life may
depend on the passage.[63]

Räisänen's 1983 study proved prophetic in raising many of the issues
that continue to dominate discussion of Paul and the Law.[64] The advances
in recent research no longer justify Räisänen's conclusion that Paul is utterly contradictory on this topic. Of course, these seven pressure points
are by no means exhaustive. One might also inquire whether and to what
extent gentiles are "under" the Law.[65] The precise factors that led to Paul's

---

[57] ἄχρις in v. 19; πρὸ τοῦ δὲ ἐλθεῖν τὴν πίστιν in v. 23; εἰς τὴν μέλλουσαν
πίστιν in v. 23; γέγονεν in v. 24; οὐκέτι in v. 25.

[58] Westerholm, *Perspectives Old and New on Paul*, 431–39.

[59] Dunn, *Galatians*, 197–200; so also Norman H. Young, "*Paidagogos*: The
Social Setting of a Pauline Metaphor," *NovT* 29 (1987): 150–76; T. David Gordon,
"A Note on Παιδαγωγος in Galatians 3.24–25," *NTS* 35 (1989): 150–54.

[60] Das, *Paul and the Jews*, 151–55.

[61] Advocates of the Reformation's "third use of the law" in Galatians and Romans should recognize that such a position depends on the meaning of νόμος
in these crucial texts.

[62] Peter J. Tomson, *Paul and the Jewish Law: Halakha in the Letters of the
Apostle to the Gentiles* (CRINT 3.1; Minneapolis: Fortress, 1990), 97–149; Brian
Rosner, *Paul, Scripture, and Ethics: A Study of 1 Corinthians 5–7* (Arbeiten zur Geschichte des antiken Judentums und des Urchristentums 22; Leiden: Brill, 1994);
Das, *Paul and the Jews*, 176–80. In his contention that Paul does not envision a
continuing role for the Law in the Christian life, Westerholm surprisingly overlooked Tomson's and Rosner's work.

[63] Das, *Paul and the Jews*, 166–86.

[64] Heikki Räisänen, *Paul and the Law* (Philadelphia: Fortress, 1983).

[65] See John C. Poirier, "Romans 5:13–14 and the Universality of Law," *NovT* 38
(1996): 344–58. See Das (*Paul and the Jews*, 120–28) on the pronominal shifts in
Galatians and the implications for the relationship between gentiles and the Law.
One must not uncritically assume that the first-person pronouns refer to Jewish
Christians and the second-person pronouns the Galatian gentiles, especially in
view of the serious problems with this position that remain to be addressed.

approach to the Law are yet another difficult question. Pauline scholarship clearly remains a field of adventure and intrigue.

FOR FURTHER READING

Achtemeier, Paul J. "Unsearchable Judgments and Inscrutable Ways: Reflections on the Discussion of Romans." Pages 521–34 in *1995 SBL Seminar Papers*. Edited by Eugene H. Lovering, Jr. Atlanta: Scholars Press, 1995. Repr. (with corrections) in pages 3–21 of *Looking Back, Pressing On*. Edited by E. Elizabeth Johnson and David M. Hay. Vol. 4 of *Pauline Theology*. SBLSymS 4. Atlanta: Scholars Press, 1997.
Avemarie, Friedrich. *Tora und Leben: Untersuchungen zur Heilsbedeutung der Tora in der frühen rabbinischen Literatur*. TSAJ 55. Tübingen: Mohr (Siebeck), 1996.
Carson, D. A., et al., eds. *The Complexities of Second Temple Judaism*. Vol. 1 of *Justification and Variegated Nomism*. Grand Rapids, Mich.: Baker, 2001.
———. *The Paradoxes of Paul*. Vol. 2 of *Justification and Variegated Nomism*. Grand Rapids, Mich.: Baker, 2004.
Das, A. Andrew. *Paul and the Jews*. Library of Pauline Studies: Peabody, Mass.: Hendrickson, 2003.
———. "Paul and Works of Obedience in Second Temple Judaism: Romans 4:4–5 as a 'New Perspective' Case Study." *CBQ* (forthcoming).
———. *Paul, the Law, and the Covenant*. Peabody, Mass.: Hendrickson, 2001.
Dunn, James D. G. *Jesus, Paul, and the Law: Studies in Mark and Galatians*. Louisville, Ky.: Westminster/John Knox, 1990.
———. *The New Perspective on Paul: Collected Essays*. WUNT 185. Tübingen: Mohr Siebeck, 2005.
———. *Paul and the Mosaic Law*. WUNT 89. Tübingen: Mohr (Siebeck), 1996.
Eskola, Timo. "Paul, Predestination and 'Covenantal Nomism'—Re-Assessing Paul and Palestinian Judaism." *JSJ* 29 (1997): 390–412.
———. *Theology and Predestination in Pauline Soteriology*. WUNT 2.100. Tübingen: Mohr (Siebeck), 1998.
Gathercole, Simon J. *Where Is Boasting? Early Jewish Soteriology and Paul's Response in Romans 1–5*. Grand Rapids, Mich.: Eerdmans, 2002.
Gundry, Robert H. "Grace, Works, and Staying Saved in Paul." *Bib* 66 (1985): 1–38.
Hollander, Harm W. "The Meaning of the Term 'Law' (ΝΟΜΟΣ) in 1 Corinthians." *NovT* 40 (1998): 117–35.

116   A. Andrew Das

Martyn, J. Louis. "*Nomos* plus Genitive Noun in Paul: The History of God's Law in Paul." Pages 575–87 in *Early Christianity and Classical Culture: Comparative Studies in Honor of Abraham J. Malherbe.* Edited by J. T. Fitzgerald et al. NovTSup 110. Leiden: Brill, 2003.

Meyer, Paul W. "The Worm at the Core of the Apple: Exegetical Reflections on Romans 7." Pages 62–84 in *The Conversation Continues: Studies in Paul and John in Honor of J. Louis Martyn.* Edited by Robert T. Fortna and Beverly R. Gaventa. Nashville: Abingdon, 1990.

Räisänen, Heikki. *Jesus, Paul, and Torah: Collected Essays.* Translated by David E. Orton. JSNTSup 43. Sheffield: Sheffield Academic Press, 1992.

———. *Paul and the Law.* 2d ed. WUNT 29. Tübingen: Mohr (Siebeck), 1986.

Roo, Jacqueline C. R. *"Works of the Law" at Qumran and in Paul.* Sheffield: Sheffield Phoenix, 2007.

Sanders, E. P. *Paul and Palestinian Judaism.* Minneapolis: Fortress, 1977.

———. *Paul, the Law, and the Jewish People.* Philadelphia: Fortress, 1983.

Schreiner, Thomas R. *The Law and Its Fulfillment: A Pauline Theology of Law.* Grand Rapids, Mich.: Baker, 1993.

Snodgrass, Klyne R. "Spheres of Influence: A Possible Solution to the Problem of Paul and the Law." *JSNT* 32 (1988): 93–113.

Talbert, Charles H. "Paul, Judaism, and the Revisionists." *CBQ* 63 (2001): 1–22.

Thielman, Frank. *From Plight to Solution: A Jewish Framework for Understanding Paul's View of the Law in Galatians and Romans.* NovTSup 61. Leiden: Brill, 1989.

———. *Paul and the Law.* Downers Grove, Ill.: InterVarsity Press, 1994.

Tomson, Peter J. *Paul and the Jewish Law: Halakha in the Letters of the Apostle to the Gentiles.* CRINT 3/1. Minneapolis: Fortress, 1990.

VanLandingham, Chris. *Judgment and Justification in Early Judaism and the Apostle Paul.* Peabody, Mass.: Hendrickson, 2006.

Westerholm, Stephen. *Perspectives Old and New on Paul: The "Lutheran" Paul and His Critics.* Grand Rapids, Mich.: Eerdmans, 2004.

Wright, N. T. *Climax of the Covenant: Christ and the Law in Pauline Theology.* Minneapolis: Fortress, 1991.

6

Paul and Judaism: Why Not Paul's Judaism?

Mark D. Nanos

When NT scholars address the topic of Paul and Judaism, the conjunction generally signals an adversative: Paul or Judaism; Paul against Judaism; Paul outside of Judaism; or Paul, not Judaism. Traditionally, the emphasis is on the distance between Paul's new religion based upon Jesus Christ and Judaism, his former religion.[1] The level of continuity or discontinuity assessed differs from interpreter to interpreter, but a shared perception remains assumed, if not argued: the religious life of Paul's communities, Paulinism, and the religious life of Jewish communities, Judaism, including Jewish Christianity, represent two fundamentally different religious systems.[2] One does not hear or read

---

[1] E.g., Hans Dieter Betz, *Galatians: A Commentary on Paul's Letter to the Churches in Galatia* (Hermeneia; Philadelphia: Fortress, 1979), 251: "the Galatians have to choose between Paul and Judaism."

[2] That there is a geo-ethnic dimension to Jewish identity, hence, Judeanness, is not to be dismissed, but the discussion about Paul focuses on the religio-ethnic dimension of the life of the Jewish communities and the various ways that each person or group or subgroup interpreted the Scriptures and traditions of their heritage, by which Paul's teachings and life are measured. In English usage, "Jew" and "Jewish" carry ethnic and religious meanings, including connotations of birth, while "Judean" signifies only geographical location, place of origin, or residence. Judeanness can be particularly salient when discussing Jews from places other than Judea proper, such as of the Diaspora, or even Galilee, who are nevertheless still described as *ioudaioi* (Acts 2:5–11), or Israelites, even when the land was not Israel but Judea (1 Macc 7:13; Rom 9:4; Acts 2:22; 4 Macc 18:5). At the same time, the significance of the geo-political (i.e., the land of Israel/Judea) remains salient in the terms "Jew" and "Judaism" as well, as witnessed in the role of Israel in the contemporary Judaism and in theology, prayers, and aspirations throughout the centuries. Rabbinic literature remained concerned to define proper behavior in the land and temple. Hence, this chapter will generally refer to Jews and Jewish and Jewishness or Judaism, unless the geo-ethnic element of Judeanness is perceived to

about Paul's Judaism, or Pauline Judaism, of Judaism or Jewishness as the propositional basis of Paul's way of life, or that of the communities he establishes and addresses.

Most interpreters today pronounce that Paul had been a Jew and that he remained one. Yet few have or would argue that Paul continued to practice and promote Judaism as an expression of covenant faithfulness after his experience of Jesus Christ. When Paul is upheld to be a Jew it thus signifies a kind of ethnic identity independent of the religious elements

---

be specifically more salient (note: non-Jews could also be Judeans, just as non-Jews can be Israelis). That there was a religious dimension to Judean/Jewish ethnicity properly named Judaism seems to me evident from relevant sources for discussing Paul's period; it arises in Paul's language in Gal 1:13–14 (discussed below). In the Maccabean literature, Judeans can either leave or return or observe in different ways and to different degrees the traditional religious practices of this people. For example, in 2 Macc 6:1–11, there are those in Judea who are described to be prohibited "even from confessing themselves to be *Ioudaioi*," which would make less sense to translate "Judeans" rather than "Jews" (cf. 2 Macc 9:13–17, where Antiochus IV Epiphanes is described as willing to become a *Ioudaios*, which most likely means Jew, not Judean, for he was not giving up his role as the Seleucid king). Philo, *On the Special Laws* 1.186, notes the range of observance among Jews but is not describing their level of Judeanness. Josephus, *Ant.* 20.34–48, relates that Izates, the king of Adiabene, seeks to live a Jewish lifestyle guided by Scripture, apparently independent of participation in a Jewish community, or role in ruling Judea or a Judean satellite nation, or even any idea of relocating to Judea. His interests and practices make more sense to classify as Judaism, even after his circumcision, although the geo-ethnic element is relevant, as witnessed by the concern about how his subjects will react (more discussion below). Moreover, note that the teacher advocating circumcision (Eleazar) is described as coming from Galilee, not Judea, so he is not arguably a Judean, although he is described as a *Ioudaios* (43), while the other one (Ananias) is not described in terms of coming from somewhere but yet as a *Ioudaios* merchant. See Daniel R. Schwartz, "'Judaean' or 'Jew'? How Should We Translate *ioudaios* in Josephus?" in *Jewish Identity in the Greco-Roman World* (ed. Jörg Frey et al.; Ancient Judaism and Early Christianity 71; Leiden: Brill, 2007), 3–27; Margaret H. Williams, "The Meaning and Function of *Ioudaios* in Graeco-Roman Inscriptions," *Zeitschrift für Papyrologie und Epigraphik* 116 (1997): 249–62; Shaye J. D. Cohen, *The Beginnings of Jewishness: Boundaries, Varieties, Uncertainties* (Hellenistic Culture and Society 31; Berkeley: University of California Press, 1999), 69–139; David Goodblatt, *Elements of Ancient Jewish Nationalism* (Cambridge: Cambridge University Press, 2006); Siân Jones and Sarah Pearce, eds., *Jewish Local Patriotism and Self-Identification in the Graeco-Roman Period* (JSPSup 31; Sheffield: Sheffield Academic Press, 1998); Anders Runesson, "Inventing Christian Identity: Paul, Ignatius, and Theodosius I," in *Exploring Early Christian Identity* (ed. Bengt Holmberg; WUNT; Tübingen: Mohr Siebeck, forthcoming). Among those arguing instead for use of "Judean" throughout, see, e.g., Philip F. Esler, *Conflict and Identity in Romans: The Social Setting of Paul's Letter* (Minneapolis: Fortress, 2003), 19–76; Steve Mason, "Jews, Judaeans, Judaizing, Judaism: Problems of Categorization in Ancient History," *JSJ* 38 (2007): 457–512.

of ethnicity related to covenant standing, a Jew or Judean who does not behave Jewishly. He is the leader if not the founder of a new religious movement, one functioning outside the boundaries of Judaism. Although some other Christ believers, like James and Peter, may be considered to remain within the circle of Judaism, so-called Jewish Christianity, Paul's churches gathered not in synagogues but in house churches of believers in Jesus Christ that were clearly distinguishable from Jewish gathering places or meetings.[3] These new communities consisted primarily of non-Jews, with perhaps a few former Jews. They represented a new religious movement that was distinguished from Judaism, namely, Christianity, even if that name had not yet been coined.[4]

Furthermore, Paul has been traditionally understood to be antagonistic toward Torah identity and practice. Some propose that he was instead simply "indifferent" (ἀδιάφορος; although Paul's letters do not contain the term).[5] Others grant that he observed Torah to various degrees, but not as an expression of faith. But either way, Paul believed that the era of

---

[3] E.g., Francis Watson, *Paul, Judaism, and the Gentiles: A Sociological Approach* (SNTSMS 56; Cambridge: Cambridge University Press, 1986), argues that Paul's strategic goal was to create "Gentile Christian communities in sharp separation from the Jewish community" (19; passim); Esler, *Conflict and Identity in Romans,* 89–97, 120–25, maintains that the policy of creating house churches was by definition a clear differentiation from synagogue gatherings; John M. G. Barclay, *Jews in the Mediterranean Diaspora: From Alexander to Trajan (323 B.C.E.–117 C.E.)* (Edinburgh: T&T Clark, 1996), 386: "In social reality Paul's churches were distinct from the synagogues, and their predominantly Gentile members unattached to the Jewish community"; Alan F. Segal, *Paul the Convert: The Apostolate and Apostasy of Saul the Pharisee* (New Haven: Yale University Press, 1990), 6–7, argues that Paul represents "a new apocalyptic, Jewish sect," yet writes of him living "in a Hellenistic, gentile *Christian community* as a Jew among gentiles" (emphasis added). I argue that the communities Paul addresses in Rome and Galatia are meeting as subgroups within the Jewish communities in *The Mystery of Romans: The Jewish Context of Paul's Letter* (Minneapolis: Fortress, 1996); idem, *The Irony of Galatians: Paul's Letter in First-Century Context* (Minneapolis: Fortress, 2002).

[4] Betz, *Galatians,* 179: "Paul draws a line between being a Jew and being a Christian. Of course, this line of demarcation is polemical, but, as Romans shows (Rom 9–11), it was in no way intended to establish a new religion. Yet the establishment of a new religion is in effect what happened. If the validity of the Jewish Torah ends for the Jew when he becomes a Christian, there is no point or basis for Gentiles as well as for Jews to adhere to the Jewish religion. Since those Christians no longer regard themselves as pagans, a new religion has *de facto* come into existence." See Runesson, "Inventing Christian Identity," for a new paradigm challenging this traditional understanding.

[5] E.g., Hans Joachim Schoeps, *Paul: The Theology of the Apostle in the Light of Jewish Religious History* (trans. Harold Knight; Philadelphia: Westminster Press, 1961), 197–200.

Torah had ended, being made obsolete, or fulfilled, or superseded in the work of Christ. He did not regard Jewish covenant identity or behavior to have any "soteriological" significance.[6] To the degree that he observed Torah occasionally, it simply reflected cultural conditioning from which he had not yet been liberated, having been born and raised a Jew.[7] Or it demonstrated the chameleon-like behavioral extremes to which he would go to win other Jews to his convictions. The latter view relies largely upon the prevailing interpretations of 1 Cor 9:19–23, wherein Paul describes becoming all things to all people in order to win them to the gospel of Christ, and specifically, of becoming to Jews and to those under law like a Jew and like one under law, and alternatively, of becoming lawless or without law as well as weak to those who are lawless or without law or weak.

The role of 1 Cor 9:19–23 in Pauline studies is significant and provides a useful place to define the topics that generally arise in discussion of Paul and Judaism. Donald Hagner speaks for many when he writes: "Paul regards himself as no longer under the law," since he "obeys it now and then. Paul thus feels free to identify with the Gentiles and not to remain an observant Jew. Incidentally, how remarkable it is that the Jew Paul can speak of himself as an outsider: "To the Jews I became as a Jew"! This implies a "break with Judaism," and "it is clear, furthermore, that observing or not observing the law is an unimportant issue before God. The position taken by Paul is one of complete expedience: he will or will not observe the law only in relation to its usefulness in the proclamation of the gospel. Before God the issue of obeying the commandments is in the category of adiaphora."[8] Heikki Räisänen declares the implications for the consensus

[6] Donald A. Hagner, "Paul as a Jewish Believer—According to His Letters," in *Jewish Believers in Jesus: The Early Centuries* (ed. Oskar Skarsaune and Reidar Hvalvik; Peabody, Mass.: Hendrickson, 2007), 97–120 (113).

[7] E.g., C. H. Dodd, *The Epistle to the Romans* (London: Hodder & Stoughton, 1932), 43; E. P. Sanders, *Paul, the Law, and the Jewish People* (Philadelphia: Fortress, 1985), 103, 198–99, discusses Paul's struggle to reconcile revelation with "his native convictions"; Hagner, "Paul as a Jewish Believer," 114, observes that while Paul may have continued to behave in some ways like a Jew, it was "by habit, if for no other reason . . . as an expression of his ethnic Jewishness, and as a matter of convenience because of the fact that he moved among Jews so frequently. This conduct no longer had any soteriological significance, however, nor was he under compulsion to obey the commandments. His conduct was now solely under the sway of Christ."

[8] Hagner, "Paul as a Jewish Believer," 113; see also Gordon D. Fee, *The First Epistle to the Corinthians* (New International Commentary on the New Testament; Grand Rapids, Mich.: Eerdmans, 1987), 427; James D. G. Dunn, *The Theology of Paul the Apostle* (Grand Rapids, Mich.: Eerdmans, 1997), 577; Richard B. Hays, *First Corinthians* (Interpretation; Louisville, Ky.: John Knox, 1997), 153–54; Segal, *Paul the Convert*, 228, 238.

view quite clearly: "1 Cor 9.20 f. is absolutely incompatible with the theory of an observant Paul."[9]

This interpretive tradition overwhelmingly upholds that Paul subscribed to a policy of mimicking the behavior of non-Jews, on the one hand, and of Jews, including fully Torah-observant Jews, or proselytes, on the other. I write "mimicking," because, while the negative aspect of this behavior that such a term conveys is not generally highlighted, it nevertheless represents what is signified for "becoming like" in the arguments made. "Becoming like" is not interpreted to mean Paul becomes the same as or like each, for he is not portrayed to subscribe to the propositional bases of the behavior he appears to adopt. Those whom he mimics presumably behave as they do to express their worldview and convictions. But he is understood merely to imitate the outward behavioral trappings when in the company of each of these different people or groups: it is not internalized, not of the heart. He does not "become" in the true sense, the sense that he wishes for them to "become" Christ believers by conviction and to live that way thereafter inwardly as well as outwardly, like himself. Paul merely adjusts his conduct to fit the lifestyle of different people and groups in order to gain the trust of each of them in the gospel.[10]

What is not often discussed is that such a policy, supposedly calculated to persuade people with entirely different behavioral patterns and cultural premises, would instead over time almost certainly alienate all of them. Surely some Jews would hear rumors of his non-Jewish eating behavior, for example, when with non-Jews, and others would no doubt witness this behavior. The same is true about non-Jews witnessing Jewish behavior when he was among Jews. This would especially be the case within the context of communal gatherings, which many also suppose this passage to address, that is, the winning of Christ-believing Jews and non-Jews to a more mature life in Christ.[11] In such settings, where push comes to shove, Paul is understood to forgo Jewish practices.[12] Why? Because he did not subscribe to Jewish behavior as a matter of conviction anyway, so he can hardly be expected to choose Torah, if that would imply to non-Jews that the gospel was in some way yoked to Torah. However

---

[9] *Paul and the Law*, 75n171.

[10] For the consensus view, see, e.g., Peter Richardson, "Pauline Inconsistency: 1 Corinthians 9:19–23 and Galatians 2:11–14," *NTS* 26 (1979): 347–62 (347); Mark D. Given, *Paul's True Rhetoric: Ambiguity, Cunning, and Deception in Greece and Rome* (Emory Studies in Early Christianity 7; Harrisburg, Penn.: Trinity Press International, 2001), 105–17; and those noted in the footnotes discussing this passage below.

[11] E.g., Hays, *First Corinthians*, 155.

[12] Sanders, *Paul, the Law*, 177–78, 185–87.

conceptualized, Paul's behavior, when interpreted along this traditional line, would eventually be observed by those who found it to be the opposite of what they supposed him to sustain for himself. Hence, the effect would be the opposite of that which he intends. To Jews he would quickly appear to be (become) like a non-Jew, to non-Jews he would quickly appear to be (become) like a Jew.

On this popular reading, Paul is understood to have, for example, eaten like non-Jews when in their company and like Jews when in theirs. To gain them, he behaved like them. But he did so disingenuously, especially when playing the part of a practicing Jew.[13] For this policy obscured the fact that Jews who valued Torah observance enough for Paul to adopt this behavior in order to gain their trust, would be, if they accepted his message, commencing on a faith journey characterized by the renunciation of Torah faith, yet unbeknown to them. It follows that if converted, they too would adopt this chameleon-like expedient behavior thereafter on the same terms, that is, only to dupe other Jews, creating a spiral of duplicity, a culture wherein misunderstanding and continued immature or weak notions of the value of Jewish practice among Jewish believers in Christ would be self-perpetuating.

John Barclay recognizes this logical element in the traditional construction of Paul but upholds it nevertheless to be the correct interpretation, cleverly comparing Paul's theology with "a Trojan horse which threatens the integrity of those who sought to live according to the law."[14] Many Jewish interpreters, accepting the traditional Christian construction, have observed the duplicity of Paul's strategy, and it has been used to substantiate the arguments of those wishing to expose suspect values at the heart of nascent Christianity.[15] At the same time,

---

[13] For most of these interpreters, Paul did share the propositional base of non-Jews about food, because he is understood to eat like a Gentile, since his behavior is supposedly no longer governed by Torah; hence, he only mimicked Jewish behavior. The lack of precision in the traditional definition of "becoming" as mere imitation of outward behavior is thereby magnified.

[14] John M. G. Barclay, "'Do We Undermine the Law?': A Study of Romans 14.1–15.6," in *Paul and the Mosaic Law* (ed. James D. G. Dunn; Grand Rapids, Mich.: Eerdmans, 2001), 287–308 (308).

[15] The history of a line of Jewish critique turning around Paul's "opportunist" subversion of Torah to gain converts as portrayed by Christian interpreters, often as if a positive trait, subjecting everything to the highest value of evangelism, is discussed by Nancy Fuchs-Kreimer, "The 'Essential Heresy': Paul's View of the Law according to Jewish Writers: 1886–1986" (Ph.D. diss., Temple University, 1990), 63–82. See also Hyam Maccoby, *The Mythmaker: Paul and the Invention of Christianity* (New York: Harper & Row, 1986), 151–57, 166–67, and David Klinghoffer, *Why the Jews Rejected Jesus: The Turning Point in Western History* (New York:

many Christian interpreters do not mention the problematic subversion of Paul's integrity this interpretation creates or explain how they reconcile it with the high moral standing otherwise attributed to Paul's life and teaching.

This interpretive approach is also popular among those who seek to reconcile the Torah-observant Paul presented by Luke in Acts with the Paul of his letters, where he is generally understood to be indifferent to Torah observance, if not opposed to it. For them, Paul's adoption of Torah in Acts exemplifies his missionary strategy as expressed in 1 Cor 9:19-23, wherein he supposedly undertakes Torah observance sometimes in the expedient pursuit of a value championed to be superior, evangelism, regardless of and generally without discussion of the moral problematic of duplicity: "The undisputable fact that he was raised as a law-observant Jew makes it reasonable to assume that he often observed Jewish customs in his daily life—as long as they did not blur the gospel. For the historical Paul, traditional law-observance was certainly subordinated to the preaching of the gospel and his concern for the salvation of mankind."[16]

Even when Paul is understood to encourage respect for Jewish behavior among Christ believers, it amounts to little more than patronizing. For example, when Paul urges those who were secure in their faith to respect the sensibilities of the "weak in faith" in Rome, they are portrayed to be Jewish believers in Jesus who still "fail to trust God completely and without qualification," that is, they have not freed themselves from Torah practice as integral to Christ faith.[17] In Corinth, although Paul is understood to call for the "knowledgeable" to refrain from eating idol food for the sake of those who object to it as a matter of conscience, or consciousness, it is understood to be but a temporary concession, because in the long run Paul is believed to share the values of those Christ believers who would eat idol food as a

---

Doubleday, 2005), 106-10. Fuchs-Kreimer also discusses some Jewish scholars do not read Paul in this way. See also Daniel R. Langton, "The Myth of the 'Traditional View of Paul' and the Role of the Apostle in Modern Jewish-Christian Polemics," *JSNT* 28 (2005): 69-104; Stefan Meißner, *Die Heimholung des Ketzers: Studien zur jüdischen Auseinandersetzung mit Paulus* (WUNT 2.87; Tübingen: Mohr Siebeck, 1996).

[16] Reidar Hvalvik, "Paul as a Jewish Believer—According to the Book of Acts," in *Jewish Believers in Jesus: The Early Centuries* (ed. Oskar Skarsaune and Reidar Hvalvik; Peabody, Mass.: Hendrickson, 2007), 121-53 (153); cf. Hagner, "Paul as a Jewish Believer," 113.

[17] James D. G. Dunn, *Romans 9-16* (WBC 38B; Dallas: Word, 1988), 798. This common understanding of Paul's language, e.g., in Rom 14—15 is challenged in Nanos, *Mystery of Romans,* 85-165, 345-47 (88-95, for "Luther's trap," where comments such as this one by Dunn are discussed).

matter of indifference to Jewish covenant food conventions.[18] According to the prevailing interpretation of Phil 3:3–7, Paul counted the value of Jewish identity and behavior to amount to nothing more than "crap [σκύβαλα]."[19]

According to the consensus of Pauline scholars, while Paul may have resisted the logical conclusion that he was no longer a representative of Judaism or a Jew in good standing but rather an apostate, one who now represented a new religion, that was an assessment hardly shared by others, including those who represented so-called Jewish Christianity.[20] He may have thought of himself as a good Jew, but no other practicing Jews would have. To the degree that Judaism continued to be lived in a meaningful way by Christ believers—as an expression of personal and communal faith and lifestyle, of kavannah (kawwanah from the root kwn; intention)—this was reserved for so-called Jewish Christianity, represented by James or Peter. That was a way of interpreting the meaning of life after the resurrection of Jesus Christ that Paul ostensibly opposed, because the Mosaic legislation no longer expressed God's purpose for humankind, either because with the work of Christ the Mosaic covenant had successfully completed its purpose or because it had failed to do so and was rendered thereafter obsolete.

In short, when NT scholars speak of Paul's religious life and values, of Paulinism or Pauline Christianity, with its "law-free gospel," most mean to signify a Judaism-free way of living because of faith in Jesus Christ.

THE NEW PERSPECTIVE ON PAUL AND JUDAISM

In recent years, the so-called New Perspective on Paul has challenged the traditional characterizations of the Judaism of Paul's time to be

---

[18] E.g., C. K. Barrett, ed., *Essays on Paul* (Philadelphia: Westminster Press, 1982), 40–59 ("Things Sacrificed to Idols"). Challenges to this reading are mounted by Peter J. Tomson, *Paul and the Jewish Law: Halakha in the Letters of the Apostle to the Gentiles* (CRINT 1; Assen: Van Gorcum, 1990); Alex T. Cheung, *Idol Food in Corinth: Jewish Background and Pauline Legacy* (JSNTSup 176; Sheffield: Sheffield Academic Press, 1999); Mark D. Nanos, "The Polytheist Identity of the 'Weak,' and Paul's Strategy to 'Gain' Them: A New Reading of 1 Corinthians 8:1–11:1," in *Paul: Jew, Greek, and Roman* (ed. Stanley E. Porter; Pauline Studies 5; Leiden: Brill, forthcoming; see also http://www.marknanos.com/Polytheist-Corinth-1-15-08.pdf).

[19] This prevailing view of Paul's polemic is challenged in Mark D. Nanos, "Paul's *Reversal* of Jews Calling Gentiles 'Dogs' (Philippians 3:2): 1600 Years of an Ideological Tale Wagging an Exegetical Dog?" *BibInt* (forthcoming; see also http://www.marknanos.com/Phil3Dogs-Reverse-1-17-08.pdf).

[20] John M. G. Barclay, "Paul among Diaspora Jews: Anomaly or Apostate?" *JSNT* 60 (1995): 89–120, for a construction of Paul whose assimilation is understood to leave only himself supposing he is not an apostate.

legalistic and arrogantly self-righteous.[21] Instead, interpreters upholding this view recognize that Judaism of Paul's time was focused on responsible behavior (Torah observance) undertaken in a spirit of gratitude appropriate to the expression of faith (i.e., loyalty) by those called by a gracious God to a covenantal relationship (covenantal nomism). In other words, these observations reflect the ideals prized by Christians in positive terms usually reserved to describe Christianity but traditionally denied to Judaism.

Taking Judaism on its own terms is the precious advance made by its proponents, largely based on the ability of Krister Stendahl's and E. P. Sanders's arguments,[22] and those made by others since, to succeed where those making similar observations had been previously unable to convince Pauline scholars and Christians in general.[23] This historically more viable and cross-culturally more respectful development, with its new level of sociological and rhetorical sensitivity, has done little, however, to alter the traditional view that Paul, as apostle, did not practice the Judaism of his day. Even a leading voice of the New Perspective, James Dunn, who generally emphasizes that Paul always regarded himself to be a Jew, nevertheless still writes also that Paul did not "think of himself as a Jew," emphasizing that he did not observe Torah as a matter of conviction, and that "insofar as 'Jew' was an ethnic identifier (and insofar as he was an ethnic Jew), Paul wished neither to be known as such nor to identify himself as such. Insofar as 'Jew' denoted a lifestyle, a commitment to the ancestral

---

[21] The position and coining of the phrase by Dunn is well summarized in "The New Perspective on Paul," *BJRL* 65 (1983): 95–122 (reprinted with additional notes in James D. G. Dunn, *Jesus, Paul, and the Law: Studies in Mark and Galatians* [Louisville, Ky.: Westminster/John Knox, 1990], 183–214). "The Paul Page" is dedicated to discussion of this topic: <http://www.thepaulpage.com/>.

[22] Krister Stendahl, *Paul among Jews and Gentiles, and Other Essays* (Philadelphia: Fortress, 1976); E. P. Sanders, *Paul and Palestinian Judaism: A Comparison of Patterns of Religion* (Philadelphia: Fortress, 1977).

[23] See, e.g., Hans Joachim Schoeps, *The Jewish-Christian Argument: A History of Theologies in Conflict* (trans. David E. Green; London: Faber & Faber, 1965), 40–52, 165, published in German in 1961 (idem, *Israel und Christenheit: Jüdisch-christliches Religionsgespräch in neunzehn Jahrhunderten* [Munich: Ner-Tamid, 1961], 57–59. Note that the first edition contains this same language: *Jüdisch-Christliches Religionsgespräch in 19 Jahrhunderten: Geschichte einer theologischen Auseinandersetzung* [Berlin: Vortrupp, 1937], 49–61, 152). Similar observations are in Schoeps, *Paul*, 168–218, 280–93. There were naturally others who anticipated these positive developments, and some examples such as G. F. Moore, W. D. Davies, and S. Sandmel, as well as central protagonists of the traditional negative biases, are discussed by Sanders, *Paul and Palestinian Judaism*, 33–59; see too Susannah Heschel, *Abraham Geiger and the Jewish Jesus* (Chicago Studies in the History of Judaism; Chicago: University of Chicago Press, 1998); Langton, "The Myth of the 'Traditional View of Paul,'" 69–104.

customs of the Jews, Paul wished neither to exercise such a commitment nor to insist that other Jews be true to their ethnic-religious identity."[24] This trajectory was anticipated in Dunn's initial discussion of the new possibilities for interpreting Paul that he discovered through Sanders's work. Regarding Gal 2:16, Dunn observed that he detected in Paul a "crucial development for the history of Christianity taking place": "the transition from a form of Jewish Messianism to a faith which sooner or later must break away from Judaism to exist in its own terms."[25]

Moreover, most New Perspective interpreters still find fault with Judaism, albeit emphasizing different reasons, or at least with Judaism as Paul (mis)understood it. Paul is portrayed to have transcended Jewish particularism, expressed in nationalism, in specific boundary-marking behavior such as circumcision, Sabbath, and food conventions (cf. Dunn; N. T. Wright). Or they find fault with Paul, in that he seems to have misunderstood his "former" religion (Sanders, and earlier, e.g., H. J. Schoeps) or to have failed to reconcile it with his new "Christian" religion (Räisänen), leaving an irreconcilable contradiction in his theology.[26]

---

[24] Dunn, "Who Did Paul Think He Was? A Study of Jewish-Christian Identity," *NTS* 45 (1999): 174–93 (182). On 179, Dunn argues that "of course Paul did not cease to be a Jew—how could he? Nor did he convert from one religion ('Judaism') to another ('Christianity'), since the term 'Christianity' did not yet exist, and the Nazarene movement was still within the matrix of Second Temple Judaism." He nuances the definition of Jew, emphasizing the religious dimension, and of Judaism, inscrutably from my perspective, to denote for Paul only "the national-religious identity which emerged particularly as a result of the Maccabean crisis and revolt. He meant Judaism identified by its zeal for the law and its willingness to use the sword to prevent the dilution of its national-religious distinctiveness. That Judaism was, however, only one part (or aspect?) of what we now call Second Temple Judaism" (184). In his conclusions, 192, Dunn argues that Paul would not give a straight no to his identity as a Jew, as long as it was qualified "to come from within and not from without, and that the trappings of Jewish identity, most explicitly the practice of circumcision and food laws, could be equally taken on or put off without affecting the integrity of that Jewishness either way." But he would give a clear no to being "in Judaism": "the term had become too much identified with ethnicity and separation from other nations; and Paul's self-understanding on just these points had been too radically transformed by his conversion . . . for 'Judaism' to continue to define and identify himself or his apostolic work."

[25] "New Perspective," in *Jesus, Paul*, 198.

[26] Cf. the observations and criticisms of Neil Elliott, *Liberating Paul: The Justice of God and the Politics of the Apostle* (Maryknoll, N.Y.: Orbis, 1994), 66–72, 108. On the problem of a continued logical negative valuation of Judaism in recent intermural Christian approaches pitting Paul against Jewish Christianity, and thus claiming to avoid the traditional Paul against Judaism judgments, see Mark D. Nanos, "How Inter-Christian Approaches to Paul's Rhetoric Can Perpetuate Negative Valuations of Jewishness—Although Proposing to Avoid that Outcome," *BibInt* 13 (2005): 255–69.

Thus, as several interpreters have noted, what has been named the New Perspective on Paul arguably represents not so much a new perspective on Paul as a new perspective on Judaism. The effort of Christian scholars to make sense of Paul's arguments in new terms has instead often resulted in a new level of confusion about Paul, or better, about the traditional construction of Paul, a construction of Paul that still generally prevails for the proponents of the New Perspective. Especially problematic is how to reconcile the implications that follow from recognizing Judaism to be grace- and faith-based with the role that Paul's voice has traditionally played in the critique of Judaism, as well as the foundations of Christian theology, wherein defining terms like "faith" and "grace" and "works" has always taken place in comparison to what they were perceived to represent in Judaism, the misguided religion of the other. But if Judaism is based on grace, then why did Paul find something wrong with it? Or did he? What does this imply about the role of Jesus for Jews?[27] Is not Pauline Christianity necessarily something other than Judaism? If not, what kind of Judaism was it, or should it be?

Naturally, not all Pauline interpreters believe that these positive reevaluations of Judaism are warranted, much less the efforts toward new interpretations of Paul or Christian origins they provoke. Many continue to view both Judaism and Paul through traditional Christian, especially Reformation-ground lenses,[28] or the bifocals shaped by F. C. Baur,[29]

---

[27] E.g., although beyond the scope of this chapter, many debates now turn around the New Perspective emphasis on reading the language of justification by faith to refer to the inclusion of non-Jews as equals rather than addressing personal salvation of everyone, as traditionally interpreted, which logically brings up the topic of whether from Paul's perspective Jews also need to believe in Jesus Christ, in particular, to be saved.

[28] E.g., Donald A. Hagner, "Paul and Judaism—The Jewish Matrix of Early Christianity: Issues in the Current Debate," *Bulletin for Biblical Research* 3 (1993): 111–30; Seyoon Kim, *Paul and the New Perspective: Second Thoughts on the Origin of Paul's Gospel* (Grand Rapids, Mich.: Eerdmans, 2001); A. Andrew Das, *Paul, the Law, and the Covenant* (Peabody, Mass.: Hendrickson, 2001); Simon J. Gathercole, *Where Is Boasting?: Early Jewish Soteriology and Paul's Response in Romans 1–5* (Grand Rapids, Mich.: Eerdmans, 2002); D. A. Carson et al., eds., *Justification and Variegated Nomism*, vol. 2, *The Paradoxes of Paul* (Tübingen: Mohr Siebeck, 2004); Stephen Westerholm, *Perspectives Old and New on Paul: The "Lutheran" Paul and His Critics* (Grand Rapids, Mich.: Eerdmans, 2004). A detailed bibliography of the New Perspective and its critics is available in Michael F. Bird, *The Saving Righteousness of God: Studies on Paul, Justification and the New Perspective* (Paternoster Biblical Monographs; Milton Keynes, U.K.: Paternoster, 2007), 194–211; idem, "The New Perspective on Paul: A Bibliographical Essay," on *The Paul Page*, webmaster Mark Mattison: http://www.thepaulpage.com/Bibliography.html.

[29] F. C. Baur, *Paul the Apostle of Jesus Christ: His Life and Works, His Epistles and Teachings* (2d ed; ed. Eduard Zeller; trans. Allan Menzies; repr., Peabody,

through which the superiority of Pauline Christianity can be clearly seen.[30] It is also notable that Jewish interpreters of Paul, who do not generally share the traditional Christian perspectives on Judaism, nevertheless often adopt the traditional interpretations of Paul.[31] The valuations that Christians have championed in this construal of Paul are easily viewed from an oppositional perspective to highlight, interestingly enough, the inferiority of Pauline Christianity.[32]

Ironically, the lack of substantial newness in the way Paul is portrayed or understood to relate to what is newly perceived about Judaism is signaled in the research that arguably inaugurated the so-called New Perspective on Paul. In his often repeated statement, Sanders cleverly poses

---

Mass.: Hendrickson, 2003); James Carleton Paget, "The Definition of the Terms Jewish Christian and Jewish Christianity in the History of Research," in *Jewish Believers in Jesus: The Early Centuries* (ed. Oskar Skarsaune and Reidar Hvalvik; Peabody, Mass.: Hendrickson, 2007), 22–52.

[30] In sharp contrast to the critique offered here, which largely revolves around the relative lack of newness in the perspectives on Paul that have been offered, those resisting the New Perspective are critical of its newness, of its departure from traditional and especially Reformation interpretations of Paul as well as of Judaism, however minor the changes proposed may be in the case of Paul. The efforts to undermine the New Perspective are frequently occupied with showing that Judaism is as Christianity has interpreted Judaism to be through the traditional interpretation of Paul's rhetoric, thereby confirming that Paul has been interpreted properly to be offering a very different religious system from that of Judaism.

[31] Although some have grouped me among New Perspective interpreters, this category represents Christians who newly discovered that Judaism is not as it has been polemically constructed in Christian tradition, which does not apply in the same way for a Jewish person who did not hold to the traditional Christian views of Judaism in the first place, or of Paul, and thus did not undergo the changes signified by the label "New Perspective." Previous to Sanders, a number of Jews and Christians unsuccessfully sought to inform the Christian tradition that Judaism was and is grace-based and that acts of righteousness are undertaken in terms of covenant loyalty, and so on; thus the change of perspective on Judaism is indeed new and welcome. For me, it made it possible to enter the discussion of redefining Paul without also undertaking the task of redefining Judaism along this line first, which, when I first imagined this task in the 1970s, appeared too daunting a course to pursue. When I learned of the New Perspective and its impact in the 1980s, I could then reconsider offering a new interpretation of Paul, although one that is in many ways significantly different from the Paul of the New Perspective on Paul proper. Since then, I have certainly been engaged in offering a new perspective on Paul, if not also Judaism, on some points.

[32] Cf. Langton, "The Myth of the 'Traditional View of Paul,'" which includes a discussion of how my work differs from the main lines the traditional Jewish perspectives on Paul have followed; and see the above discussion of Jewish reactions to the prevailing interpretations of 1 Cor 9:19–23, on which my views are briefly set out below.

the matter in starkly contrasting terms: "*this is what Paul finds wrong in Judaism: it is not Christianity.*"[33] Sanders defines this problem not as a critique of "the means of being properly religious" but of "the prior fundamentals of Judaism: the election, the covenant and the law; and it is because these are *wrong* that the means appropriate to 'righteousness according to the law' (Torah observance and repentance) are held to be wrong or are not mentioned."[34]

To my knowledge, what has gone largely unrecognized in Sanders's turn of phrase, and in much of the work by New Perspective interpreters, is the traditional assumption that remains necessary to it. For Sanders's statement requires the institutional development of Christianity to make sense, however historically unlikely that remains, and regardless of how often the formation of Christianity in Paul's time is otherwise denied.[35] This results in a great deal of confusion in recent discussions about Paul and Judaism. Initial claims that there was no such thing as Christianity are regularly emptied of significance as the arguments proceed. It becomes evident that the interpreter is still working with a perception of Paul and his communities as something other than Judaism. This includes the problem of the continued use of nomenclature like "Christian" and "Christianity" to refer to him, his teachings, and his communities.[36]

---

[33] Sanders, *Paul and Palestinian Judaism*, 552 (emphasis his).

[34] Ibid., 551–52 (emphasis added).

[35] Stanley Kent Stowers, *A Rereading of Romans: Justice, Jews, and Gentiles* (New Haven: Yale University Press, 1994), 24–25, similarly notes this problem.

[36] Dunn regularly notes that Paul was not converted to a new religion and that he precedes what can be properly denoted as Christianity (James D. G. Dunn, *The Partings of the Ways: Between Christianity and Judaism and Their Significance for the Character of Christianity* [London: SCM Press, 1991], 116–19, 135). Even after the Antioch incident, which Dunn takes to represent a monumental realization of incompatibility, he still conceptualizes the eventual developments to be "as much a parting of the ways *within* the new movement as *between* Christianity and Judaism, or better, as within Judaism" (emphasis his). And he challenges the idea that Paul should be defined only in discontinuity with Judaism, as opposite to it (James D. G. Dunn, "How New Was Paul's Gospel? The Problem of Continuity and Discontinuity," in *Gospel in Paul: Studies on Corinthians, Galatians, and Romans* [ed. L. Ann Jervis and Peter Richardson; Sheffield: Sheffield Academic Press, 1994], 385). Yet Dunn also writes, "we must be careful about defining Pauline Christianity simply as a kind of Judaism" (385; in the same sentence upon which my prior sentence was based). Note that here we see that it is Christianity that Paul is described as doing (although he refers to denoting Jew and Christian as "anachronistic" for Paul's time on 387), and moreover, he observes that it is not Judaism. How does one square this with the idea that Paul precedes Christianity and did not convert to a new religion or abandon Judaism? Similar logical problems on these topics are common in New Perspective arguments, just as they remain common in tradition-oriented arguments: after denying that Christianity had begun or that anyone was

Moreover, Sanders's phrase requires the construction of a Paul who finds something wrong with Judaism. It is with the pillars of Jewish identity and religious values that Paul finds fault: election, covenant, Torah, and repentance. And he does so from outside Judaism rather than from on the inside, since the problem lies in the prior fundamentals of Judaism.

The problem for Sanders's Paul is not with some or other Judaisms, not with some Jewish people[37] or ideas or institutions or practices, not with some or other Christ-believing Jews or Jewish groups[38] or their ways of interpreting the meaning of Jesus Christ—but with and in Judaism per se, which Paul "*opposed.*"[39] Granted, this is not because Judaism was legalistic or based on achieving righteousness by fulfilling commandments rather than by grace, as the traditional views that Sanders criticizes maintained, because he recognized that these were not how Judaism operated. But for Sanders, Paul does not level his critique from within Judaism: he is not engaged in prophetic speech based upon an appeal to the noble values

---

yet known as a Christian, the conceptualizations expressed in language choices and argumentation do not follow this logic out or express a viable alternative at work. Hagner, "Paul as a Jewish Believer," 97–120, proceeds similarly, which I critiqued in Mark D. Nanos, "Have Paul and His Communities Left Judaism for Christianity? A Review of the Paul-Related Chapters in *Jewish Believers in Jesus* and *Jewish Christianity Revisited*" (Jewish Christianity Consultation of the SBL; San Diego, 17 November 2007; available at http://www.marknanos.com/SBL-07–Jewish-Chrstnty.pdf).

[37] Lloyd Gaston, *Paul and the Torah* (Vancouver: University of British Columbia Press, 1987), 140, makes a similar observation: "this is what Paul finds wrong with other Jews: that they did not share his revelation in Damascus."

[38] I prefer not to use the terms "Christian" and "Christianity" except where it is necessary to the discussion and refer to, e.g., Christ believers and Christ-believing Jewish coalitions in an effort to avoid perpetuating this problem. I hope my readers will be encouraged to do so too, although I recognize that the change of terminology can be taxing, creating cumbersome language—and that these choices are still not perfect. Likewise, I try to minimize the use of "Gentile(s)" to label the non-Jew(s), because it obscures the implied "not-ness" of the Hebrew and Greek terms for the non-Jewish (and non-Israelite) other, a way of conceptualizing the world still present in Paul's choice of language and thus with some relevance to the historical interpretive task. In this same direction, it would be clearer, although even more taxing, to refer to "a member of the nations other than Israel" when ἔθνος is translated, and for the plural, "nations," or "members of the other nations," that is, other than *the* nation, Israel.

[39] Sanders, *Paul, the Law,* 156 (emphasis his). Posing the question in a slightly different way, Daniel Boyarin, *A Radical Jew: Paul and the Politics of Identity* (Berkeley: University of California Press, 1994), 52, observes: "What was *wrong* with Jewish culture in Paul's eyes that necessitated a radical reform? And what in the culture provided the grounds for making that critique? The culture itself was in tension with itself, characterized both by narrow ethnocentrism and universalist monotheism."

of these fundamental Jewish ideals, accusing competing Jewish groups or Judaisms of compromising them. Rather, Paul devalues or challenges the ideals themselves, and he does so from outside Judaism. In this sense, the New Perspective view of Paul remains similar to traditional approaches, including the views expressed by those challenging them for ostensibly compromising traditional notions held to be fundamental to certain Christian truths.

Sanders does mention the limitation of referring to "Paul and Judaism" in a way that fails to suggest something other than "Paul and *the rest* of Judaism" but concludes that "the traditional terminology would seem to be justified by his being engaged in a mission which *went beyond the bounds of Judaism.*"[40] For Sanders, Paul's problem remains with or in Judaism as a system that does not offer salvation in Jesus Christ. But does it not do so? Is it not precisely within Judaism where Paul as well as all of the other Jewish and Judean believers in Jesus Christ understood themselves to find him? Did not Paul persecute (i.e., seek to discipline) groups within Judaism for failing to exemplify Jewish values according to his Jewish group's terms, and then later, was it not instead those persecuted groups' values that he upheld to be the most representative of Judaism—Judaism as it should and will be when the end of the ages has arrived, having now, however, in specifically Jewish communal terms, already dawned? Is it not Judaism's ideals as represented in Judaism's Scriptures to which he appeals in order that his addressees will "hear Torah" aright (Gal 4:21), that is, according to Paul's interpretation? Was he not disciplined as a Jew within Judaism?

Interestingly, Sanders argues as much when discussing Paul's thirty-nine lashings five times as evidence that Paul remained within the orbit of synagogue authority, for receipt of this disciplinary action logically implies Paul's continued presence in synagogues.[41] This fact involves voluntarily yielding to the jurisdiction of local Jewish authorities who would not be able to wield such authority over former Jews, those who have chosen to leave the community and the practice of Judaism. Reaching across Jewish communal lines to discipline those outside the community would run afoul of prevailing Roman conventions.

---

[40] Sanders, *Paul and Palestinian Judaism,* 1 (emphasis added).

[41] Sanders, *Paul, the Law,* 192, interestingly enough, in this later work (although without engaging the earlier contrary viewpoint he expressed), writes of Paul as still attending synagogue, that is, as Jewish in socially measurable terms, and argues that Paul and all of the parties, including his non-Jewish addressees as well as those who opposed Paul's work, understood the "Christian movement" they were involved in to be within "the bounds of Judaism. *Punishment implies inclusion*" (emphasis his).

COMPARING VIEWS OF JUDAISM FOR NON-JEWS (GENTILES) VERSUS FOR EVERYONE

I do not wish to downplay the many innovative developments in Pauline scholarship, as a result of which many advances in the study of Paul as well as Judaism have been made, for which I am deeply grateful, and certainly not the contribution of Sanders or Dunn or any of the other scholars whom my discussion engages and from whom I have learned much. At the same time, I would like to focus attention on a few issues that seem to remain unaddressed or confusing in a way that obstructs the gains that might be made in the direction of rereading Paul within the framework of the Judaism (or Judaisms) of his time. My aim is to prod the Pauline interpretive community to paradigmatic change. To begin this process, let us look a little closer at what Sanders wrote.

Sanders compared "how *one* gains righteousness" in Paul's religious system to that of so-called Palestinian Judaism.[42] He found that the Paul he constructed did not share many of the values of the Jewish systems to which Sanders compared him. Besides approaching Paul as outside Judaism, this is a decisive move that continues to reverberate not only in the work of those who constitute the so-called New Perspective and its variations but also in the work of those who oppose it, in that he seeks to measure how one gains righteousness in these two systems.

That approach poses the topic in universal terms for everyone. However, this formulation does not exemplify how either Paul or the other Jewish groups approached social reality, which for them consisted of Jews and non-Jews, who were understood to stand in a different relationship to God and to each other from birth (cf. Gal 2:15; 1 Cor 7:17–24; Rom 3:29–30).[43] The question requires a more precise formulation: How does

---

[42] Sanders, *Paul and Palestinian Judaism,* 12 (emphasis added).

[43] For recent discussions of the problems with the way Paul's voice has been understood in universalizing terms, including being set in contrast to Jewish particularism as its foil, including often more positive terms for understanding Paul's relationship with Judaism, see, e.g., Anders Runesson, "Particularistic Judaism and Universalistic Christianity? Some Critical Remarks on Terminology and Theology," *ST* 54 (2000): 55–75; Kathy Ehrensperger, *That We May Be Mutually Encouraged: Feminism and the New Perspective in Pauline Studies* (New York: T&T Clark International, 2004); Denise Kimber Buell and Caroline Johnson Hodge, "The Politics of Interpretation: The Rhetoric of Race and Ethnicity in Paul," *JBL* 123 (2004): 235–51; Pamela Eisenbaum, "Paul, Polemics, and the Problem of Essentialism," *BibInt* 13 (2005): 224–38; William S. Campbell, "Perceptions of Compatibility between Christianity and Judaism in Pauline Interpretation," *BibInt* 13 (2005): 298–316; idem, *Paul and the Creation of Christian Identity* (Library of New Testament Studies 322; London: T&T Clark, 2006); Caroline Johnson Hodge, "Apostle

one not born Jewish gain equal standing among the righteous ones (i.e., Israelites, Jews, children of Abraham, people of God)?

In other words, Sanders errs when posing the soteriological concerns of the rabbis in such universal terms as "when a man."[44] The question, to the degree that male circumcision is central to the discussion, should be either, "when a Jewish man," or in this case, since it is to be compared with the "when a non-Jewish man" context of Paul's rhetoric, "how does a non-Jewish man gain standing among the righteous ones." Naturally, apart from circumcision, the implications apply to women as well as men.

When Sanders does look specifically at the question of the inclusion of non-Jews as righteous ones both in this age and in the age to come, he readily admits that unlike the literature addressing the members of the covenant from which he develops the notion of covenantal nomism, "the Gentiles are dealt with only sporadically, however, and different Rabbis had different opinions about their destiny."[45] Recognition of this fact should profoundly alter the interpretive landscape for comparing Paul and Judaism.[46] That move is further accentuated if one attends to Second Temple Jewish literature rather than the rabbis.[47]

Consider Josephus's account of the two very different opinions about how the non-Jewish King Izates should proceed in the present age to worship God and express pious adherence to a Jewish (Judean) way of life, either by becoming circumcised or not. These opinions are espoused by two different Jewish informants, Ananias and Eleazer, and, interestingly enough, within a Diaspora setting during Paul's period (*Ant.* 20.17–96). Ananias not only emphatically opposes the circumcision of Izates but also proposes that Izates' resolve to practice the Jewish life completely represented a way of worshiping God that was more highly valued than circumcision, given his present situation (20.38–42). I have not noticed any secondary source refer to the teaching against the circumcision of Izates as representing a religious viewpoint arising from outside of Judaism or from a "former" Jew, one who no longer observed Torah. Rather, the conceptualizations are stretched to encompass the breadth of Jewish

---

to the Gentiles: Constructions of Paul's Identity," *BibInt* 13 (2005): 270–88; idem, *If Sons, Then Heirs: A Study of Kinship and Ethnicity in the Letters of Paul* (New York: Oxford University Press, 2007).

[44] Sanders, *Paul and Palestinian Judaism*, 75.

[45] Ibid., 207.

[46] Cf. Gaston, *Paul and the Torah*, 23.

[47] See Terence L. Donaldson, *Judaism and the Gentiles: Jewish Patterns of Universalism (to 135 C.E.)* (Waco, Tex.: Baylor University Press, 2007).

views that just such an incident makes necessary.[48] Josephus and his interpreters treat both Ananias and Eleazer as Jews who espouse different
points of view on the role of circumcision for conversion, as well as on
how God should be properly worshiped by a non-Jew, on the basis of their
interpretations of how to apply Jewish Scripture and tradition to the situation of this non-Jew, the king of a non-Jewish nation. Both find something
wrong with the solution proposed by the other. In other words, it is the
interpreter's definitions of Judaism that are challenged by this case: one
must find a way to explain this example within the boundaries of Judaism,
rather than suppose that one or the other participant stood outside of it
or found something wrong with or in Judaism itself.

Unfortunately, to date the distinction between a proposition discussing righteous standing with God for Jews and one discussing the topic for
non-Jews continues to be obscured in the manner that the issues are posed.
But since this is a subject about which Paul specifically writes and around
which a variety of Jewish views can be expected to emerge, it should be
central to the "Paul and" debates.

The Role of Ethnic Distinction
in Paul's Argumentation

If Paul's rhetoric does not collapse the ethnic boundary defining Jew
and non-Jew, then why do interpreters not maintain that difference when
seeking to compare Paul and other Jewish voices on any given issue? Thus
we do not read of "Paul against Torah observance for non-Jews (as if they
were under Torah on the same terms as are Jews)" but of "Paul against
Torah-observance," inferring "Paul against Torah-observance for all humankind." The normal shorthand for calling up this paradigmatic understanding of that for which Paul stands is "Paul's law-free gospel." That
phrase is so common as to seem unremarkable, beyond requiring defense.
But should that be the case?

If we were to limit comparisons to those within the realm of Paul's
rhetorical (i.e., argumentative) concerns, that is, to the matter of righteous
standing for non-Jews, we would find that other Jewish sources also do

---

[48] As a case in point, the note to this comment in the Loeb volume, edited
and translated by Louis Feldman, 22 n. a, discusses a possible rabbinic parallel
(no less!) wherein Rabbi Joshua argues in *b. Yebamot* 46a that circumcision was
not required for a convert, just baptism, according to Bamberger and Klausner. In
addition, a logical reason for this teaching by a Jew and within Judaism is offered:
the policy of exception for circumstances where life would be endangered.

not believe that non-Jews are obliged to observe Torah on the same terms as Jews.[49] We would find differences emerge around the question of the standing of non-Jewish people within the community of the people of God in the present age. But this would be different from a discussion about the age to come, because according to some Jewish voices the righteous non-Jew can gain equal or even higher standing then (Isa 66:18–20; Zeph 3:9; Zech 2:15; Tob 13:11; 14:5–6; cf. *t. Sanhedrin* 13.2; *b. Megillah* 13a). Are such views to be classified then as law-free? Or are they qualified as related specifically to non-Jews, those not by definition under Torah on the same terms as Jews, and thus, not universalized to apply to "everyone"?

---

[49]See Terence L. Donaldson, *Paul and the Gentiles: Remapping the Apostle's Convictional World* (Minneapolis: Fortress, 1997), 60–74, for discussion of various expectations for non-Jews, including a natural law non-Jew who turns from idolatry but is not identified with circumcision and other special laws for Israelites, e.g., observing dietary customs; righteous Gentiles; and eschatological pilgrimage scenarios. Examples include Josephus, *Ant.* 20.41 (34–48); Philo, *Questions and Answers on Exodus* 2.2; *On the Life of Moses* 2.4; *On the Life of Abraham* 3–6, 60–61; *On the Virtues* 102, 181–182, 212–219; *On the Special Laws* 1.51; 2.42–48; 4.178; *Joseph and Aseneth*; *t. Sanhedrin* 13.2. Cf. Paula Fredriksen, "Judaism, the Circumcision of Gentiles, and Apocalyptic Hope: Another Look at Galatians 1 and 2," in *The Galatians Debate: Contemporary Issues in Rhetorical and Historical Interpretation* (ed. Mark D. Nanos; Peabody, Mass.: Hendrickson, 2002), 236–47; Michael Wyschogrod, *Abraham's Promise: Judaism and Jewish-Christian Relations* (Radical Traditions; Grand Rapids, Mich.: Eerdmans, 2004), 162–63, 190–95.
At the same time, as the case for Ananias, one of the teachers of Izates, exemplifies—in contrast to the other teacher, Eleazer, who upholds that unless he is circumcised the Torah will not benefit him—there are Jews who upheld that members of the nations are called to Torah apart from becoming Jews (*Ant.* 20.34–48). Even the outrage expressed by Eleazer arguably demonstrates that he views Izates breaking the very laws he reads in Scripture, if he remains uncircumcised, although Izates is at this point a non-Jew reader. Both cases, however, may demonstrate that Izates is not simply a non-Jew but of a special category, a non-Jew who seeks to worship the God of the Jews, and thus he is obliged to a different level of Torah adherence. The view that Gentiles are in some way obligated to Torah observance is also expressed in a few rabbinic texts, although a minority view (e.g., *Mekilta de R. Yismael* [Bahodesh 1], on Exod 19:2; *Sifra* to Lev 18:1–5; M. Hirshman, "Rabbinic Universalism in the Second and Third Centuries," *HTR* 93 [2000]: 101–15), and aspects of this notion are implicit in the very idea of the apostolic decree of Acts 15, and the Noahide commandments (*t. Abodah Zarah* 8.4). Magnus Zetterholm, "Paul and the Missing Messiah," in *The Messiah: In Early Judaism and Christianity* (ed. Magnus Zetterholm; Minneapolis: Fortress, 2007), 33–55, applies the tension between these views to an interpretation of Paul, with Paul taking the side of those who uphold that Torah belongs only to Israel; hence, non-Jews in Christ are taught not to seek to observe it as if Jews, in contrast to other Christ-believing Jews who are teaching non-Jews in Christ to observe Torah, because Gentiles too are under obligation to Torah.

Moreover, Paul's argument is time specific, claiming something new
has transpired in the midst of the present age. It is on the matter of what
is appropriate now regarding non-Jews turning to Judaism's God that a
comparison of Paul's Judaism with other Judaisms exhibits a salient difference of opinion. His Jewish coalition claims that the end of the ages
has already dawned, and thus that the re-identification of non-Jews now
takes place on the awaited-age terms. *That* proposition is unique to the
Christ-believing Jewish groups.[50] It revolves around a different answer
to the question, "What time is it now?" on the basis of a different belief
about the meaning of Jesus Christ, and in particular, based on the claim
that God has already raised him from the grave.

We thus encounter a familiar difference arising between Jewish
groups, one that turns around eschatological convictions. The issue is
not whether the Torah obtains, but how it functions in the present age
for non-Jews, in contrast to Jews. Differences of opinion are contested
between these groups over where humankind is presently standing on
God's timeline, and thus, about what kind of behavior is appropriate now,
and more importantly, in the case of Christ-believing groups, over what
to do about the identity of the non-Jews who have turned to Christ. It was
because of different answers to these kinds of questions from the ones
offered by those who controlled the Jerusalem temple that the Dead Sea
Scrolls community of the Righteous Teacher apparently withdrew from
the temple worship of its time.[51] It was because of a different and controversial answer to the question of what God was doing among the nations that the Christ-believing Jewish groups suffered for upholding that
non-Jews were full and equal members of the righteous ones apart from
proselyte conversion. Neither group opposed Torah observance, but they
disagreed with the way that other Jewish groups interpreted how Torah
was to be observed, given the present circumstances.[52]

---

[50] Depending on how one reads Acts and Paul, it is a propositional truth shared
by the other apostles of this movement; cf. Mark D. Nanos, "Intruding 'Spies' and
'Pseudo-brethren': The Jewish Intra-Group Politics of Paul's Jerusalem Meeting
(Gal 2:1-10)," in *Paul and His Opponents* (ed. Stanley E. Porter; Pauline Studies
2; Leiden and Boston: Brill, 2005), 59-97; idem, "What Was at Stake in Peter's
'Eating with Gentiles' at Antioch?" in *The Galatians Debate: Contemporary Issues
in Rhetorical and Historical Interpretation* (ed. Mark D. Nanos; Peabody, Mass.:
Hendrickson, 2002), 282-318. Exceptions that appear to prove the rule among
other Jewish groups include the Izates story, just discussed, and may be implied
in Philo's criticism of some Jews in Alexandria (*On the Migration of Abraham* 92).
[51] Cf. Ps 37:33; 4QMMT C 25-32; 4QpPs^a 1-10 iv 7-9; 1 QpHab 8:10-13;
11:2-8; 1 Macc 10:21.
[52] Cf. James D. G. Dunn, "Echoes of Intra-Jewish Polemic in Paul's Letter to the
Galatians," *JBL* 112 (1993): 459-77 (467). It is interesting to note the subtle shifts

Here is a simple suggestion. To be more faithful to the contextual usage of Paul's language, the interpreter of Paul's rhetoric should add, "for non-Jews" as well as "believers in Jesus Christ" to the end of virtually every sentence in his letters about these matters, certainly so when he is specifically addressing non-Jews within them.[53] As historical critics, why not keep the specificity of the case before us? "Why did Paul oppose circumcision?" misses the point. It implies that he opposed it in principle for all Christ believers, and thus for Jews as well as for non-Jews. It leads to hermeneutical applications of supposed universal values for everyone. Admittedly cumbersome, one should ask instead, "Why did Paul oppose the circumcision of non-Jewish believers in Jesus Christ?" Then theological propositions that appeal to Paul's language have a better chance of reflecting Paul's contextual perspective, and likewise each hermeneutical application can better reflect the tension between what he meant and what it might mean for the later interpreter.[54]

There is no reason to believe that Paul opposed circumcision of children born to Jewish parents, and good reason to suppose that he did not.[55] And there is no reason to suppose that he opposed circumcision of

in language that betray the way that Jewish groups other than Christ-believing ones, such as those exemplified by the Dead Sea Scroll community's conflicts with other Jewish groups, are understood to revolve around different views of how to properly interpret Torah on the matter at hand ("the *correct* and only *legitimate* enactment of what the Torah laid down at these points"), but when the dispute is within groups of Christ-believing Jews or between them and other Jewish groups, the terms change to how much Torah applies ("the *extent* and *detail* of Torah obligation"; emphases added). If Paul was practicing his faith in Christ within Judaism, however, we would expect him to argue that his position exemplifies the ideals of Torah in contrast to other interpretations no less than do the writers of the Dead Sea Scrolls or the authors of any other Jewish literature of his time.

[53] This is a major topic in contemporary Pauline studies. Many interpreters now highlight that in his letters, including the most important ones bearing on these topics, like Galatians and Romans, while there may be Jews in the audience, his encoded or implied audience is the non-Jewish Christ believers.

[54] Cf. Stendahl, *Paul among Jews and Gentiles*, 35–36, 74–75, 125, for the programmatic call to never ask merely "What does it mean?" without adding ". . . to whom?"; idem, "Biblical Theology, Contemporary," in *The Interpreter's Dictionary of the Bible* (ed. George A. Buttrick; Nashville: Abingdon, 1962), 1:418–32.

[55] Many suppose that in Rom 2:25–29, Paul dismisses the role of bodily circumcision for Jews. But this language as well as that in Rom 3 represent diatribe, and the questions that follow immediately in 3:1 indicate that Paul is here writing to non-Jews about how Jews should behave in view of their circumcision, with circumcised hearts as well as bodies. If they do not, they fail to represent the real meaning of the circumcision of their bodies. The point is not that non-Jews become Jews, as if they somehow gain the real objective for which Jews are circumcised. And they do not become "true" or "spiritual" Jews; they remain non-Jews.

non-Jews who were not Christ believers. At many points the logic of his position suggests that Jewish believers in Christ, including Paul, observed his instruction to remain in the state in which they were called, keeping the commandments of God (1 Cor 7:17–24), which, for a Jewish person, involved guarding the whole Torah, by Paul's own admission (Gal 2:15; 5:3, 6:13; discussion below). And it makes sense to suppose that Paul, like the Christ-believing Jews described by James in Acts 21, would be zealous in his observation of halakhic behavior and take the steps necessary to demonstrate this fact and dispel any rumors that he did not do so. Thus, Luke presents Paul to undertake a Nazarite vow in the temple, which involved a burnt offering (Acts 21:19–26).

If Paul does not observe Torah, he leaves himself open to the easiest objection to his proposition that Jesus is the Christ that can be leveled by the very Jews he seeks to convince, an accusation that has been made ever since the construction of Paul and Paulinism as Torah-free was invented.[56] If Paul did not himself represent the highest ideals of the Judaism which maintained the hope of just such a day, how could he expect to reach Jews, much less non-Jews, with his message that the awaited restoration of Israel and of the rest of the nations (of creation itself) had begun with the resurrection of Jesus?

Pursuing clarification of Paul's teaching and the implications for Jews is not the same task as investigating the meaning of Paul's rhetoric for non-Jews, the members of the nations other than Israel whom he directly addresses.[57] For example, note that in Gal 5:11, Paul does not argue that he is persecuted for failure to observe Torah, for failing

---

Only Jews are circumcised in order to indicate in their bodies the dedication to God of their whole person, to living according to the precepts God has given for right living, and not merely to teaching them to others. Only they can become in that sense "true" or "spiritual" Jews. That identity is particular to Jews, to those of the nation Israel, whose dedication to the one God includes circumcised bodies as well as it should involve circumcised hearts, unlike non-Jews, non-Israelites, which the addressees remain. Their non-Jewish hearts, however, can be "like" the circumcised hearts of Jews (the circumcised): directed toward God, and living right, not merely professing the precepts of right living (Rom 12:1–2).

[56] Cf. W. D. Davies, *Paul and Rabbinic Judaism: Some Rabbinic Elements in Pauline Theology* (rev. ed.; New York: Harper & Row, 1967), 73–74.

[57] Boyarin, *Radical Jew,* 17, evaluates Paul's critique of Judaism as dissatisfaction with Jewish difference: "the quintessentially 'different' people for Paul were Jews and women." Leaving aside the topic of women, as a "Jew from birth" (Gal 2:14), which Paul claimed to be, the "different" should be expected to be non-Jews, and indeed Paul's rhetoric addresses how non-Jews, who are different from Jews/Israelites, now fit into God's universal plan for humanity (the rest of the nations) by way of Israel's service and Messiah. I think Boyarin's point is correct, however, with regard to the constructed Paul of traditional Paulinism, which has been populated

to keep a Jewish diet or Sabbath or uphold circumcision for Jews, but specifically for the policy of not teaching non-Jewish Christ believers to become proselytes. Note that his letters do to not concern themselves with answering other charges.

Many point to the implications of 1 Cor 9:19–23 to undermine the proposition of a Torah-observant Paul, as discussed above, but I understand Paul to be expressing a rhetorical strategy, not a change of halakhic behavior. As noted, the consensus interpretation understands Paul's becoming like the different parties to signify mimicking each, not actually becoming like them in the sense of sharing their convictional bases for their behavior that he merely imitates temporarily in order to seek to gain them to an entirely different set of convictions. But I propose that "becoming like" signifies "arguing from the premises" of each.[58]

When seeking to win Jews to the message of good in Christ, he argues from Jewish premises; that is easy enough for him to do, because he shares them. He argues from law-based premises when among those "under law," a phrase that can be variously understood. When he mentions causing himself to become like the "lawless" or "sinner" (νόμος), often translated "without law," it is no more likely that he means he abandons halakhic behavior or acts like a sinner than it is that Jesus behaved

---

by non-Jewish Christians for whom the Jew is the different other. But should that be expected to be the vantage point of Paul?

[58] Understanding Paul to signify rhetorical conduct to various degrees—although not proposing that Paul maintained Torah-observant behavior—or that he specifically is communicating that he appealed to their various argumentative premises, see Henry Chadwick, "'All Things to All Men' (1 Cor. IX.22)," *NTS* 1 (1954–1955): 261–75; idem, "St. Paul and Philo of Alexandria," in *History and Thought of the Early Church* (ed. Henry Chadwick; London: Variorum Reprints, 1982; original: *BJRL* 48 [1965–1966]), 297–98 (286–307); Richard N. Longenecker, *Paul, Apostle of Liberty* (New York: Harper & Row, 1964), 244; Clarence E. Glad, *Paul and Philodemus: Adaptability in Epicurean and Early Christian Psychagogy* (NovTSup 81; Leiden: Brill, 1995), esp. 1, 240, 273, 327; Johnson Hodge, *"If Sons, Then Heirs,"* 124–25. Margaret M. Mitchell, "Pauline Accommodation and 'Condescension' (συγκατάβασις): 1 Cor 9:19–23 and the History of Influence," in *Paul beyond the Judaism/Hellenism Divide* (ed. T. Engberg-Pedersen; Louisville, Ky.: Westminster John Knox, 2001), 197–214, traces some language in the church fathers, esp. Chrysostom and Origin, that points in this direction, although it is not clear that they did not also believe Paul's language included changing conduct too. Fee grants that Paul *may* have accommodated the content of the message for different audiences but concludes that 1 Cor 9:19–23 itself is about conduct, not content (*First Epistle to the Corinthians*, 428n36; 432–33). Given holds that Paul's modus operandi was to accommodate rhetorically in both content and conduct (e.g., *Paul's True Rhetoric*, 36–37, 97), but his discussion of 1 Cor 9:19–23 focuses almost exclusively on conduct and reflects the consensus interpretation (103–15). See also below, note 62.

like a prostitute or tax collector to relate to them.[59] Paul is a self-confessed slave to righteous living. Communicating the message of Christ to sinners does not entail behaving sinfully in order to do so, but quite the contrary: it behooves one seeking to influence them to the message of good in Christ, to membership among the righteous ones of God, and to righteous lifestyles, to behave righteously as a matter of conviction and at all times.

Paul is not here admitting to compromising Jewish behavioral practices when among non-Jews but explaining how he relates the message of Christ to them on their own terms. In the midst of his discourse throughout chapters 8–10, wherein he explains why the Christ believers in Corinth cannot eat idol food, Paul relates his strategy toward non-Christ believers in 9:19–23. Just as he explains to the "knowledgeable" in Corinth why they must respect the sensibilities of the "weak" or "impaired" (ἀσθενής), and not eat according to their theoretical "rights," his argument nevertheless aims to convince them not to exercise those rights.[60] They cannot eat at the table of the Lord and the table of demons; they cannot eat food that they know to be idol food, whether from the market or at someone's home.

Although Paul solicits the support of scriptural precedent, he does not proceed as he would if a Jew asked him about eating idol food. He does not simply cite Torah against eating idol food to make this case; at least not initially. Rather, he argues from their own worldview as non-Jewish Christ believers. He begins his argument in terms of their own premises, but he drives them to a very different conclusion than they have otherwise arrived at on their own: they must flee from anything that can be understood to represent idolatry.[61]

Paul does not act like the knowledgeable, but he argues in a way that they might. In that sense he "causes himself to become like" the knowledgeable, to convince them to become like himself, one who regards idol

---

[59] See also David Jacob Rudolph, "A Jew to the Jews: Jewish Contours of Pauline Flexibility in 1 Corinthians 9:19–23" (Ph.D. diss.: Selwyn College, University of Cambridge, 2006; forthcoming in revised version, Mohr Siebeck).

[60] See Nanos, "The Polytheist Identity."

[61] Apparently Paul did not anticipate that former polytheists would reason that since they no longer believed idols represented gods, that there was no reason to abstain from eating food that was being or had been offered to them, regarding it to be profane, perhaps even that doing so with indifference demonstrated the strength of their new convictions. Although Jews had long ago declared that idols did not represent real gods, this nevertheless was accompanied by the very different conclusion that anything associated with idolatry is by definition out of bounds, and that eating idol food would instead show their lack of conviction; see Nanos, "The Polytheist Identity."

food as anathema.[62] This approach is exemplified in Acts 17:16–34, where Luke portrays Paul appealing to a statue (idol) to the Unknown God in order to make his case to polytheists, even though Paul did not believe that such statues should be made. This exemplifies becoming like a polytheist to make his point to polytheists but in no way becoming a polytheist or practicing idolatry to do so. He appeals to their logic of their own premises to seek to bring them to a very different conclusion than they have drawn. He seeks thereby to win them to the message of good in Jesus Christ.[63]

PAUL'S JUDAISM

Let us look at how Paul used the term Ἰουδαϊσμός (Judaism) to see if my proposition can be sustained in that context. Paul uses this

---

[62] *Pace* Given, *Paul's True Rhetoric*, 105–17. Although I appreciate the argument against interpretations that seek to protect Paul's integrity, on 111, after he concludes that Paul's "becoming like" signifies eating or otherwise behaving like each of the groups (in concert with the prevailing views), nevertheless, Given's interpretation does not represent "the realm of being" rather than "that of seeming" any more than do the viewpoints he criticizes (Glad in particular). For Given imagines only the behavior of mimicking: not subscribing to the philosophical basis of the various behaviors, not *being* like them but merely *seeming* to be like them. On 112, Given uses "appearing as" synonymously with "becoming like." At the same time, I do not think that Given's reading need be far from the one I propose, if dropping *acting* like but keeping *speaking* like, for on 117 he concludes that Paul shapes his "insinuative rhetorical strategy similar to that imagined by Luke with respect to Jews and Gentiles."

[63] Although on this interpretation Paul is still involved in a persuasive enterprise, and thus does not necessarily believe in the premises that he adopts as the basis for initiating arguments but merely seeks to manipulate the listener by beginning from their premises, such rhetorical behavior does not require the compromise of integrity that the traditional interpretation of his change of behavioral conduct necessitates. Philosophical and religious arguments between people and groups approaching a topic with different points of view are understood by each to proceed by way of the tactic of beginning from the opposition's presuppositions and premises in order to undermine their conclusions and lead them to one's own. There was a lively debate stretching back to Antisthenes about whether Odysseus should be interpreted along this line, as exemplifying a polytrope, one who adapted his figures of speech to his various audiences, such as the Stoics and Cynics sought to do, rather than as an unethical chameleon who changed his behavior in a way that compromised his moral character. See W. B. Stanford, *The Ulysses Theme: A Study in the Adaptability of a Traditional Hero* (Dallas: Spring Publications, 1992), 90–101; Fernanda Decleva Caizzi, ed., *Antisthenis Fragmenta* (Milan: Instituto Editoriale Cisalpino, 1966), 24–28, 43–44. For application to Paul, although not to the same conclusion I am drawing, see Abraham J. Malherbe, *Paul and the Popular Philosophers* (Minneapolis: Fortress, 1989), 91–119; Glad, *Paul and Philodemus*, 21–22, 26, 28–29, 251, 272–73.

terminology only two times, and both cases are in Gal 1:13–14. He writes of "my former way of living in Judaism" (τὴν ἐμὴν ἀναστροφήν ποτε ἐν τῷ Ἰουδαϊσμῷ). The clause appears in the midst of a sentence describing a certain feature of his former way of living Jewishly with which his addressees are familiar. That way of living was specifically as one who persecuted the Jewish subgroup communities of believers in Jesus Christ. In further describing that time, he writes that he advanced in the Judaism of his former way of life beyond many of his contemporaries in his ethnic group (προέκοπτον ἐν τῷ Ἰουδαϊσμῷ ὑπὲρ πολλοὺς συνηλικιώτας ἐν τῷ γένει μου), because he possessed more zeal for the "traditions of my fathers." Note that Paul writes of his relationship to the traditions in such personal terms, as "of my fathers" and not simply "of the fathers." Does Paul betray here that his identity continues to be bound up with a particular interpretive tradition that he still considers himself to represent, albeit in some way that no longer brings the approval that he formerly enjoyed from the members of this group?

Traditionally, interpreters have understood Paul to be describing himself as now no longer living in Judaism. But the language Paul uses here arguably describes a certain way of living in Judaism that no longer characterizes the way he lives in Judaism now.[64]

Paul's former way of living included a more zealous approach than that of his fellows to protecting "the traditions of the fathers," a catch phrase almost certainly denoting Pharisaic Judaism.[65] And it may be, although it is not certain, that the specific area in which his zeal for the traditions of the fathers was demonstrated to be greater than his peers was in his taking action against what he considered to be a threat posed by the Christ-believing Jewish subgroups. This could imply that he has moved within Pharisaism, from a group of Pharisees that approved of his zeal to destroy these groups to a group of Pharisees[66] (or a coalition of groups

---

[64] Paul's language is analogous to a Christian speaking of his former way of living as a Christian when remaining a Christian, but of a different kind. This language is then employed to represent, for example, moving between denominations or faith traditions, such as from Catholic to Protestant and vice versa, or between subgroups of a denomination, such as to or from charismatic or some other similar subgroup identity within a larger denominational body.

[65] Josephus, *Ant.* 13.297, 408; 17.41; cf. Albert I. Baumgarten, "The Pharisaic Paradosis," *HTR* 80 (1987): 63–77. Paul refers to himself as a Pharisee in the context of referring to his zeal to persecute the Christ believers (Phil 3:5–6).

[66] According to Acts 15:5, there were Christ believers who belonged to the sect of the Pharisees, and Paul is portrayed as affiliated with Pharisaism in his proclamations of Christ (Acts 23:6; 26:5). This arguably aligns with the self-identity he still asserts to express that this identity, although advantageous in Jewish communal comparative terms, does not make him better than those Christ believers

including Pharisees) that now expressed the aspirations of those groups. More likely, it signifies that he has moved from his particular Pharisaic group's appeal to the traditions of the fathers as the ultimate authority on this topic to a different group's ultimate source of authority in Jesus Christ, to Christ-believing Judaism.[67]

Paul claims to have had a revelation that his peers have not experienced, and I understand this to be the background for his dissociating statement that his good news message and authority as an apostle are "not from human agents or through human agency, but through God" (Gal 1:1, author's translation). In contrast to the prevailing views, I think it likely that his references to "humans" and the "flesh and blood" from whom he does not gain approval or seek advice (1:1, 10–12, 16) are not to the other apostles who knew Jesus personally but to his contemporaries from whom he had won great approval, until he changed course following the revelation of Christ (1:13–16). Although he also expresses relative independence from the other apostles for many years, he makes this point to argue for their ultimate unanimity on the matters at hand, even though arrived at independently (1:17—2:10). Hence, Paul is not indicating that he formerly lived in Judaism but no longer does so, but that he has changed the way he lives within Judaism, his social location relative to his former group and its approval, probably the particular Judaism to which he owes allegiance, that is, his Pharisaic group.[68] Behaving so as

---

who cannot make the same claims to identity. His self-deprecation appears to target cases where the non-Jews may be suffering marginality in Jewish communal terms for not having become proselytes and thus to be paying for failure to substantiate their claims to full membership on the prevailing terms for conversion (Phil 3:3–11, esp. v. 5; Nanos, "Paul's Reversal"; cf. Gal 6:12–15; idem, *Irony of Galatians*, 226–33).

[67]Cf. Segal, *Paul the Convert*.

[68]The reference to the "flesh and blood" with whom he does not confer has traditionally been understood to refer to the apostles who knew Jesus in a human sense that Paul did not share, but that is unlikely in my view; rather, Paul believes they all work from shared grace and revelation (cf. Gal 2:2, 7–8; 1 Cor 15:5–8). Although he arrived at his understanding without consulting the Jerusalem apostles, when he did go to them later, he admits he was seeking their approval (Gal 2:1–2). Thus, rather than a redundant reference to flesh and blood and the other apostles, I suggest they are two different parties he did not immediately consult, neither his former group, Pharisees, nor his new group leaders, the apostles in Jerusalem. In the first case, Paul is referring to not having conferred with the leaders of his Pharisaic group. Flesh and blood may refer to the traditions handed down among the Pharisees which are attributed to the fathers and constitute their own special group rulings, or perhaps may imply that the rabbinic policy of the rule of the majority of sages was characteristic of the Pharisees already, but that he did not subject his new convictions to their deliberation, or that he avoided returning

to gain the approval of those peers no longer characterizes the way he is living in Judaism, Jesus-Christ-based-Judaism, now.[69]

Paul does not specify what the Christ-believing Jewish groups were doing that he deemed to be so threatening; thus interpreters must fill in a proposition to make sense of Paul's earlier life and change of course. Interpreters have generally understood Paul's opposition to be to a lax attitude toward Torah observance, perhaps even outright renunciation—proto-Paulinism, you might say.[70] The issues of the letter, and the topic of his calling as described in Gal 1:16, to proclaim God's Son to the nations, suggest that Paul objected specifically to the policy of regarding non-Jews who believed in Jesus Christ to be full equal members without having become Jews, as children of Abraham apart from the traditional convention of proselyte conversion to gain that standing.[71] That policy is

---

and thereby violating the Pharisees' policy of not contesting the views of the elders, which his new conviction would be expected to challenge (cf. Josephus, *Ant.* 18.12). Paul is indicating that he did not immediately seek to win formal approval of this revelation and call to bring this message to the nations from the Pharisaic group among whom he had previously held high esteem. The purpose of this for the Galatians is likely to relate to them in their own circumstances: if they follow Paul's teaching and resist proselyte conversion, they will need to stand alone against the opinions of the local Jewish communal leaders too. Paul understands this, having stood alone for this truth claim. But it is also the position of the other apostles to which he calls them, even if he initially arrived at this understanding independently. His rhetorical purpose is to relate to the vulnerability of his Galatian audience: he wants them to know that he understands what it is to stand alone and be marginalized for the gospel's proposition, just as his Galatian audience is now experiencing. It is what all Christ-believing group leaders uphold (cf. Nanos, "Intruding 'Spies'"; idem, "What Was at Stake?"; idem, *Irony of Galatians*. On the rabbinic policy of majority rule, see *b. Baba Mezia* 59b; on the topic of interpretive authority and the role of revelation during this period, see Ben Sira 24; 39.1–8; 1QS 5; 8; George W. E. Nickelsburg, "Revealed Wisdom as a Criterion for Inclusion and Exclusion: From Jewish Sectarianism to Early Christianity," in *"To See Ourselves as Others See Us": Christians, Jews, "Others" in Late Antiquity* [ed. Jacob Neusner and E. Frerichs; Chico, Calif.: Scholars Press, 1985], 73–82).

[69] Martin Goodman, "A Note on Josephus, the Pharisees and Ancestral Tradition," *Journal of Jewish Studies* 50.1 (1999): 17–20, makes an interesting case for recognizing that the Pharisees were not characterized only by distinctive theological ideas such as resurrection, but that they upheld proper behavior according to ancestral customs that were not necessarily Pharisaic. If so, this would fit well with the issue at hand in Paul's opposition to the traditional convention for non-Jews to gain membership via proselyte conversion. It is not just Pharisaic tradition that is being challenged, but general Jewish tradition, which the Pharisees uphold more zealously than other interest groups (from Paul's point of view).

[70] Traditional views and her interesting proposal are described by Fredriksen, "Judaism," 248–55.

[71] The topic of Nanos, *Irony of Galatians*.

the one for which he claims to be persecuted later, namely, for not "still" preaching circumcision of non-Jews (Gal 5:11). While Paul championed this move, he probably did not initiate it. Rather, since before the dramatic revelation of Christ in him and the call to bring this message to the nations, he was the most vicious opponent of this policy, it is likely that this policy of including non-Jews as full members was a propositional truth for Christ-based groups that predated his change of course. If so, what motivated Paul's zealous response was not a failure by Jewish members of the Christ groups to observe Torah per se. They were observing, for example, Sabbath and dietary customs, and circumcising their sons. At issue was a change of policy based on an alternative interpretation of Torah for defining the inclusion of non-Jews as full and equal members based on the claim that God has in Christ initiated the age to come kingdom with just such expectations for members of the rest of the nations to join alongside Israel in the worship of the one God.

Unlike the conventions in place in all Jewish groups of the time of which we are aware, these non-Jews were being identified not merely as guests, however welcome and celebrated, as in other Jewish groups. They were instead being treated as members in full standing, on the same terms as proselytes, children of Abraham, and yet at the same time not proselytes, not members of Israel, but representatives of the other nations bearing witness to the proposition that the end of the ages had dawned in Christ.[72] They were celebrating a kind of messianic banquet expected in the age to come within the midst of the present evil age.

In other words, it seems likely that what Paul and his fellow group members objected to were rumors of insurrectionist agendas among some Jewish groups proclaiming the seditious message that there was already a ruler anointed to rule Israel and the nations other than Caesar. This was made manifest by the new way Jews and non-Jews were interacting within these groups as if the awaited banquet of all nations

---

[72] I am suggesting here an alternative that Fredriksen, "Judaism," does not discuss, although a variation of one she dismisses (251) on the grounds that it was not objectionable for Jewish groups to include Gentiles. The difference is that she is dealing with a proposition that these Gentiles remained merely guests, while I am proposing that the Gentiles in these groups were being identified and treated as full members in a way that other Jewish groups reserved for proselytes. At the same time, I do not believe that they were being classified by Paul as proselytes (contra Donaldson, *Paul*). Rather, it was important to Paul's proposition that they remain representatives of the other nations but in membership standing on a par with proselytes, indeed, with natural-born Jews as well, so that the "new creation" community consisted of members of Israel *and* the rest of the nations with one voice worshiping the one God of all humankind (cf. Rom 3:29–30; 10:12; 15:5–13; Gal 3:28; cf. Nanos, *Mystery of Romans*, 179–92).

worshiping together as equals under God's reign had begun. Jews and
non-Jews were eating together as equal members of the righteous ones,
as brothers and sisters in the family of Abraham. Such a stance threatened
to undermine the way that the political exigencies of compliance with
Roman rule were understood to be best expressed by Paul's Pharisaic
group and other Jewish interest groups to which they answered, such
as the temple authorities, who did the bidding of the Roman regime.[73]
Hence, as their representative seeking to sustain the ostensible gains
of maintaining the status quo, he had sought "to destroy" the Jesus-as-
Christ/Lord confessing groups.

Paul refers to a specific way of living Jewishly, within Judaism, that is,
among those Jews who looked to the traditions of the fathers for authority. Based upon his arguments throughout Galatians, and especially the
dissociating of his authority as directly from God and not human agencies
and agents, I believe that Paul seeks to remind the addressees that what
he taught them ran against the prevailing views of Jewish groups that
looked to "the traditions of the fathers" on the matter at hand, the place
of proselyte conversion for non-Jewish believers in Christ. In the present
age, those who protect this convention among Jewish groups may have
the authority to compel compliance, but the non-Jewish addressees are
to resist that authority and to suffer any consequences required, awaiting
God's vindication of their righteous standing according to the message he
had proclaimed (Gal 5:5). Paul argues that he too suffers for this policy,
but he does not alter his course to seek the relief that could be gained by
relaxing it (5:11). Now they are to join him in suffering for challenging
the prevailing conventions, looking to the suffering of the one in whom
they have believed (3:1; 4:12; 6:14).[74] "Do [they] not hear Torah" rightly
(4:21)—that is, with Paul?[75]

Although Paul believes it should be otherwise, he does not yet expect
Jewish authorities who do not share his faith in Jesus to legitimate his
way of incorporating non-Jews according to the revelation of Christ. He

---

[73] Cf. Nanos, "Intruding 'Spies,'" 59–97; Martin Goodman, *The Ruling Class
of Judaea: The Origins of the Jewish Revolt against Rome, A.D. 66–70* (Cambridge:
Cambridge University Press, 1987).

[74] Cf. Dieter Mitternacht, "Foolish Galatians?—A Recipient-Oriented Assessment of Paul's Letter," in *The Galatians Debate: Contemporary Issues in Rhetorical
and Historical Interpretation* (ed. Mark D. Nanos; Peabody, Mass.: Hendrickson,
2002), 408–33.

[75] Note that Paul does not write "Do not hear Torah," as if Torah was no longer
the authority on the matter at hand, that is, as if its role for Christ believers was
finished (which undermines the usual interpretations of Paul's statement earlier,
in Gal 3:23–25, when taken to mean that the role of Torah is finished with the
coming of Christ).

tells this story to serve as an example to his non-Jewish addressees: they should not yet expect approval of their identity claims by them either.[76] Instead, they must resist pressure to comply with or conform to prevailing conventions to gain undisputed standing among the righteous ones: they must "out of faithfulness to the Spirit wait for the hope of righteousness" (Gal 5:5, author's translation). This intragroup disapproval extends not only to Paul, however independent his ministry among the non-Jews has been, but to the other apostles of this coalition too, who stand up for the same principle truth of the message Paul delivered to the Galatian addressees, albeit sometimes a bit too tentatively for Paul's taste (cf. 2:1–21).[77]

In Christ-believing-based Judaism, non-Jews do not become proselytes after becoming believers in Jesus Christ, for doing so would undermine the propositional truth upon which their faith is based, namely, that with the resurrection of Jesus Christ the end of the ages has dawned. Incorporating non-Jews into the people of God in the present age as proselytes according to the traditions of the fathers is no longer halakhically warranted. That is not because Paul or the non-Jewish addressees are no longer a part of Judaism but because they are members of a particular Judaism, or alternatively, of a Jewish coalition which understands itself in the role of the remnant representing the interests and eventual destiny of the whole cloth, of every Jewish group and way of living Jewishly. In other words, regardless of how triumphalistic it may be, these Christ-believing Jews—and non-Jews!—live on behalf of Judaism and every Jewish person, not against them (Rom 9–11; esp. 11:11–36).[78]

In this service, these Christ-believing Jews do not reject Torah but develop halakhot that articulate the appropriate way to observe Torah now, in view of the revelation of Christ that the representatives of the nations are not to become Israelites but to join with Israelites in a new community

---

[76] Paul's hostile rhetoric betrays that he believes those influencing his addressees should instead accept the truth claims of his proclamation of the gospel (cf. Gal 1:6–9; 3:1; 4:17–18; 5:7–12; 6:12–13; cf. Nanos, *Irony of Galatians*, 226–33), and that they will, when the course of his two-step ministry of proclaiming Christ to the representatives of Israel in each location and then decisively turning to the nations also ("the fullness of the nations begins") has reached its climax, when the rest of those of Israel will reconsider, and "all Israel will be saved" (Rom 11, as explained in Nanos, *Mystery of Romans*, 239–88).

[77] Nanos, "What Was at Stake?"; idem, "Intruding 'Spies.'"

[78] Mark D. Nanos, "Broken Branches: A Pauline Metaphor Gone Awry? (Romans 11:11–36)," paper presented on Romans 9–11 at the Interface between the 'New Perspective on Paul' and Jewish-Christian Dialog (Göttingen, Germany, 1–4 May 2008). Forthcoming (eds. R. Wagner and F. Wilk; Tübingen: Mohr-Siebeck); see also http://www.marknanos.com/BrokenBranches-8-1-08.pdf).

adumbrating the restoration of all humankind.[79] Otherwise, Paul's question in Rom 3:29, "Or is God of the Jews only, and not also of members of the other nations?" could not be answered to affirm the inclusion of anyone but Jews. However, Paul's answer was: "Yes, God is the one God of the members of the other nations also." According to Paul's logic, the alternative would have been to argue instead that God is only the God of Israel, and anyone from the other nations wanting to become part of God's people must become Jewish proselytes, as was the case for the present age before the death and resurrection of Jesus Christ changed what was appropriate, within Judaism, to age-to-come terms.

To put this another way, Paul understands the oneness of God in view of the faith of/in Christ to warrant a change of perspective on the way to incorporate non-Jewish people into the righteous ones, into the family of Abraham without joining the family of Jacob/Israel. That change, Paul argued, is according to the teaching of Torah, according to the declaration of God's oneness, according to the expectations of the prophets.[80] To maintain otherwise is to experience "stumbling" instead of enjoying Israel's special privilege (alongside Paul) of bringing light to all of the nations when that day has come (Rom 11:13–36).[81] It is Israel that has been entrusted with the words of God for the nations (3:2; 10:14—11:12).

---

[79] When Sanders writes, "He [Paul] seems to have 'held together' his native view that the law is one and given by God and his new conviction that Gentiles and Jews stand on equal footing, which requires the deletion of some of the law, by asserting them both without theoretical explanation" (Sanders, *Paul, the Law*, 103), because of the inscrutability of 1 Cor 7:19 in Sanders's system, his view overlooks the option I am trying to articulate here. From the oneness of the particular Lord of Israel and the universal God of all the rest of the nations, one can claim equal footing for Israelites and members of the other nations without requiring "the deletion of some of the law." By regarding the Torah to be particular to Israel, to Jewish observance, the need arises for halakhic developments to incorporate non-Jews as equals within this subgroup/coalition. Likewise, when Sanders states that circumcision, Sabbath observance, and dietary restrictions, although clear to Paul as prescribed in Scripture, "are not binding on those in Christ" (103), he again does not make the distinction that I uphold, that is, that they are binding on the Jew in Christ but not on the non-Jew. Moreover, making halakhic decisions for Jews who live in view of faith in Christ that may require some deviation from prevailing conventions being upheld by other Jewish groups is not the same thing as deleting laws. The making of halakhah is a dynamic enterprise.

[80] Cf. Pinchas Lapide, "The Rabbi from Tarsus," in *Paul, Rabbi and Apostle* (ed. Pinchas Lapide and Peter Stuhlmacher; Minneapolis: Augsburg, 1984), 31–55 [48–49].

[81] Paul seeks to provoke his fellow Jews to jealousy "of his *ministry*" (v. 13), not because non-Jews are being included per se but because they are not participating in this awaited task (i.e., "ministry") of bringing light to the nations too (Rom 3:2; 10:14–17; cf. Nanos, *Mystery of Romans*, 247–51; idem, "The Jewish Context of

It is interesting to note that Rashi, who writes around halfway between Paul's time and our own, finds in the repetition of God's name in the Shema the anticipation of a day not unlike that which Paul argues to have arrived:

> The Lord who is our God now, but not (yet) the God of the (other) nations, is destined to be the One Lord, as it is said, "For then will I give to the people a pure language, that they may all call upon the name of the Lord, to serve Him with one consent" (Zeph 3:9). And (likewise) it is said, "And the Lord shall be King over all the earth; on that day shall the Lord be One and His name One" (Zech 14:9).[82]

This logic helps us to understand how all of the parties present in Antioch when Paul confronted Peter could be eating according to prevailing Jewish diets but not arranged at the table according to prevailing conventions that discriminated seating or food distribution or in other ways that demonstrated relative status based upon identity as Jew or non-Jew (Gal 2:11–14).[83] Non-Jews were not under Torah; they were nevertheless obliged to observe the appropriate halakhah for this association as equals to take place. That is an idealistic notion within the constraints of the present age, when discrimination ineluctably accompanies difference.[84] But Paul believed the age to come had dawned, changing the terms, so that discrimination was to be eliminated by way of living according to the Spirit, that is, according to the age-to-come-way-of-life the Spirit made

---

the Gentile Audience Addressed in Paul's Letter to the Romans," *CBQ* 61 (1999): 283–304 [300–304]). The charge of failure to be persuaded and the assessment of those Jews who have not yet joined Paul in his faith in Christ as stumbling but not fallen bespeak the position of one who views himself and his coalition to be upholding the righteous standing of Israel in the sense of the remnant preserving the certain destiny of the whole cloth. The issue for Jews, unlike non-Jews, is not getting in, contra Sanders, but staying in, now by way of response to Christ. Even the culpability for failing to yet make that decision is mitigated by the admission that God is involved in a complicated scheme to include the nations that will eventually include the restoration of all Israel, for which some of Israel is vicariously suffering presently (cf. Nanos, *Mystery of Romans*, 239–88).

[82] Translation from Norman Lamm, *The Shema: Spirituality and Law in Judaism as Exemplified in the Shema, the Most Important Passage in the Torah* (Philadelphia: Jewish Publication Society, 2000), 31. See too *Sifre* on Deut 6:4 (Piska 31); and D. Hoffmann, ed., *Midrasch Tannaim zum Deuteronomium* (Berlin, 1908-1909; repr., Jerusalem: n.p., 1984), 190–91 from Gaston, *Paul and the Torah*, 200 n. 27): "But Israel said to the Holy One, blessed be He: out of all these gods we have chosen only you, as it is said: 'The Lord is my portion, says my soul.'"

[83] Nanos, "What Was at Stake?"

[84] Cf. Michael A. Hogg and Dominic Abrams, *Social Identifications: A Social Psychology of Intergroup Relations and Group Processes* (London: Routledge, 1988).

possible within this community, if they will dedicate themselves to walk-
ing in the Spirit. Hence, Paul can write of equality of Jew and non-Jew in
Christ, and of keeping the commandments of God as paramount, without
negating any of Torah. Within this community, the ethnic or national difference between Jew/Israelite and non-Jew/member of the nations, and
therefore their different relationships to the Torah, remain, but not the
present age discrimination inherently concomitant with such distinctions.

For Paul, it is fundamental to the truth of the gospel that difference
remains, that social boundaries are acknowledged, but that discrimination
does not, in this age, as in the age to come. It is an age which, according
to that gospel, has dawned in Christ and should thus be made evident in
the body of those who are committed to that trust when they meet and
live together in community. For everyone is to live in a way respecting the
different other, in love as the perfect expression of the commandments of
God, of Torah for Jews, and the law of Christ for Jews and non-Jews too.
Figuring out how to make this work constitutes establishing halakhah for
Paul, not its elimination.[85] And the difficult reality of exemplifying this
challenge in the present evil age is realized in Paul's constant appeal to live
in "faith working through love," which is defined by Torah but energized
by the work of God in them through the Holy Spirit, embodying the life
of the age to come and not that of human conventions that instead legitimate discrimination where difference is found, amplified, for example, by
the creation of norms by which to measure each other hierarchically. In
Christ's body, they are to be equals in rank but otherwise different, extending even to the ways that God's Spirit is manifest in their lives, including
how their different gifts and ministries are manifest. Like a body, they all
represent different parts but contribute those parts to the health of the
whole (Rom 12; 1 Cor 12–14). Otherwise, the whole would be but one
part. As there is a place for Gentiles in that body, so too there is a place
for Jews, and thus, for Torah.

Contextualizing Paul's Torah Observance and Rhetoric for Non-Jews

To evaluate Paul's rhetoric we must decide or otherwise assume what
his audience knows about him, often firsthand. Paul's interpreters have
proceeded on the basis that his addressees know him to live a Torah-free
life. However, the opposite hypothesis should be tested. If Paul writes from

---

[85]Contra Sanders, *Paul, the Law,* 144.

within Judaism, if, for example, he is Torah observant, then his polemical language would carry very different implications for those it addressed. To name a few important indicators, I understand him to eat according to prevailing halakhic conventions for Diaspora Jews in each location he visits,[86] to respect the ideals of temple worship in the ways that religiously observant Diaspora Jews would, such as attempting to travel to Jerusalem in time to celebrate Shavuot/Pentecost, which marks the receipt of Torah by Moses (1 Cor 16:8);[87] to make a collection for those in Jerusalem suffering economic hardship for upholding the policy of Gentile inclusion apart from proselyte conversion (Rom 15:25–31; Gal 2:7–10); and, according to Luke's account, to take a Nazarite vow in the temple, in order to confirm that he lives and teaches according to Torah, in the face of rumors that he does not (Acts 21).

Consider Gal 5:3, where Paul seeks to undermine the addressees' confidence that they have proper motives for assessing the social advantages proselyte conversion appears to offer, at the same time putting in doubt the motives of those influencing them, implying that they have not made a full disclosure of the obligations concomitant with the re-identification that they are promoting. Paul argues that if these non-Jewish Christ believers are circumcised they will be responsible to "observe the whole Torah." This has been understood to mean that Paul is against Torah observance, that he sees it as a burden to be avoided. But if he is himself Torah observant, and known to be such by his Christ-believing Gentile audiences, it would signal a very different meaning. It would seek to expose and undermine the lack of integrity in the rival message. That message promotes the ostensible good to be gained by undertaking proselyte conversion and thereby to overcome the marginality that non-Jews claiming full standing as righteous ones apart from such conversion suffer in both the larger (but still minority) Jewish and overarching pagan communities in which they live, communities that do not share their conviction about the meaning of Christ. Paul's rhetorical approach subverts its proponents'

---

[86] In my view, certain texts that have been traditionally understood to suggest that Paul opposed a Jewish diet for himself, and by implication, for other Jewish believers in Christ, imply instead that Paul observed Jewish dietary customs and was understood by his non-Jewish addressees to do so (see my arguments related to Rom 14, in Nanos, *Mystery of Romans*, esp. chs. 3 and 4; related to the Antioch incident, in Nanos, "What Was at Stake?" and related to idol food at Corinth, in Nanos, "The Polytheist Identity").

[87] I understand the calendar Paul opposes in Gal 4:10 to be a polytheistic calendar, one that does not contain the distinctive mark of the Jewish calendar, "weeks," by which Paul's groups should mark time (Nanos, *Irony of Galatians,* 267–68; Troy Martin, "Pagan and Judeo-Christian Time-Keeping Schemes in Gal. 4:10 and Col. 2:16," *NTS* 42 [1996]: 120–32).

projected neglect to disclose that this step involves more than an identity solution but also necessarily involves the obligations of Torah identity. The tone of ironic rebuke here and throughout the letter seeks to expose the naïveté of his non-Jewish audience, much as does the ironic rebuke of a parent aimed at a teenager for failure to calculate the long-term cost of the short-term aims they seek to gain under peer pressure.[88]

Moreover, to carry weight, this rhetoric bespeaks knowledge of Paul as a Torah protector, since he is a Jewish person by birth, one who has, in keeping with his teaching, remained in that circumcised state in which he was called (1 Cor 7:17–24; 2 Cor 11:22; Phil 3:4–7). Otherwise, his non-Jewish audience would be expected to reply that they simply want what Paul has achieved, the advantage of traditionally accepted social identity for those claiming to be full members within these Jewish groups, without the obligation to observe the Torah. Consistent with this observation, Paul instructs his non-Jewish addressees to remain in their non-Jewish state, although, importantly, in a way that represents righteousness according to Jewish norms for defining human behavior (further evidence of his continued perspective from within Judaism). Even the love to which they are called to work out their faith is an articulation of the Torah: note, not by love working through faith but by "faith" or "faithfulness working through love" (Gal 5:6, 13–14, author's translation).[89] In doing so, they represent the nations turning from idolatry to worship Israel's Lord as the one God of all humankind (cf. Rom 3:29–31; 6:15–23; 13:8–14; 15:15–16; 1 Cor 10; 1 Thess 1:9).

One then wonders, why does Paul employ rhetoric that seemingly qualifies the advantages of being a Jew and having Torah? It is not hard to understand this development if Paul's non-Jewish addressees are suffering

---

[88] The topic of Nanos, *Irony of Galatians*; Dieter Mitternacht, *Forum für Sprachlose: Eine kommunikationspsychologische und epistolär-rhetorische Untersuchung des Galaterbriefs* (Coniectanea Biblica New Testament Series 30; Stockholm: Almqvist & Wiksell, 1999).

[89] This is but one of many indications throughout Galatians that Paul is not challenging a rival proposition upholding Torah observance for his addressees or proposing a sharp distinction between faith and works of righteousness, for then he would have presumably been more careful to write "love working through faith" here and to avoid the many other instructions about striving to undertake to behave righteously, or else not be among those who are of the kingdom of God (Gal 5:21). This implication is even present when Paul warns them that adopting proselyte conversion involves the obligation to observe the whole Torah (5:3), for his warning implies that the rival message is not teaching Torah observance but simply the benefits to be gained by proselyte conversion, which Paul seeks to undermine as a half-truth. These and other elements pointing in this direction are discussed at length in Nanos, *Irony of Galatians*.

status uncertainty and disadvantage because they have accepted the proposition that they have become equal members of Abraham's family without becoming equal members of Israel via proselyte conversion, because now God is shown in Christ to be the one God of members of the other nations as well as of Israel. These non-Jews have discovered the bad news social consequences in the present age for believing and acting according to the good news proposition of the dawning of the age to come. Paul and those whose teaching has brought about this painful identity dissonance and social disadvantage need to qualify their own advantage as Israelites, Jews who have the privilege of the promises, of covenant, of Torah and temple (cf. Rom 9:4–5; Gal 2:15; Phil 3:4–6). That was just what was at stake in the Antioch incident (Gal 2:11–14). The problem, Paul tells Peter, is not that the faith of these Jews in Jesus Christ has brought them down to the standing of non-Jews, but the proposition that the non-Jews have been brought up to equal standing with Jews (Gal 2:15–21).[90] From this follows the need to qualify their relative advantages, and by implication, the relative advantages of those Jews who do not accept this re-identification proposition apart from proselyte conversion. Hence, Paul asks in Romans, is God the God of Jews only? Of course not, he answers, because God is one (Rom 3:29–30). Note that Paul's argument here for the place of non-Jews depends upon the prior assumption of the place of the Jews as God's own. That is not what is being contested, but instead forms the basis for extending the logic to the inclusion of members of the other nations also.

That these comments are not to be taken apart from their rhetorical function as arguments for relative equality among Jews and non-Jews in Christ is logically demonstrated in Paul's many negative answers to the questions he poses in the midst of these arguments, "Much in every way" is the "advantage of the Jew" and "of the circumcision," he pronounces in Rom 3:1–2, because they "were entrusted with the oracles of God" (author's translation), the special prophetic privilege of bringing God's word to the rest of the nations (cf. Rom 10–11). "May it never be" that we "overthrow the Torah by this faith," he thunders at the end of that chapter's argument (Gal 3:31). Moreover, what many overlook are his many positive statements about the Torah that should make the traditional portrait of Paul nonsensical but that have usually been ignored, downplayed, or reasoned away.[91] For Paul not only writes that what matters is the "keeping of the commandments of God" (1 Cor 7:19) but also that "the Torah is holy and the commandment is holy and just and good" (7:12); he even argues

---

[90] Nanos, "What Was at Stake?"

[91] Gaston, *Paul and the Torah,* and John G. Gager, *Reinventing Paul* (Oxford: Oxford University Press, 2000), have criticized this tendency.

that "the Torah is spiritual" (v. 14)! How many dissertations, monographs, or even essays have been written on these un-Pauline-like declarations; indeed, how many sermons have ever been delivered on them?

Paul's rhetoric is rhetorical.[92] When it is isolated from its argumentative context for non-Jews within the first century and Jewish communal and conceptual concerns, and made into universal whatever-the-context truths for every person, for all times, interpretations run a high risk of missing entirely what the historical Paul and his Judaism represented to them, the good news along with the bad. If we approach Paul with the hypothesis that he was a figure within Judaism, indeed, propagating a particular Jewish community-forming viewpoint to Diaspora Jews and non-Jews throughout the lands north of the Mediterranean, and one whom his addressees know to observe Torah as a matter of faith, many possibilities emerge.

We can begin to read his letters as expressions of Judaism pre-Christianity, however deviant that form of Judaism was and came to be regarded to be by the other Jewish groups that survived. If we keep in focus that the issue for his addressees was their relative identity within Judaism without having to become Jews, their seeking of full member rather than merely guest standing within the Jewish community, then the issues of identity that circle around undertaking proselyte conversion (the "work of law" that turns a non-Jew into a Jew),[93] and why Paul denies this option to his addressees, need not be confused with Torah observance for Jews

---

[92] Cf. Lauri Thurén, *Derhetorizing Paul: A Dynamic Perspective on Pauline Theology and the Law* (WUNT 124; Tübingen: Mohr Siebeck, 2000).

[93] I understand "works of law" to function as a synonym for "circumcision," and both of these terms as metonyms in Paul's arguments to signify the role of proselyte conversion, by which non-Jews undertake the rite (hence, "act" or "work") by which, according to the traditional interpretation of the Torah, they can become children of Abraham's covenant on the same standing with (male) Jews from birth, who are circumcised as children. In my view, then, works of law = circumcision = proselyte conversion. Contra the traditional view, works of law does not refer to observing Torah, which non-Jews are not obliged to observe as if Jews, and contra Dunn's view, it does not include observance of special boundary-marking behavior such as Sabbath and food laws, which are also for those already defined as Torah people, that is Israelites, Jews, which Paul's addressees are not. It is, however, boundary marking in the sense of referring to the process of identity transformation, the behavior associated with completion of the rite of conversion (circumcision, in agreement with this point by Dunn), referring to the behavior that renders a non-Jew a Jew (a non-Israelite an Israelite), in keeping with the topic in view throughout Galatians. But that is different from the behavioral requirements that follow conversion, when they are re-identified as Jews and thus as obliged to observe Torah fully, just like all other Jews (cf. Gal 5:3). Thus the boundary mark of circumcision is different from the Torah obligations of Sab-

or with some kind of fault along the usual lines discussed, whether works righteousness, or nationalism, or exclusivism, and so on.[94]

Paul argues for the propositional views of this Jewish group in tension with the views that prevail among other Jewish groups and in the larger non-Jewish society in which all of these Jewish groups functioned as minority groups and subgroups, often specifically with how to identify non-Jews as either guests or members and thus with how they should be obliged to behave, including how Jews are to interact with them. It is to be according to the rules of the anticipated feast for all the nations who turn to worship God alongside Israel in the age to come, which has dawned, according to Paul, in Jesus Christ.

CONCLUSION

The investigation of Paul and Judaism has traditionally proceeded as if what was written was Paul or Judaism, with the understanding that these referents represent two different religious systems. That has not really changed with the development of the New Perspective. In the sense of Paul within or for or representing Judaism (or even a particular Jewish group), little work has been done to date. Interpreters do not often, if ever, write of converts to Paul's Jewish communities, of Paul's Judaism or Pauline Judaism, of the Judaism of Paul,[95] or of the Judaism of Paul's communities.[96] Never do I remember reading of Judaism's Paul. The two

---

bath and food laws for those who have been circumcised, and thereby are in the category of being obliged to observe Torah.

[94] Often interpreters run together the categories of identity and behavior, of circumcision and Torah observance for Jews as well as non-Jews, for example, when discussing what Paul opposes in Galatia. But Paul's argument is not with Torah observance, and he even appeals to it as that which follows after the identity transformation involved in proselyte conversion (circumcision), as discussed above, indicating that it is not Torah observance that is at issue in Galatia but identity transformation.

[95] Although, see, e.g., John G. Gager, "Paul, the Apostle of Judaism," in *Jesus, Judaism, and Christian Anti-Judaism: Reading the New Testament after the Holocaust* (ed. Paula Fredriksen and Adele Reinhartz; Louisville, Ky.: Westminster John Knox, 2002), 56–76; Jörg Frey, "Paul's Jewish Identity," in *Jewish Identity in the Greco-Roman World* (ed. Jörg Frey et al.; Ancient Judaism and Early Christianity 71; Leiden: Brill, 2007), 285–321.

[96] In a forthcoming introduction to Paul, Anders Runesson and I have been working with the phrase "Apostolic Judaism" to denote the larger movement among Christ believers, including Paul and his co-workers and communities as well as the other apostles such as James and Peter and their communities.

terms are different, and something must be wrong with one or the other side of the equation, or else they would not be so essentially antithetical.

This "essentializing" of difference between Paul and Judaism, and the concomitant requirement to find fault with one or the other, is influenced by the interpreter's ideological vantage point.[97] It will likely continue to be perpetuated implicitly, when not explicitly, to the degree that the ethnic division that Paul maintains within Christ-believing Judaism between Jews and Gentiles, between Israel and the other nations, is approached by his interpreters as if drawn between Judaism and Christianity instead (whether using the term "Christianity" or not), or between Jewish and Pauline Christianities.[98]

Christianity has had much invested in the tradition of Paul against Judaism, providing a counternarrative against which to measure its own unique fulfillment of God's expectations, whereas the Judaism it has fashioned in this meaning-making is portrayed to have failed. Interestingly, Jewish interpreters have become invested in the same construction of Paul, although turning the meaning upside down. This is all the more evident since the nineteenth-century reclamation of Jesus as a faithful Jewish figure, when Paul becomes the distorter of Jesus and antagonist even of the Judaism that he had represented.[99] Since it is so obvious that Paul did not understand his former religion and no longer recognized its value, it was easy to trivialize and blame Paul for the misunderstandings and ill will that Christianity so often expressed toward Jewish people and religion. There was no reason to take him or those who appealed to his authority seriously, and certainly no reason to look for Judaism at work in him, or in Paulinism.[100]

---

[97] See Pamela Eisenbaum, "Paul, Polemics, and the Problem of Essentialism," *BibInt* 13 (2005): 224–38.

[98] Nanos, "How Inter-Christian Approaches."

[99] See Heschel, *Abraham Geiger*; Langton, "Myth of the 'Traditional View of Paul'"; Pamela Eisenbaum, "Following in the Footnotes of the Apostle Paul," in *Identity and the Politics of Scholarship in the Study of Religion* (ed. Jose I. Cabezon and Sheila G. Davaney; New York: Routledge, 2004), 77–97. The trend continues in recent works: e.g., Klinghoffer, *Why the Jews Rejected Jesus*; Amy-Jill Levine, *The Misunderstood Jew: The Church and the Scandal of the Jewish Jesus* (New York: HarperSanFranscisco, 2006).

[100] Interestingly, the traditional portrait of Paul against Torah has also played a role in disputes between Jewish groups about the relative merits and demerits of so-called progressive policies toward Torah (see Jonathan D. Brumberg-Kraus, "A Jewish Ideological Perspective on the Study of Christian Scripture," *Jewish Social Studies* 4 [1997]: 121–52; Daniel R. Langton, "Modern Jewish Identity and the Apostle Paul: Pauline Studies as an Intra-Jewish Ideological Battleground," *JSNT* 28 [2005]: 217–58). The implications of reading Paul as a Torah-observant Jew for modern Jewish/Christian relations are addressed in Mark D. Nanos, "A

I have argued that successfully challenging the implicit as well as explicit negative valuations of Judaism that arise in the study of Paul requires attending to the particular contexts of Paul's language, written to non-Jews. Instead of treating this language as if universal, as if it addressed everyone, for example, Jews also, we should approach his rhetoric as highly situational and specific and not designed to offer a balanced view for everyone, on everything, forever. Sufficient historical-critical work on Paul has made it clear that the particular should not be confused with the absolute. Instead of proceeding as if Paul finds fault with Judaism, we should test the hypothesis that to the degree that he finds fault, it is to be understood in nuanced social contexts. Paul's rhetoric, addressed to non-Jews, is often developed in conflict with rival Jewish groups and their interpretations of how to best live Jewishly, which emerge because of his Jewish coalition's claim that non-Jews, by way of their response to the gospel of Christ, have become included in the Jewish communities, in Judaism, as equal members, apart from them becoming Jews, that is, without undertaking proselyte conversion. But it is to the non-Jewish members of his audiences, to address their identity and behavioral concerns, that Paul explains the implications of this Jewish group's positions.

Paul faulted some Jews for failure to agree with him that the expectations of Judaism were being realized in the work of proclamation in which he and his Jewish coalition were engaged, for failure to recognize that the end of the ages had dawned in Jesus Christ, and for not joining him in announcing this glad tiding to all of the scattered of Israel and to all of the nations in which they were to be found (Rom 9–11; 15:30–32). Even more so, Paul found fault with those who sought to prevent him from making this announcement (1 Thess 2:15–16). He wished a curse upon those who marginalized his fellow non-Jewish coalitionists for believing his message and thus expecting communal inclusion on an unprecedented level (Gal 1:8–9; 5:12).

Paul's criticism was not of Judaism. It was for the failure of some Jews and Jewish groups to be all that Judaism promised to be when the end of the ages had dawned.[101] This day he proclaimed to have arrived in the news of good in Jesus Christ, made manifest in the community of Jews and non-Jews who gathered as equal members to proclaim God's name in one voice. The awaited universal participation of all humankind in this joint praise

Torah-Observant Paul? What Difference Could It Make for Christian/Jewish Relations Today?" paper presented at the Christian Scholars Group for Christian/Jewish Relations, Boston, 4–6 June 2005 (available at http://www.marknanos.com/Boston-Torah-obs-5-9-05.pdf).

[101] Cf. Davies, "Paul and the People of Israel," in *Jewish and Pauline Studies* (Philadelphia: Fortress, 1984), 123–52 (136, 142).

was what he believed all Jews should agree to now by way of including non-Jewish Christ believers to be equal co-participants in Abraham's family, in the community of the righteous ones, and to live accordingly. What separated his particular way of living in Judaism was that he believed that everyone should be persuaded by this proposition now. Yet many other Jews and Jewish groups (or Judaisms) did not believe that awaited day had arrived. They believed that non-Jews were welcome as guests, but to be included as equal members in the present age required membership in Israel, which involved completing the rite of proselyte conversion. His stance was thus, *mutatis mutandis*, as ethnocentric and particularistic in its application of the universalistic proposition of the meaning of Christ for humanity as that of any Jewish group which did not believe this proposition to be true yet and thus maintained the particularistic requirement of proselyte standing for non-Jews to be included on equal terms. Neither proposition made sense independent of Judaism, independent of a particular people and way of living that proposes to know the will of the Creator, and thus to represent the ultimate interests of all humankind.

Paul explains in Rom 11, when confronting potential arrogance on the part of non-Jewish Christ believers, that he regarded his fellow Jews rejecting this message or its reception among the non-Jews to be "stumbling" but still within the covenant, insisting that they have not yet fallen (vv. 11–36). He believed that within his lifetime his fellow Jews would eventually be steadied again as a result of his ministry. That ministry also included the role of the non-Jews to whom he wrote. He sought to make them realize that generosity of spirit rather than triumphalism or indignation was warranted. Their lives must represent the righteous ideals of the age to come that they proclaim to have dawned in Christ: Judaism as it should be lived. They are to understand the momentary out-of-balance state of these Jewish brothers and sisters not to be a final judgment but rather to represent vicarious suffering on their behalf. Paul believed that bringing this message to the rest of the nations would ultimately result in the restoration of all Israel, as well as the salvation of the other nations, even if he only came to that conclusion with the passing of time and the disclosure of a mystery (vv. 25–26, 33–36).[102]

Whether one judges Paul's Judaism—or Pauline Judaism if you will—to be right about these claims, or in its criticisms of other Jews and Jewish

---

[102] Nanos, *Mystery of Romans*, 239–88; idem, "Challenging the Limits That Continue to Define Paul's Perspective on Jews and Judaism," in *Reading Israel in Romans: Legitimacy and Plausibility of Divergent Interpretations* (ed. Cristina Grenholm and Daniel Patte; vol. 1 of Romans through History and Culture Series; Harrisburg, Penn.: Trinity Press International, 2000), 217–29.

points of view, is another matter entirely. But in my view, this is what Paul would find wrong in Paulinism: it is not Judaism.

For Further Reading

Barth, Markus. "St. Paul—A Good Jew." *Horizons in Biblical Theology* 1 (1979): 7–45.

Boyarin, Daniel. *A Radical Jew: Paul and the Politics of Identity.* Berkeley: University of California Press, 1994.

Campbell, William S. *Paul and the Creation of Christian Identity.* Library of New Testament Studies 322. London: T&T Clark, 2006.

Davies, W. D. *Paul and Rabbinic Judaism: Some Rabbinic Elements in Pauline Theology.* Rev. ed. New York: Harper & Row, 1967.

Ehrensperger, Kathy. *That We May Be Mutually Encouraged: Feminism and the New Perspective in Pauline Studies.* New York: T&T Clark International, 2004.

Eisenbaum, Pamela. "Is Paul the Father of Misogyny and Antisemitism?" *Cross Currents* 50 (2000–2001): 506–24.

Elliott, Neil. *Liberating Paul: The Justice of God and the Politics of the Apostle.* Maryknoll, N.Y.: Orbis, 1994.

Frey, Jörg. "Paul's Jewish Identity." Pages 285–321 in *Jewish Identity in the Greco-Roman World.* Edited by J. Frey et al. Ancient Judaism and Early Christianity 71. Leiden: Brill, 2007.

Gager, John G. *Reinventing Paul.* Oxford: Oxford University Press, 2000.

Gaston, Lloyd. *Paul and the Torah.* Vancouver: University of British Columbia Press, 1987.

Harink, Douglas Karel. *Paul among the Postliberals: Pauline Theology beyond Christendom and Modernity.* Grand Rapids, Mich.: Brazos, 2003.

Johnson Hodge, Caroline. *If Sons, Then Heirs: A Study of Kinship and Ethnicity in the Letters of Paul.* New York: Oxford University Press, 2007.

Kinzer, Mark. *Postmissionary Messianic Judaism: Redefining Christian Engagement with the Jewish People.* Grand Rapids, Mich.: Brazos Press, 2005.

Langton, Daniel R. "The Myth of the 'Traditional View of Paul' and the Role of the Apostle in Modern Jewish-Christian Polemics." *JSNT* 28 (2005): 69–104.

Lapide, Pinchas. "The Rabbi From Tarsus." Pages 31–55 in *Paul, Rabbi and Apostle.* Edited by P. Lapide and P. Stuhlmacher. Minneapolis: Augsburg, 1984.

Munck, Johannes. *Paul and the Salvation of Mankind.* Translated by F. Clarke. Richmond: John Knox, 1959.

Nanos, Mark D. *The Irony of Galatians: Paul's Letter in First-Century Context.* Minneapolis: Fortress, 2002.

———. *The Mystery of Romans: The Jewish Context of Paul's Letter.* Minneapolis: Fortress, 1996.

Sanders, E. P. *Paul and Palestinian Judaism: A Comparison of Patterns of Religion.* Philadelphia: Fortress, 1977.

Schweitzer, Albert. *Paul and His Interpreters: A Critical History.* Translated by W. Montgomery. New York: Macmillan, 1951.

Segal, Alan F. *Paul the Convert: The Apostolate and Apostasy of Saul the Pharisee.* New Haven: Yale University Press, 1990.

Stendahl, Krister. *Paul among Jews and Gentiles, and Other Essays.* Philadelphia: Fortress, 1976.

Tomson, Peter J. *Paul and the Jewish Law: Halakha in the Letters of the Apostle to the Gentiles.* CRINT 1. Section 3: Jewish Traditions in Early Christian Literature. Assen: Van Gorcum, 1990.

Wyschogrod, Michael. *Abraham's Promise: Judaism and Jewish-Christian Relations.* Radical Traditions. Grand Rapids, Mich.: Eerdmans, 2004.

Yoder, John Howard. *The Jewish-Christian Schism Revisited.* Radical Traditions. Grand Rapids, Mich.: Eerdmans, 2003.

Zetterholm, Magnus. "Paul and the Missing Messiah." Pages 33–55 in *The Messiah: In Early Judaism and Christianity.* Edited by Magnus Zetterholm. Minneapolis: Fortress, 2007.

7

Paul and Women:
Telling Women to Shut Up Is More
Complicated Than You Might Think

Deborah Krause

The most important development in critical scholarship on Paul and women is that the subject itself is defunct. At the base what is defunct in all biblical research is the treatment of Paul as a decontextualized religious figure whose stand on various topics from women to the law to homosexuality merits intense investigation to arrive at some precise conclusion of how Paul thought about them. In this sense, much of what is new about "Paul and women" is in keeping with what has been new in the study of Paul and his letters for the last century or more, namely, the work of understanding the man and his writings within the complexities of their historical, rhetorical, social, cultural, political, economic, and religious contexts.

Just as scholars have developed more culturally engaged critical analyses of Paul's letters, so too, the study of women within ancient literature has been influenced by developments within the fields of feminist criticisms, gender studies, and women's history. Scholars in these disciplines have engaged Paul's writings and rhetoric about women not as a segregated issue within the literature of Paul but as a part of his cultural, religious, political way of being and context. These projects have shifted from the more traditional approach of selecting pertinent passages to the "problem" of women in Paul's letters (e.g., 1 Cor 11:2–16 and 1 Cor 14:34–36) to a more comprehensive investigation of the relation of Paul's letters and the churches they represent with the history of women within the Hellenistic world. As such newer approaches to the subject of Paul and women have moved from investigations into particular problematic passages and determinations of whether Paul is "pro" or "anti" woman (whatever that would mean) to a more thoroughgoing investigation into the histories of women within Hellenistic cultures and in relation to the cultural, religious, and political realities at work in the communities of Paul's churches. In this sense the study of Paul and women has developed from investigations that seek to establish Paul as a male chauvinist or a feminist, to investigations that seek to determine what his letters might reveal about the everyday life of women within the Hellenistic world and early Christian origins.[1]

In Christian belief and practice Paul is an enduring authoritative figure in matters regarding the church and its administration. His letters, while originally intended to address particular issues within terminal congregations, were circulated and copied as sources of instruction and wisdom for the church in general. This generalized version of "Paul" more than the historical figure or his particular letters has been the target of feminist critical engagement. This is so because what "Paul" says about women is not consistent. At one time he seems to uphold women's leadership and full participation within the community of faith (e.g., Rom 16:1), and at other times he seems to deny women's leadership (e.g., 1 Cor 14:34–35; 1 Tim 2:8–15).

Early feminist treatments of the subject made most headway in refuting "Paul's" prohibition of women's leadership in the church, for instance, by placing his rhetoric in its social and historical context.[2] For this reason, early feminist treatments of the subject of "women and Paul" critically engaged what had become a generalized perspective on Paul and his views on women. Paul's likely "authentic" letters were divided from those letters written decades later in his name.[3] Seemingly contradictory claims,

---

[1] Several essays trace these developments. Excellent overviews of this history of scholarship are Luise Schottroff, "How Justified Is the Feminist Critique of Paul," in *Let the Oppressed Go Free: Feminist Perspectives on the New Testament* (trans. Annemarie S. Kidder; Louisville, Ky.: Westminister/John Knox, 1993), 35–59; and the volume of essays edited by Ross Shepard Kraemer and Mary Rose D'angelo, *Women and Christian Origins* (New York: Oxford University Press, 1999), especially Margaret Y. Macdonald, "Reading Real Women through the Undisputed Letters of Paul," 199–220, and "Rereading Paul: Early Interpreters of Paul on Women and Gender," 236–53.

[2] For an example of an important early feminist treatment of the subject of women in Paul toward an apologetics for women in ordained ministry positions, see Krister Stendahl, *The Bible and the Role of Women: A Case Study in Hermeneutics* (Philadelphia: Fortress, 1966). Importantly, Stendahl's contribution underscores the fact that feminist criticism is the purview of all scholars who are committed to human liberation and is not essentially circumscribed to women. In other words, not all women are feminists, and men are perfectly capable of being both male and feminist.

[3] Romans, 1 Corinthians, 2 Corinthians, Galatians, Philippians, 1 Thessalonians, and Philemon are referred to as the "undisputed" letters of Paul or the

such as the call for women to be silent in 1 Cor 14:34–35, were argued to be interpolations by later redactors of the Pauline tradition. In this sense, the historical critical study of Paul's letters has been an essential tool for apologists who have argued for women's full leadership (e.g., ordination) and personhood within church and society. In this perspective, the historical Paul is championed for his inclusion of women within the ministries and leadership of the church. Only the later interpreters of his tradition (within the practice of pseudepigraphy) are seen as responsible for commanding women's silence and submission to men.

In this period of study on the subject of "Paul and women" the question of whether Paul believed women to be of equal status to men within the church was asked of the surface of the text. The primary goal of such investigation was to determine whether commands against women's leadership (1 Cor 14:34–35 and 1 Tim 2:8–15) were the historical Paul's words. This surface investigation of the subject of "Paul and women" changed in 1983 with the publication of Elisabeth Schüssler Fiorenza's feminist theological reconstruction of Christian origins, *In Memory of Her*.[4] In her study of Paul's letters and the letters of the Pauline tradition, Schüssler Fiorenza examines Paul's letters as tendentious rhetorical constructions from which women's history must be mined. As such, whether she is examining the pre-Pauline baptismal formula of Gal 3:28 (and its altered application in 1 Cor 12:13) or the roles of various named women within Paul's letters (e.g., Phoebe, Rom 16:1) Schüssler Fiorenza treats Paul's letters not as representative of the conditions of women within the early church but as rhetorical constructions within the convention of letter writing that coincidentally—unwittingly—convey artifacts of women's history, a history in the first few centuries of the common era in which there was much contention about women's roles and place in church and society.

"seven authentic" letters of Paul. The remaining letters written in Paul's name are to a greater or lesser extent understood by critical scholars to be parts of the pseudepigraphical tradition, representing writings in Paul's name by interpreters of the Pauline tradition in the generations following Paul (e.g., Colossians, Ephesians, 2 Thessalonians, 1 Timothy, 2 Timothy, and Titus).

[4] What is most important to me about Schüssler Fiorenza's work is that it is now a standard of early Christian history. No longer is it treated as a women's book or a feminist book; it resides on the shelf with other historical treatments of Paul and the early church. Even male colleagues of mine who teach critical introductions to the NT use the volume as a textbook, not simply as women's history but as a viable historical reconstruction of the early church in general. In this sense, the influence of feminist scholarship is transforming the practice of biblical scholarship in general.

Patriarchalization of the early Christian movement and ascendancy of the monarchical episcopacy not only made marginal or excluded women leaders in the early church but also segregated and restricted them to women's spheres, which gradually came under the control of the bishop. Nevertheless it must be emphasized again that the writings suggesting this kind of patriarchal dynamic are *prescriptive* rather than *descriptive*, since the male clergy were often dependent upon wealthy and influential women even into late antiquity. Ideological prescription and social reality do not always correspond.[5]

With Schüssler Fiorenza's work came a shift to the approach to the subject of women in the letters of Paul. No longer a debate about whether the historical Paul silenced women or curtailed their leadership, the study of women in Paul's letters became a project of reading between the lines to hear the embedded histories and implied perspectives at work in prescriptive rhetoric. The shift was no doubt indebted to the historical work of Walter Bauer in *Orthodoxy and Heresy in Earliest Christianity*, which proposes that rather than an original orthodoxy from which later Christianity fell, the early church was originally and regionally diverse in belief and practice.[6] Such an insight produces the capacity to discern the prescriptive rhetoric of Eph 5 or 1 Tim 2 as representing particular perspectives within diverse and contentious Christianities of the late first- and early second-century church. Between the lines of the prescriptions one may hear alternative stories of women's lives. For example, calls for women's submission likely arise from contexts in which women were asserting their authority, and commands for women's silence likely come from contexts in which women were talking. In other words, you do not tell someone to shut up unless she is talking! Needless to say, this historical lens offers Schüssler Fiorenza and others the opportunity to discern that, in spite of the claims of certain early Christian texts, women were leaders of Pauline communities and that these women were often in conflict with Paul and those who interpret his legacy within the canonical epistles.[7]

---

[5] Elisabeth Schüssler Fiorenza, *In Memory of Her: A Feminist Theological Reconstruction of Christian Origins* (New York: Crossroad, 1983), 310.

[6] First published in German in 1934 as *Rechtgläubigkeit und Ketzerei im ältesten Christentum*, Bauer's work in English is *Orthodoxy and Heresy in Early Christianity* (trans. Robert Kraft; Philadelphia: Fortress, 1971).

[7] An example of a work in this same vein is Dennis MacDonald, *The Legend and the Apostle: The Battle for Paul in Story and Canon* (Philadelphia: Westminster Press, 1983), in which MacDonald compares the rhetoric of 1 Timothy, 2 Timothy, and Titus with that of the noncanonical The Acts of Paul, particularly around the legend of Thecla. The comparison exposes the tensions between the lines of mandating of women's silence and prohibition of their teaching (1 Tim 2:8–15) is in direct contrast with Thecla whom Paul ultimately commissions to preach and teach the word.

In concert with the historical work of Schüssler Fiorenza, Bernadette Brooten in 1985 called for a study of women and Christian origins that would shift from examining "male attitudes toward women" to a vision of putting women at the center of historical study to understand their lives.[8] Brooten picked up this work in her study of women in early Judaism, and Schüssler Fiorenza, Luise Schottroff, and many others pursued the study of the everyday life of women in relation to early Christianity. These studies are ongoing, evidenced particularly in the work of Margaret MacDonald in her contribution to the Ross Kraemer and Mary Rose D'Angelo edited volume *Women and Christian Origins*. This work has moved to examine the lives of women in the ancient world—of Hellenism—in relation to their religions, Judaisms, Christianities, Greco-Roman religions, as whole people within complex cultures. Such advances within the study of early Christian origins have pursued the study of Paul and women in Paul's letters along two important fronts—rhetorical and discourse analyses of Paul's letters.

An early innovative and ambitious engagement of Paul with regard to his use of rhetoric in relation to women is Antoinette Wire's *The Corinthian Women Prophets: A Reconstruction through Paul's Rhetoric*.[9] Rather than the traditional approach of exegeting the "problem" passages for women in 1 Corinthians, Wire interprets 1 Corinthians as Paul's rhetorical struggle with women prophets within Corinth. As if responding directly to Brooten's challenge to place women at the center of exegetical examination, Wire radically shifts the focus of the study of women and Paul from 1 Cor 11:2–16 and 1 Cor 14:34–35 to the letter as a whole. Using a method understood as the "new rhetoric" and sociological analysis, Wire sees Paul's letter through a model of conflict, with his writing targeted to persuade and discredit those whom Wire reconstructs as women prophetic leaders within the Corinthian church. Wire's work offers a new angle on Paul that sees his message not as a necessary or natural articulation of the gospel of Jesus Christ but rather as a particular theological construction with particular investments that engaged other theological and ecclesial articulations of his day. Wire engages Paul's emphasis on the cross and suffering of Christ as one aspect of his particularity. She wonders how this

---

[8] Bernadette Brooten, "Early Christian Women and Their Cultural Context: Issues of Method in Historical Reconstruction," in *Feminist Practices of Biblical Scholarship* (ed. Adela Yarbro Collins; Chico, Calif.: Scholars Press, 1985), 65–91.

[9] Antoinette Wire, *The Corinthian Women Prophets: A Reconstruction through Paul's Rhetoric* (Minneapolis: Fortress, 1990). Evoking Wire's reinterpretation of Paul's Corinthian correspondence in light of women's religious and social experience is the recent exploration of Galatians by Tatha Wiley, *Paul and the Gentile Women: Reframing Galatians* (New York: Continuum, 2005).

teaching would have been heard by women within the Corinthian church who had begun to taste the new social freedom that baptism into Christ had afforded them. With regard to the subject of women, the study of Paul has been enriched by Wire's insights. Rather than a sideline or particular "problem issue," women were a vital part of the early house church and missionary movements. Seeing the complexity of the Corinthian women in relation to Paul is one important way to recover the diverse and contentious nature of early Christianity.

Contemporary with Wire's publication, Elizabeth Castelli engaged Paul's letters as constructions of power.[10] Rather than a sociological analysis of Paul's rhetoric, Castelli engages Paul's use of mimesis from the angle of ideological criticism and cultural criticisms, influenced in particular by the work of Michel Foucault. Much like Wire, Castelli understands that Paul's rhetoric is not "natural" or "necessary" but constructed. As such she scrutinizes his use of the call to "imitate him as he imitates Christ" as a particular construction of power within his churches. This construction of power, Castelli argues, is forged in an ideological commitment to sameness that resists difference and seeks to deny the presence of tension and conflict. Such may be Paul's desire, Castelli avers, but in fact his letters protest "too much." In this sense she explores Paul's letters as sites in which can be discerned a struggle for social control and political conformity within a larger cultural context of heterodox identities and competing ideologies. With Castelli, as with Wire from a different angle, the study of Paul's rhetoric and its relation to women comes firmly into the social and political realm.

The issue of identity with regard to women in the letters of Paul is further complicated and broadened by Daniel Boyarin in his important study *A Radical Jew: Paul and the Politics of Identity*.[11] Boyarin, like Castelli and Wire, examines Paul's letters as rhetorical constructions that reveal his own commitments and location as a particular kind of theologian and ecclesial leader within the complexities of his culture/world. Boyarin as a Jewish scholar is particularly interested in how Paul constructs his understanding of identity with regard to his christological claims and his understanding of Judaism. This understanding, much like Castelli's analysis of Paul's discourse of power regarding imitation, takes on Paul's understanding of the "universal" human new being that is borne in one's baptism into Christ. Boyarin argues that Paul's understanding of

---

[10] Elizabeth Castelli, *Imitating Paul: A Discourse of Power* (Louisville, Ky.: Westminster/John Knox, 1991).

[11] Daniel Boyarin, *A Radical Jew: Paul and the Politics of Identity* (Berkeley: University of California Press, 1994).

this "human" obliterates difference—both Jewish and female—as it denies the realities of enfleshed existence and seeks an ideal, spiritual, universal expression that is for Paul, of course, normed as Christian and male. In this regard Boyarin, as Castelli, complicates the traditional apologetic of Paul's inclusive vision in Gal 3:28—in Christ there is no Jew or Greek, slave or free, male and female, for all are one in Christ Jesus. Such a vision may seem to create a basis for socially egalitarian community, but as such a culturally unbiased and socially homogeneous expression is not possible "in the flesh" it denies the heterogeneity and multi-vocal reality of human community. In this sense, even where Paul has seemed to be an ally toward women's full inclusion within the rhetoric of early Christianity, critics such as Boyarin offer a caution about the social and cultural implications of this radical vision. Sometimes what looks to promise equality can in fact function as a structure of conformity and, even more, a historical reality that obliterates ethnic, religious, biological, or sexual difference.

In a recent and important contribution to the social construction of gender in 1 Corinthians, Jorunn Økland articulates the contrast of approach between seeing Paul as a unified subject who authors his letters out of his ideas about women, the law, grace, and so on, to understanding 1 Corinthians within the "broader discourses" of Corinthian culture of which Paul is a part.[12] In such an approach, contradictions in Paul's writings are not so much problematic as they are full of potential for better understanding the complexities of the cultural context in which Paul is writing. Like Castelli and Boyarin, Økland understands Paul's texts as replete with meaning beyond his control. With regard to women's lives this approach is not so much concerned with what Paul thought about women as it is with what Paul's writings reveal about gender construction within the cultural context of Corinth. "Real" historical women, just as the "real" historical Paul, fade from view as the rich complexity of gendered social discourse as it relates to the Corinthian community comes to the fore.[13] In exploring the discourses of gender and space in Corinth, Økland discerns that what seem to be contradictions in Paul's rhetoric about Corinthian women and their place and activity may in fact be indications of the fluidity of social relations and gender roles. In 1 Cor 11, women are identified as having prophetic roles within sanctuary space. In 1 Cor 14, they are commanded to silence in the assembly. In 1 Cor 12, Paul constructs a metaphor of the unity of the membership as a body, but the metaphor is gendered as male. Ultimately Økland discerns that women

---

[12] Jorunn Økland, *Women in Their Place: Paul and the Corinthian Discourse of Gender and Sanctuary Space* (London: T&T Clark, 2004), 22–23.

[13] Ibid., 217–23.

occupy a potentially subversive "no man's land" in Corinth and Paul's affirmation or denial of the space and role of the real women named in 1 Cor 11–14 (and Rom 16) does not exist because of Paul's inclusive ideas about women but because Paul is flexibly and contextually navigating gendered constructions of social space in which women's place is not settled.[14]

Margaret Macdonald's engagement of historical issues related to women's lives in *Early Christian Women and Pagan Opinion*[15] and her essays on Paul and the canonical interpreters of Paul in the above named Kraemer and D'Angelo volume offer a rapprochement between the theoretically driven analyses of Castelli, Boyarin, and Økland and the more historical work of scholars like Schüssler Fiorenza and Schottroff. MacDonald places the rhetoric of Paul about women and their activities in conversation with the rhetoric of critics of early Christianity, such as Celsus, in order to understand how the historical fact of women's leadership within early Christian prophetic movements, house churches, and missionary movements became such a problem and embarrassment to writers such as Paul and his interpreters.[16] In this analysis, MacDonald assesses how the broad Greco-Roman cultural bias that women's religious experience was prone to excess and hysteria influenced the development of early Christian movements and found expression in their writings. In this sense, traditional apologies for Paul's restriction on women's teaching in 1 Cor 14:33–34 or of the restrictions on women's ecclesial leadership in the Pastoral Epistles are challenged. Rather than seeing this Christian rhetoric as reflecting a necessary evil of the cultural accommodation of the church to its larger culture, MacDonald sees the rhetoric as participating in the construction of women's religious excesses alongside the broader popular cultural rhetorical construction of women's experience. In the ancient world, male rhetoricians regularly characterized women of Jewish, Greco-Roman, and Christian religious communities as excessive. Importantly, this insight holds that Christian women were not unique in their assumption of religious leadership. Women of different religious ex-

---

[14] Ibid., 222–23. Ongoing research in the exploration of gender and social discourse in Paul's letters can be found in works such Joseph A. Marchal's *The Politics of Heaven: Women, Gender, and Empire in the Study of Paul* (Minneapolis: Fortress, 2008).

[15] *Early Christian Women and Pagan Opinion: The Power of the Hysterical Woman* (Cambridge: Cambridge University Press, 1996).

[16] For a similar type of treatment of women in Paul's writings and the ancient world, see Bruce W. Winter, *Roman Wives, Roman Widows: The Appearance of New Women in the Pauline Communities* (Grand Rapids, Mich.: Eerdmans, 2003); Gillian Beattie, *Women and Marriage in Paul and His Early Interpreters* (London: T&T Clark, 2005).

pressions both assumed religious leadership and were disparaged in their popular cultural discourse for it. Seen in this context, Paul's letters, and those of his interpreters in Ephesians, Colossians, 1 Timothy, 2 Timothy, and Titus, are expressions of their culture (not exceptions to it), and as such they reflect the ongoing cultural, political, and social struggles of the culture. The Pauline letters thereby function as a site for the excavation of Christian women's histories—not in some ideal utopian sense but in the sense of recovery of the complexity of women's everyday lives in relation to their religious experiences. MacDonald examines how women such as Chloe and Junia, Phoebe, Euodia, and Syntheche are placed within this complex cultural mix to appreciate not only how Paul's rhetoric would have sounded to them but also how in between the lines we might see and understand something about their history.

The newer approaches to Paul in scholarship regarding women represent a broadening of the field of analysis from a few select texts to the culture in general. As such, all the topics covered in this volume pertain to the subject of Paul and women. From this perspective, the texts of the canon are more than mere descriptions of the life of the early church. They are more than the sum of their author's thoughts on the problem or issue of women. They are contentious discourses about the nature of human community in relation to religious experience and the institutions that order it. The history of the church is an ongoing argument about women, yes, and men, sexuality, authority, identity, and many other vexing human problems. Paul's letters reveal this argument from an early part of the church. Letters within the Pauline tradition (e.g., Ephesians, Colossians, 2 Thessalonians, 1 Timothy, 2 Timothy, and Titus) demonstrate how this argument developed into the late and early second century.

WOMEN'S SPEECH IN THE PAULINE TRADITION

There are two direct prohibitions of women's speech within in the Pauline writings: 1 Cor 14:34–36 and 1 Tim 2:11–12. Until recently, much scholarly analysis of these texts surrounded questions of whether the prohibitions are authentic to the historical Paul. The goal of such investigation has been to cast doubt upon whether Paul actually made these claims, particularly in light of the seemingly contradictory evidence of women's leadership within his churches (e.g., the reference to women prophesying in 1 Cor 11:5 and the commendation of Phoebe to the Roman church as a deacon of Cenchreae in Rom 16:1). As such, some scholars have argued that 1 Cor 14:34–36 is in fact an editorial interpolation into 1 Corinthians by the author of 1 Timothy.[17] Through this insight, advocates for women's leadership within the contemporary church have been able to marginalize the prohibitions of women's speech in the church to the particular claim of the late first- or early second-century church leader who wrote the Pastoral Epistles. In this vein, interpreters have been able to claim that women's leadership within worship and administration of early churches is well evidenced and that prohibitions to women's speech in church are not original to Paul's churches but a later development of a part of the church in its accommodation to Greco-Roman culture.

As outlined above, recent scholars of women's lives within the letters of Paul have broadened the concern of their research from determining the intention of the historical Paul to understanding Paul's writings as expressions of the culture and history from which they come. In this interpretive approach, prohibitions to women's speech are examined as social-political rhetorical claims that function less to describe the state of churches within the Pauline tradition on the subject of women and more to intervene in broader ongoing arguments within these churches and cultures about human social relationships, identity, authority, and religious experience. When read in this vein, the claims from 1 Cor 14:34–36 and 1 Tim 2:8–15 are, as Schüssler Fiorenza has said, prescriptive and not descriptive of women's experience. In this light the texts take on a depth and texture that calls for investigation of more than simply the single voice and will of their author. It calls for a reading of the context (literary and historical) of the text and for a hearing of that which is not said—that which is between the lines of the text.

1 Corinthians 14:34–36

The text is preceded in 1 Cor 14:33 by a universal context for the teaching on women's silence ("as in all the churches of the saints," NRSV). Nowhere else in 1 Corinthians or his other letters does Paul set this broad a vision of the church as a context for a teaching. As the text concludes there is another universal claim in 1 Cor 14:35: "it is shameful for a woman to speak in church" (NRSV). As totalizing as these introductory and concluding claims against women's speech in church may seem, if you place them together they begin to trouble one another somewhat. If women's silence in church is a norm in "all the churches of the saints," then how is it known that for women to speak in church is shameful? The combination of claims begins to suggest that perhaps the writer is less confident about his claims to "all the churches" than he may seem.

---

[17] MacDonald, *The Legend and the Apostle*, 85–89.

In addition to shaken certainties about what is practiced in "all the churches," the passage reveals a division in thinking between the public and the private behavior of women and men. What is remarkable about this delineation is that it seems to suggest that women are perfectly capable of knowing and understanding (they have the "desire to know") but that this desire is only appropriately acted upon by women in relation to their husbands within their homes and not the churches ("let them ask their husbands at home"). In this division the letter writer reveals that the issue with women's speech is not that it is ignorant but that it is disruptive—disruptive of the public space of church leadership. For this reason, the writer of the letter sends the women and their desire to know home. The direction is parallel to Paul's teaching in 1 Cor 11:22 where in challenge to those who come to church for the Lord's Supper and get drunk while others go hungry, Paul corrects: "Do you not have homes to eat and drink in?" (NRSV). Order in the church is maintained through the division of the community between church and home, between public and domestic arrangements of power and relationship. While universal claims are made and authoritative laws are cited to prescribe women's silence, Paul constructs particular spaces of "church" and "home" for the maintenance of a particular kind of order. Paul's rhetoric appeals to that which is universally true but constructs that which is particularly necessary to enforce it.

Seen in this light, the teaching in 1 Cor 14:33–34 is not about women's incapacity to know and learn but about a strategy for containing their speech related to their knowing and learning in a realm removed from the administration of the church. As a discourse of power the text reveals the struggle for controlling speech within Corinth (or some later part of the church) and the challenge of the speech of women to the established order of the church. In spite of the author's intention to ground the command to women's silence in church as a universal ("as in all the churches"), the text read as discourse begins to reveal the particularity of his concerns about women's speech and his strategies to control it.

1 Timothy 2:8–15

As noted above, the predominant scholarly engagement with 1 Tim 2:8–15 from the subject of Paul and women is to argue that Paul did not write it. As an artifact of ancient pseudepigraphy, the writing (along with 2 Timothy and Titus) claims the name of Paul in order to direct and inform the interpretation of the Pauline tradition in the late first- or early second-century church. As such, the command to women's silence and the exegetical rationale for the command in 1 Tim 2:13–15 are viewed as not original to Paul's churches and as evidence of the later accommodation of the church to Greco-Roman culture.

When the text is examined, however, from the perspective of a discourse of power, like 1 Cor 14:33–34 it reveals less the certain rhetoric of the prohibition of women's speech and more the tense negotiation of women's leadership and presence within the church. As with the claim in 1 Cor 14:33 that women should direct their desire to learn toward their husbands within the domestic realm, 1 Tim 2:12 notes, in the midst of the command to silence, that women are capable of learning. Moreover, when the writer exclaims, "I permit no woman to teach or to have authority over a man" (NRSV), he reveals that women may well teach and have authority in other arenas. The trouble that teaching outside of the realm of the church may cause for the writer seems to be suggested in 1 Tim 5:13 when he characterizes the activity of younger widows (women unattached to men) as "gadding about from house to house, and they are not merely idle, but gossips and busybodies, saying what they should not say" (NRSV). Seen from the context of a rhetorical construction within a negotiation of power, 1 Tim 2:8–15 reveals a leader of the church attempting to constrain an activity that is already on the loose. Rather than a historical portrait of women cowering within their homes, submissive and silent, the text, read within its literary and historical contexts, reveals a contentious community with competing claims to leadership and religious authority of which women were a vital part.

Conclusion

Newer scholarship about women in the Pauline tradition represents an expansion of the subject from the intention and person of the Apostle Paul to a broader exploration of women's lives within the Hellenistic world. The letters within this expansion are not so much a reservoir of Paul's ideas about women as they are artifacts of discourse about human relationships, gender, religious experience, and power at work in Paul's churches and the world in which they lived. Seen in this light, the letters of the Pauline tradition are not friend or foe in the cause of women for their full inclusion in leadership in the church. Rather, they are witnesses to the struggle that women and men have engaged to define the nature of the church's leadership, the shape of human community within the church, and the intersection between religious experience and the authority to speak of it. We can see from the Pauline tradition that these challenges were far from settled within the early church. We know from contemporary practices of Christian rhetoric in all its diversity that these challenges are far from settled today. In this new vein the letters of the Pauline tradition and the rhetoric of the contemporary church are witnesses to an enduring struggle within which women and men who hope for a more humane, inclusive, and just church will not necessarily take comfort but through which they might take courage.

FOR FURTHER READING

Bauer, Walter. *Orthodoxy and Heresy in Early Christianity.* Translated by Robert Kraft. Philadelphia: Fortress, 1971.

Boyarin, Daniel. *A Radical Jew: Paul and the Politics of Identity.* Berkeley: University of California Press, 1994.

Brooten, Bernadette. "Early Christian Women and Their Cultural Context: Issues of Method in Historical Reconstruction." Pages 65–91 in *Feminist Practices of Biblical Scholarship.* Edited by Adela Yarbro Collins. Chico, Calif.: Scholars Press, 1985.

Castelli, Elizabeth. *Imitating Paul: A Discourse of Power.* Louisville, Ky.: Westminster/John Knox, 1991.

MacDonald, Dennis R. *The Legend and the Apostle: The Battle for Paul in Story and Canon.* Philadelphia: Westminster Press, 1983.

MacDonald, Margaret Y. *Early Christian Women and Pagan Opinion: The Power of the Hysterical Woman.* Cambridge: Cambridge University Press, 1996.

Økland, Jorrun. *Women in Their Place: Paul and the Corinthian Discourse of Gender and Sanctuary Space.* London: T&T Clark, 2004.

Schottroff, Luise. *Let the Oppressed Go Free: Feminist Perspectives on the New Testament.* Translated by Annemarie S. Kidder. Louisville, Ky.: Westminster/John Knox, 1993.

Schüssler Fiorenza, Elisabeth. *In Memory of Her: A Feminist Theological Reconstruction of Christian Origins.* New York: Crossroad, 1983.

Shepard Kraemer, Ross, and Mary Rose D'Angelo. *Women and Christian Origins.* New York: Oxford University Press, 1999.

Stendahl, Krister. *The Bible and the Role of Women: A Case Study in Hermeneutics.* Philadelphia: Fortress, 1966.

Winter, Bruce W. *Roman Wives, Roman Widows: The Appearance of New Women in the Pauline Communities.* Grand Rapids, Mich.: Eerdmans, 2003.

Wire, Antoinette. *The Corinthian Women Prophets: A Reconstruction through Paul's Rhetoric.* Minneapolis: Fortress, 1990.

8

Paul and Rhetoric:
A *Sophos* in the Kingdom of God

Mark D. Given

The past thirty years or so have witnessed an explosion of rhetorical studies of Paul.[1] In this chapter I will first provide a brief overview of the subject of Paul and rhetoric. Then I will describe how classical rhetorical criticism is typically applied to 1 Corinthians. In the final section, I will discuss some of the distinctive characteristics of a postmodern rhetorical approach and apply some of them to an issue in the interpretation of 1 Cor 1–4 in order to illustrate how classical and postmodern rhetorical approaches differ. A classical rhetorical approach is content to describe "the rhetorical situation" Paul faced, mostly from his own point of view, and to foreground the rhetorical means he used to address it. A postmodern approach is not content with this mainly descriptive task and includes attention to ideological issues pertaining to rhetoric, power, and interpretation itself.

PAUL AND RHETORIC

Rhetoric was the queen of the arts in the ancient Greco-Roman educational system.[2] Aristotle (384–322 B.C.E.) wrote a treatise on it, and

---

[1] My title alludes to E. A. Judge's forthright designation of Paul as a sophist in his classic article on "The Early Christians as a Scholastic Community: Part 2," *Journal of Religious History* 1 (1961): 125. As we shall see, calling Paul a *sophos* is not exactly the same thing, but there are intriguing similarities.

[2] For a brief but informative discussion of the importance of ancient rhetoric, see Ben Witherington, *Conflict and Community in Corinth: A Socio-Rhetorical Commentary on 1 and 2 Corinthians* (Grand Rapids, Mich.: Eerdmans, 1995), 39–43.

many rhetorical handbooks were composed in the following centuries.[3] The mark of a well-educated person was the ability to express oneself well, and the teaching of rhetoric was associated especially with the sophists. The Oxford Classical Dictionary (2d ed.) defines the sophists as

> itinerant teachers who went from city to city giving instruction for a fee. The subjects of instruction varied somewhat in content, but always had a relation to the art of getting on, or of success in life. . . . Under the Roman Empire, particularly from the second century onwards, the word acquired a more specialized meaning and became restricted to teachers and practitioners of rhetoric, which by this time was tending to become a purely literary exercise practiced for its own sake.[4]

The sophists were often attacked by philosophers because, among other things, they tended to be philosophical relativists, but even many philosophers acknowledged that rhetorical skill was necessary.[5]

The subject of Paul and rhetoric rightly begins with Paul's own reflections on it. His earliest surviving letter, 1 Thessalonians, reveals his awareness of the differing rhetorical styles of itinerant teachers as well as their differing motives, not all of which were pure (1 Thess 2:1-12). In a 1970 article, "'Gentle as a Nurse': The Cynic Background of 1 Thessalonians 2," Abraham Malherbe argued that Paul, very much like Dio Chrysostom (ca. 40–ca. 120 C.E.), presented his modus operandi as that of a philosopher, consciously distinguishing himself from a sophist.[6] Furthermore, the Corinthian correspondence demonstrates beyond any doubt that Paul was well aware that he was being judged according to classical rhetorical

---

[3] For a full yet very readable survey of rhetoric from the pre-Socratics through the Middle Ages, see George A. Kennedy, *A New History of Classical Rhetoric* (Princeton: Princeton University Press, 1994). Kennedy also includes useful discussions of rhetoric and religion, especially Christianity.

[4] For full reference and discussion, see Mark D. Given, *Paul's True Rhetoric: Ambiguity, Cunning, and Deception in Greece and Rome* (ESEC 7; Harrisburg, Penn.: Trinity Press International, 2001), 10.

[5] Bowersock observes, "It was, in fact, possible for the professions of philosopher and rhetor to be conflated and confused. They had many tasks in common, and both were obliged to use the spoken and written word. Accordingly, as Philostratus recognized, eloquent philosophers might be numbered among the sophists" (G. W. Bowersock, *Greek Sophists in the Roman Empire* [Oxford: Oxford University Press, 1969], 11). For more on the feud between philosophy and rhetoric and its relevance to the study of Paul, see Given, *Paul's True Rhetoric*, 1–37.

[6] Abraham Malherbe, *Paul and the Popular Philosophers* (Minneapolis: Augsburg Fortress, 1989). See Given, *Paul's True Rhetoric*, 13–15, for a discussion and table that present Malherbe's comparison.

standards and found wanting by some.[7] An excellent study of this aspect of the situation in Corinth is Bruce W. Winter's *Philo and Paul among the Sophists: Alexandrian and Corinthian Responses to a Julio-Claudian Movement,* originally published in 1997 and now in its second edition.[8] While I have some reservations about Winter's approach to Paul's rhetoric, he performed the valuable service of demonstrating that the ideals of the Second Sophistic, a powerful resurgence of the sophistic movement in the early Roman Empire, were already thriving in Alexandria and Corinth by the mid first century. This, of course, increases the likelihood that they were thriving in other urban centers as well and that Paul could not have escaped interacting with them. Whether or not Paul had an advanced formal rhetorical education, in light of Winter's study there can be little doubt that he had interacted with other church leaders who used sophistic rhetoric and was capable of using some of their techniques, if only to combat them. More fundamentally, though, there can be little doubt that Paul had some basic training in rhetoric, and this is supported by the long history of biblical scholarship that has applied rhetorical analysis to Paul's letters.

Classical NT Rhetorical Criticism

A good place to pick up some of that history is Hans Dieter Betz's 1986 essay in *L'Apôtre Paul* entitled "The Problem of Rhetoric and Theology according to the Apostle Paul."[9] The first part of this essay is a survey of rhetorical readings of Paul stretching back to the church fathers. It is quite clear from this survey that the application of classical rhetoric to the study of Paul is hardly a recent phenomenon. For example, the Protestant Reformers were well aware of the rhetorical qualities of Paul's discourse.[10] A later particularly strong example of investigating classical

---

[7] It is important to realize that it is unlikely that all the Corinthians thought that Paul's rhetoric was inadequate. Rhetorical tastes varied. Some scholars fall into the trap of thinking that there was only one possible ideal for an orator; that "the Corinthians" as a whole thought Paul failed to measure up to it; and that their assessment was accurate. This represents a chain of misleading oversimplifications. See Given, *Paul's True Rhetoric,* 2n3 for examples of highly successful sophists whose personal characteristics were far from the Greco-Roman upper-class ideal.

[8] Bruce W. Winter, *Philo and Paul among the Sophists: Alexandrian and Corinthian Responses to a Julio-Claudian Movement* (2d ed; Grand Rapids, Mich.: Eerdmans, 2002).

[9] Hans Dieter Betz, "The Problem of Rhetoric and Theology according to the Apostle Paul," in *L'Apôtre Paul: Personnalité, style et conception du ministère* (ed. A. Vanhoye; BETL 73; Leuven: Leuven University Press, 1986), 16–48.

[10] Ibid., 17.

rhetorical features in Paul is Johannes Weiss's "Beiträge zur paulinischen Rhetorik," published in 1897.[11]

Augustine's early treatment of the subject is especially intriguing. A careful reading of the fourth book of Augustine's *On Christian Doctrine* (426 C.E.) will quickly dispel the oft repeated opinion that the church fathers did not see any evidence of rhetorical sophistication in the NT.[12] Augustine pursues two strategies. On the one hand, with respect to the Bible as a whole, he admits that most of its authors do not exhibit rhetorical training, but he presents many examples of impressive rhetoric that he considers the product of natural gifts and/or divine inspiration. On the other hand, he spends a lot of time on Paul, referring to him as "our great orator," giving many stylistic examples to demonstrate his rhetorical prowess. He also says,

> But perhaps someone is thinking that I have selected the Apostle Paul because he is our great orator. For when he says, "Though I be rude in speech, yet not in knowledge," he seems to speak as if granting so much to his detractors, not as confessing that he recognized its truth. If he had said, "I am indeed rude in speech, but not in knowledge," we could not in any way have put another meaning upon it. He did not hesitate plainly to assert his knowledge, because without it he could not have been the teacher of the Gentiles. And certainly if we bring forward anything of his as a model of eloquence, we take it from those epistles which even his very detractors, who thought his bodily presence weak and his speech contemptible, confessed to be weighty and powerful.[13]

Augustine is convinced that Paul had more than a nonprofessional's knowledge of rhetoric, and he certainly considers Paul rhetorically gifted. This opinion comes from someone who had studied and taught rhetoric, whose own writings are masterful rhetorical compositions, and whose own oratory moved people to tears, groans, and applause.[14] On the issue of whether Paul might have been a rhetorically gifted writer but a poor speaker, Augustine takes Paul's concession to his critics concerning his speech making abilities to be rhetorically sophisticated irony. A very literal translation of the passage preserves the ambiguity involved: "But even if I am an amateur in speech, yet I am not in knowledge" (2 Cor 11:6).

[11] J. Weiss, "Beiträge zur paulinischen Rhetorik," in *Theologische Studien* (ed. C. R. Gregory et al.; Göttingen: Vandenhoeck, 1897), 165–247.

[12] See George A. Kennedy, *New Testament Interpretation through Rhetorical Criticism* (Chapel Hill: University of North Carolina Press, 1984), 11, 30, 93–94.

[13] *On Christian Doctrine* 4.7.15 (*Nicene and Post-Nicene Fathers*, Series 1, 2:579).

[14] Ibid., 4.24.53; 4.26.56.

Augustine takes the first half of the sentence to be only a hypothetical concession to his opponents. Most modern commentators take it to be a real one. However, even some of them are not convinced that Paul intends to admit that he lacks oratorical skill. Although the word *idiōtēs* has usually been translated "rude," "unskilled," or "untrained," it is probably best translated "amateur." Winter has demonstrated that this term could be used of people who had studied advanced rhetoric but chose not to practice it as a profession.[15] So Paul may not intend to concede anything about his oratorical abilities but rather to brag about how he is willing to share his knowledge without the pretentiousness of the "super apostles," who boast in their speaking abilities and probably expect remuneration for them like professional sophists (vv. 7–21).

If one grants this possibility, then whether or not Augustine was correct about how Paul only hypothetically conceded his lack of oratorical skill, a very literal translation of the earlier passage to which he alludes makes good sense: "For they say, 'His letters are weighty and strong, but his personal presence is unimpressive, and his speech contemptible.' Let such a person consider this, that what we are in word by letters when absent, such persons we are also in deed when present" (2 Cor 10:10–11 NASB). Paul here employs the venerable contrast between word and deed, and he appears to be making the counter claim that "such a person" will soon find out that his personal presence and speech are also weighty and strong.[16] The book of Acts presents Paul as a skilful orator. It is not at all clear that this is in contrast to Paul's own assessment of his oratorical abilities.

Early as well as later medieval, Enlightenment, and early modern perspectives on NT rhetoric were mainly formalistic. Interpreters mostly commented on isolated stylistic matters such as the use of rhetorical figures. That was to change in the late twentieth century with the explosion of classical rhetorical analyses of Paul that focus on argumentative structures and rhetorical strategies. Betz's work is fundamental, along with that of George Kennedy. Betz's 1979 Hermeneia commentary on Galatians really got the ball rolling.[17] Not everyone agreed with all the details of Betz's rhetorical analysis of Galatians—Kennedy included—but few could deny that Betz was on to something with his thesis that Paul's letter was "composed in accordance with the conventions of Greco-Roman rhetoric and

---

[15] Winter, *Philo and Paul,* 225–28.

[16] Cf. 2 Cor 13:2–4 and 1 Cor 4:18–21.

[17] His 1972 monograph on Paul and the Socratic tradition is also important. Unfortunately, it was never translated into English. See Hans Dieter Betz, *Der Apostel Paulus und die socratische Tradition: Eine exegetische Untersuchung zu seiner "Apologie" 2 Korinther 10–13* (Beiträge zur historischen Theologie 45; Tübingen: Mohr, 1972).

epistolography."[18] Richard Longenecker would say a little over ten years later in his own Galatians commentary that "what Betz has done, in effect, has been to push a good thesis too hard and too far."[19] But Longenecker's approach to Galatians is thoroughly rhetorical and a testimony to just how good that thesis was.

One of Betz's critics was the classicist George Kennedy. However, what Kennedy was to do for rhetorical criticism of the NT turned out to be even more influential. In 1984, he published *New Testament Interpretation through Rhetorical Criticism* with the express intent of giving NT scholars a well-defined method for applying rhetorical analysis to any given text.[20] Kennedy's method relies heavily on ancient categories, especially those of Aristotle, but combines them with the more modern formulations of Bitzer, Perelman and Olbrechts-Tyteca, and others. It is an example of the "new rhetoric," which blossomed in the second half of the twentieth century.[21] His methodology released the floodgates. It has been combined profitably with a descriptivist sociological approach, most notably by Ben Witherington III, who has poured forth a flood of useful and instructive socio-rhetorical NT commentaries.[22]

Many NT rhetoric conferences have been held in the years since Kennedy's book was released, and many of the papers collected in numerous published volumes regularly show their debt to Kennedy's inspiration. In 2008, former students of Kennedy edited a volume of essays titled *Words Well Spoken: George Kennedy's Rhetoric of the New Testament*, which honors the ongoing influence of their teacher on NT rhetorical criticism.[23] It is also an excellent resource for current bibliography.

Postmodern Rhetorical Criticism

There is quite a bit of ferment in NT rhetorical criticism, so I would not want to give the impression that it is a unified approach. In terms of volume of scholarship, the classical or "new rhetoric" approach has dominated

---

[18] Hans Dieter Betz, *Galatians* (Hermeneia; Philadelphia: Fortress, 1979), xiv.

[19] Richard N. Longenecker, *Galatians* (WBC 41; Dallas: Word, 1990), cxi.

[20] See above, p. 175n2. The book remains in print. I have used it as one of the textbooks in an undergraduate senior seminar on rhetoric and the NT, and some students have told me that they learned more about effective communication from it than from their required general education communications course.

[21] For further discussion, see Wilhelm Wuellner, "Rhetorical Criticism" in The Bible and Culture Collective, *The Postmodern Bible* (New Haven: Yale University Press, 1995), 156–61.

[22] E.g., his *Conflict and Community in Corinth*, to which I later refer.

[23] C. Clifton Black and Duane F. Watson, eds., *Words Well Spoken: George Kennedy's Rhetoric of the New Testament* (Waco, Tex.: Baylor University Press, 2008).

rhetorical criticism of the NT. However, a more interdisciplinary and theoretically informed postmodern rhetorical criticism also exists.[24]

Vernon Robbins is a NT scholar who has had considerable methodological influence on NT rhetorical criticism, especially since the late 1980s. Whether or not he would call himself a postmodernist, his approach reflects some postmodern perspectives. In 1994, he published two books that represent an advanced stage in the evolution of his multidisciplinary socio-rhetorical method.[25] The longer of the two, *The Tapestry of Early Christian Discourse: Rhetoric, Society, and Ideology,* is the more theoretical, and most suitable for graduate students. The other, *Exploring the Texture of Texts: A Guide to Socio-Rhetorical Interpretation,* is a basic and practical how-to manual.[26] While Robbins's socio-rhetorical approach has some things in common with that of Witherington, the greater multidisciplinary content and the attention to ideological issues sets it apart. Robbins's method examines the inner texture, intertexture, social and cultural texture, ideological texture, and sacred texture of NT texts. The reader should consult his works for a fuller explanation. Also, in 2003, former students of Robbins edited a volume of essays entitled *Fabrics of Discourse: Essays in Honor of Vernon K. Robbins,* which is a valuable resource.[27]

However, even Robbins's approach has not gone far enough for some who have been discontented with NT rhetorical criticism for being out of touch with the way the study of rhetoric has evolved in the modern university. We might mention especially J. David Hester Amador, a student of Wilhelm Wuellner, who in 1999 published an aggressive critique of mainstream NT rhetorical criticism titled *Academic Constraints in Rhetorical Criticism of the New Testament: An Introduction to a Rhetoric of Power.*[28] There is a strong influence from Michel Foucault on this work, and that may be taken as emblematic of what Amador and a few others would like to see, that is, a more explicitly postmodern ideological turn in NT rhetorical criticism.[29] Amador is especially attracted to the work

---

[24] See esp. Wuellner, "Rhetorical Criticism," 149–86.

[25] Vernon K. Robbins, *Exploring the Texture of Texts: A Guide to Socio-Rhetorical Interpretation* (Valley Forge, Penn.: Trinity Press International, 1996); *The Tapestry of Early Christian Discourse: Rhetoric, Society, and Ideology* (London: Routledge, 1996).

[26] I have used it very successfully with advanced undergraduates. Robbins has even used some of it with his Sunday school class.

[27] David B. Gowler et al., eds., *Fabrics of Discourse: Essays in Honor of Vernon K. Robbins* (Harrisburg, Pa.: Trinity Press International, 2003).

[28] J. David Hester Amador, *Academic Constraints in Rhetorical Criticism of the New Testament: An Introduction to a Rhetoric of Power* (JSNTSup 174; Sheffield: Sheffield Academic Press, 1999).

[29] See also Wuellner, "Rhetorical Criticism," 149–86.

of Elisabeth Schüssler Fiorenza, the celebrated feminist biblical scholar
who has often combined rhetorical and ideological criticism.[30] Antoinette
Wire's rhetorical approach to 1 Corinthians also reflects postmodern ideological concerns.[31] I will have more to say about the characteristics of
a postmodern rhetorical approach in the final section. For now, I will
conclude this brief overview of Paul and rhetoric by observing that we
can be assured that NT rhetorical criticism will continue to thrive, evolve,
and be all things to all people.

CLASSICAL RHETORICAL-CRITICAL
READING OF 1 CORINTHIANS

In this section, I will provide an overview of what classical rhetorical
criticism typically looks like when applied to 1 Corinthians as a whole. A
full rhetorical analysis of the letter requires a book, so this only a sketch.
While not all rhetorical interpreters follow Kennedy's methodology precisely, given its enormous influence I will use it for illustrative purposes.
As summarized by Duane Watson,

> His methodology has five interrelated steps: (1) determine the rhetorical unit;
> (2) define the rhetorical situation; (3) determine the rhetorical problem or
> stasis and the species of rhetoric, whether judicial (accusation and defense),
> deliberative (persuasion and dissuasion), or epideictic (praise and blame); (4)
> analyze the invention, arrangement, and style ("invention" is argumentation
> by ethos, pathos, and logos). "Arrangement" is the ordering of the various
> components, such as the *exordium* (introduction), *narratio* (narration of the
> facts), *probatio* (main body), and *peroratio* (conclusion). "Style" is fitting the
> language to the needs of invention and includes such things as figures of
> speech and thought; and (5) evaluate the rhetorical effectiveness of the rhe-
> torical unit in meeting the exigence.[32]

Step 1: Determining the Rhetorical Unit

Discerning the overall arrangement of a discourse involves discerning
the various rhetorical units throughout. But when looking at a Pauline

[30] See especially Elisabeth Schüssler Fiorenza, *Rhetoric and Ethic: The Politics
of Biblical Studies* (Minneapolis: Fortress, 1999).
[31] Antoinette Wire, *The Corinthian Women Prophets: A Reconstruction
through Paul's Rhetoric* (Minneapolis: Fortress, 1990).
[32] Duane F. Watson, "New Testament Rhetorical Criticism," in *Methods of
Biblical Interpretation* (Nashville: Abingdon, 2004), 192.

letter as a whole, determining the rhetorical unit has been somewhat controversial.[33] Some rhetorical-critical interpreters tend to stress that these
are rhetorically informed epistles, not formal speeches, so expecting to
find a close structural match between a letter of Paul and the typical arrangement of any particular species of ancient rhetoric (judicial, deliberative, or epideictic) is misguided. Other rhetorical-critical interpreters,
however, do tend to approach the letters as speeches with epistolary frames.
In this case, the usual formal features of the letter introduction (prescript,
blessing, and thanksgiving) and closing (travel plans and greetings) are
often understood to display some intimate relationship with the introduction and conclusion of the body of the letter, which is in turn understood
to closely resemble a speech. It may well be that there is truth in both
perspectives and that one or the other may be more convincing depending
on which letter is under analysis. For example, Galatians may sound more
like a speech within an epistolary framework than does 1 Thessalonians.
One of the most often heard criticisms of some rhetorical-critical analyses
of Paul's letters is that they take the descriptions of the arrangement of
various types of speeches discussed in the ancient rhetorical handbooks
and apply them woodenly. This is no doubt true of some poor examples of
rhetorical-critical analysis, but it is certainly not true of all. On the issue
of the relationship of the epistolary frame to the letter body, my analysis
of 1 Corinthians is indebted to Margaret M. Mitchell. Throughout her
outstanding monograph on 1 Corinthians, Mitchell demonstrates how
Paul melds the epistolary genre with the deliberative species of rhetoric.[34]

Step 2: Defining the Rhetorical Situation

The rhetorical situation of 1 Corinthians might be summed up as an
unholy and divided church. These concerns are already foreshadowed in
the prescript of the letter where Paul addresses the "church of God that is
at Corinth" as "those sanctified in Christ Jesus, called to be saints, together
with all those who in every place call on the name of the Lord Jesus Christ,
both their Lord and ours" (1:2 NRSV). This prescript anticipates a concern
with both the moral/ethical issues and the lack of unity Paul has found out
about through oral (v. 11) and written means (7:1). From Paul's perspective,
the divisions are caused by pretentious arrogance and selfishness. When

---

[33] Also disputed is Kennedy's contention that rhetorical units within a discourse can have their own rhetorical situations and, in some cases, their own
dispositions, that is, *exordium, narratio, propositio,* and so on.

[34] Margaret M. Mitchell, *Paul and the Rhetoric of Reconciliation: An Exegetical
Investigation of the Language and Composition of 1 Corinthians* (Hermeneutische
Untersuchungen zur Theologie; Louisville, Ky.: Westminster/John Knox, 1993).

one contemplates the range of problems he had to address in a single letter, one appreciates how easily this letter could have turned into a heap rather than a building.[35] It is a testimony to his rhetorical skill that it did not.

Step 3: Determining the Rhetorical Problem and Species of Rhetoric

In some rhetorical situations, there is the additional complication of one or more rhetorical problems. In this case, the rhetorical problem is that the factionalism in the congregation was very likely undermining Paul's authority. With some members claiming to belong to Paul, some to Apollos, some to Cephas, and some to Christ, would Paul be able to give advice and commands to those who do not look to him as their example? This is probably why he dealt with this most extreme case of division first.

The species of rhetoric in 1 Corinthians is certainly deliberative. Judicial rhetoric is mostly encountered in the courts and has to do with accusation or defense with respect to past actions. Epideictic or demonstrative rhetoric has to do with praise or blame, usually in the present. Deliberative rhetoric has to do with persuasion or dissuasion with respect to future actions. While Paul will occasionally use a judicial or epideictic tone in the letter, his overall purpose is the deliberative one of trying to persuade the Corinthians to choose a better course in the future with respect to several matters.

Step 4: Supplying Rhetorical Analysis

The arrangement of 1 Corinthians is quite compatible with the expectations for the deliberative species. What follows is my analysis of the rhetorical structure of 1 Corinthians. My debt to Mitchell is readily apparent, although I do depart from her analysis in some significant ways.[36]

I. Epistolary Opening/Rhetorical Introduction (*exordium;* 1:1–9)

A. Prescript (1:1–3)

B. Thanksgiving (1:4–9)

II. Thesis (*propositio;* 1:10)

"I appeal to you, brothers and sisters, by the name of our Lord Jesus Christ, that all of you be in agreement and that there be no divisions among you, but that you be united in the same mind and the same purpose." (NRSV)

[35] See ibid., 184, for a delightful quotation of Godet concerning this point.
[36] For Mitchell's outline, see *Paul and the Rhetoric of Reconciliation,* 184–86.

III. Arguments (*argumentatio*)

A. Heading One: Divisive Leadership Issues (1:11–4:21)

B. Heading Two: Divisive Ethical Issues

    1. "Incest" (5)

    2. Lawsuits (6:1–8)

    3. Fornication (6:9–20)

    4. Marriage (7)

    5. Misuse of Freedom regarding Idol Meat (8–10)

C. Heading Three: Divisive Worship Issues

    1. Improper Conduct of Women Prophets (11:2–16)

    2. Improper Conduct at the Lord's Supper (11:17–34)

    3. Improper Use of Spiritual Gifts and Disorderly Worship (12–14)

D. Heading Four: A Divisive Doctrinal Issue (15:1–57)

IV. Conclusion (*peroratio;* 15:58)

"Therefore, my beloved, be steadfast, immovable, always excelling in the work of the Lord, because you know that in the Lord your labor is not in vain" (NRSV)

V. Epistolary Closing (16:1–24)

A. The Collection (16:1–4)

B. Travel Plans (16:5–12)

C. Final Appeals and Greetings (16:13–24)

The epistolary form of 1 Cor 1:1–9 is obviously that of a Greek letter opening (prescript and thanksgiving), but its rhetorical function as an *exordium* is also readily apparent. An *exordium* (Greek: *prooimion*) is the introduction of a speech where its subject and purpose are announced. While Mitchell prefers to reserve the designation "Rhetorical *prooimion*" for the thanksgiving, her exegesis confirms that Paul is already anticipating the main theme of maintaining unity within diversity in the prescript.[37] An *exordium* may prepare the way for a formal statement of the thesis (*propositio;* Greek: *prothesis*) of the speech, and that is indeed what happens in this case.

---

[37] Ibid., 192–94.

The *exordium* is also important for establishing the character (*ethos*) of the speaker and may include an effort to make the audience well disposed toward the speaker by praising them (1 Cor 1:4-7). This is often referred to as a *captatio benevolentiae*, a "taking captive the good will" of the audience. Paul's authority in the congregation is threatened by factionalism, so it may seem strange that he did not make his exordium longer and concentrate more on building up his *ethos* in the exordium. However, he probably thought that the only way to restore his authority would be in the context of arguing against the factionalism.[38] Thus, it is no accident that this issue will be addressed first in the body of his discourse.

Before that first argument, however, comes the thesis (*propositio*) in 1 Cor 1:10. The thesis is a succinct call for agreement, a unity of mind and purpose, rather than division. While this thesis seems tailor made for the immediately following argument concerning factions, by not building that specific problem into the thesis, Paul leaves it open enough to serve admirably as the thesis of the entire letter. Interestingly, the conclusion (*peroratio;* Greek: *epilogos*) of the letter is similarly succinct and generalized, making it an appropriate complement to the thesis.

Next comes the *probatio* (Greek: *pisteis*) or "proofs."[39] Kennedy uses this term, but some scholars prefer to use *argumentatio*, the "arguments," as I have done.[40] Like Mitchell, I think Paul put considerable thought into how he would organize the long list of diverse subjects he had to address. While I use simplified terminology for the "headings" and construe their functions somewhat differently than her, I agree that there are four major headings or subject groupings in the *argumentatio*. For reasons discussed below, the problems with factionalism needed to be addressed first under "Heading One." The next five subjects can be grouped together under "Heading Two" as addressing "Divisive Ethical Issues."[41] "Heading Three"

---

[38] For more on this viewpoint, see Given, *Paul's True Rhetoric*, 93-95. Joop Smit also emphasizes the *ethos* building purpose of 1 Cor 1-4 in "'What is Apollos? What is Paul?' In Search for the Coherence of First Corinthians 1:10-4:21," *NovT* 44 (2002): 231-51. He concludes that "in the last analysis the drift of 1 Cor. 1:10-4:21 can be summarized in a single rhetorical term: in this passage Paul is reestablishing his ethos" (251).

[39] Both Mitchell and Witherington consider 1 Cor 1:11-17 to be a *narratio* (narration of relevant facts) between the thesis and arguments, but I find these verses to be too well integrated with the first argument to stand alone.

[40] See Hans-Josef Klauck, *Ancient Letters and the New Testament: A Guide to Context and Exegesis* (Waco, Tex.: Baylor University Press, 2006), 219.

[41] Mitchell's fuller title for this heading is appropriate: "The Integrity of the Corinthian Community against Outside Defilement: Advice on Divisive Issues within the Group." See also Dale Martin, *The Corinthian Body* (New Haven: Yale University Press, 1995).

addresses three "Divisive Worship Issues," while "Heading Four" takes up a "Divisive Doctrinal Issue," the resurrection of the dead. Why did Paul choose to deal with this problem last? Some interpreters have argued that he probably did so because misunderstandings about resurrection and the body could have been the source of several of the moral and ethical problems in the church pertaining to the body. Another possible reason for the placement of Heading Four is its relationship to "final things." Here we might compare Romans in which, in my opinion, the *argumentatio* section ends with a discussion of eschatological matters in chapter 11.[42]

As I stated earlier, the conclusion (*peroratio*) of 1 Corinthians is, like the thesis, succinct and generalized. Indeed, the ancient rhetorical handbooks often recommend brevity in the conclusion.[43] Of 1 Cor 15:58, Mitchell rightly states,

> The conclusion is short and to the point, and amounts to a restatement of the central argument of the letter: seek the upbuilding of the church in concord, even when it entails sacrificing what appears to be to your present advantage, because this is the appropriate Christian behavior of love (τὸ ἔργον τοῦ κυρίου ["the work of the Lord"]) which will lead to eschatological advantage (οὐκ ἔστιν κενὸς ἐν κυρίῳ) ["is not in vain in the Lord"]).[44]

I would add two things about this brief *peroratio*. First, just as the thesis is generalized enough to serve as the thesis of the entire letter while having an especially close relationship with the first argument, the conclusion is generalized enough to serve as the conclusion of the discourse of the entire letter while having an especially close relationship to the last argument. Ultimately, the resurrection gives hope that one's work in the Lord is not in vain. Second, this conclusion serves as an excellent transition into the first topic of the "Epistolary Closing." The collection for the saints is an example of "the work of the Lord," a "labor that is not in vain."

After the *peroratio* comes the "Epistolary Closing" in which Paul speaks of the collection, travel plans, final appeals, and greetings.[45] There

---

[42] In an unpublished paper, "Parenesis and Peroration: The Rhetorical Function of Romans 12:1–15:13," I argue that Paul's arguments end in Rom 11 and the peroration begins in Rom 12. Although brevity is often recommended for perorations, it is not the rule in real speeches. Deciding what is the peroration of Romans or any other discourse should be decided based on the variety of functions perorations can perform, not their length.

[43] Mitchell, *Paul and the Rhetoric of Reconciliation*, 291, provides some excellent examples of very short perorations similar to that of 1 Corinthians.

[44] Ibid., 290.

[45] Witherington, *Conflict and Community in Corinth*, 313–17, includes 1 Cor 16:1–12 in the *probatio*. He considers 15:58 to be the peroration of chapter 15. Seeing an intimate connection between 15:58 and the immediately preceding

are aspects of the travel plans and final appeals that recapitulate the concerns of the thesis and the first major argument. The mention of Timothy and Apollos (1 Cor 16:10–12) and the commendation of the household of Stephanas (vv. 15–18) remind us Paul's will concerning the leadership issues, and 1 Cor 16:13–14 echo again themes in the thesis and peroration.[46]

A full rhetorical analysis would require analyzing Paul's invention and style throughout the letter. This cannot be carried out here. Invention consists of various persuasive appeals based on *ethos* (the character of the speaker), *pathos* (stirring of the emotions), and *logos* (reason). I will touch on Paul's use of these in the next major section. As for style, most modern rhetorical-critical interpreters make such observations haphazardly since the focus tends to be on the structure of the argument. The major commentaries are often a good source for such stylistic observations, especially some of the older British and European commentaries on Paul's letters.

Step 5: Evaluating Rhetorical Effectiveness

The final step is to "evaluate the rhetorical effectiveness of the rhetorical unit in meeting the exigence." This includes discussion of Paul's rhetorical strategies. Some scholars have a tendency to laud Paul with accolades for his wisdom and persuasiveness, but in most cases, we have no way of knowing how successful he was. If, as in the case of 1 Corinthians, there is evidence he did not fully succeed, the blame is often laid upon his obtuse or recalcitrant children. However, Mitchell's verdict is refreshingly blunt: "Paul's rhetoric of reconciliation in 1 Corinthians was a failure." She identifies two main reasons for this.

> First of all, it is clear from 2 Corinthians that Paul's rhetorical strategy of appealing to himself as the respected example to be imitated was not well received at Corinth, but was instead negatively interpreted as Paul's "self-commendation." Secondly, as a deliberative argument for concord, Paul's 1 Corinthians was an inherently risky undertaking. Instead of reuniting the Corinthian factions, Paul seems, by his argument in the letter, to have "incurred the enmity of both." So 1 Corinthians was a failure in its original historical setting.[47]

---

argument is natural, as I suggested above, but viewing the contents of 16:1–12 as an argument is not. Witherington himself refers to 16:1–12 as a "potpourri of various items" (313). Indeed, the fact that it is not an argument is another reason to consider 15:58 the peroration of the whole discourse.

[46]On 1 Cor 16:13–18 as a recapitulation within the epistolary closing, see Mitchell, *Paul and the Rhetoric of Reconciliation*, 294.

[47]Ibid., 303.

Mitchell's example confirms that some classical NT rhetorical criticism can be quite critical where Paul is concerned. One is left to contemplate the possibility that Paul could have done better. Nevertheless, more postmodern interpreters would not find even this level of critique satisfactory. They would say that we need to ask questions that are more penetrating about Paul's rhetoric—and our own.

POSTMODERN RHETORICAL-CRITICAL
READING OF 1 CORINTHIANS

Some of the problems with the classical or "new rhetoric" methodology are expressed well in the "Rhetorical Criticism" chapter of *The Postmodern Bible.*

> In spite of its contributions to the retrieval of an ample classical rhetoric, the new rhetoric continues in its own way to make similar reductive gestures. It reduces rhetoric to poetics, stylistics, and literary criticism generally . . . to communication studies or social studies, or to text linguistics or discourse analysis (Johanson). Another way to restrain rhetorical criticism is to reduce it to social description or to historical reconstruction . . . Rhetoric does indeed overlap with the other sciences, but the "realm of rhetoric" (Perelman, 1982) has its own integrity and its own constraints.[48]

William Wuellner, the unidentified author of *The Postmodern Bible*'s chapter on rhetorical criticism, is quite appreciative of the "new rhetoric" because it anticipates several postmodern concerns.[49] However, because it does not go far enough, what he calls for are "new" rhetorical critics who will practice postmodern rhetorical criticism. Perhaps the main characteristic of postmodern rhetorical criticism according to Wuellner is greater "self-reflexivity."[50] While I cannot reproduce every characteristic of what he means by this here, the following excerpts will give a taste of it:

> A new rhetorical theory needs to emphasize the inescapable social, political, religious, and ideological constraints that are operative before, during, and after reading. Ideology in this context may be thought of as the rhetoric of basic communication, of what counts as true or goes without saying. These new readings may then be able to take place within discursive constraints that previously could not be exposed as restrictive because they were operative simply as "truth."[51]

---

[48] "Rhetoric," in *The Postmodern Bible*, 161.
[49] Ibid., 156.
[50] Ibid., 166.
[51] Ibid.

Against the backdrop of postmodernism the "new" rhetorical critic needs to study "discursive practices" and try to understand them "as forms of power and performance" or "as forms of *activity* inseparable from the wider social relations between writers and readers" (Eagleton, 1983:205–6).[52]

"New" radically self-reflexive rhetorical critics, then, will practice rhetorical criticism in a practical way as cultural criticism. They will expose, but also employ rhetorical power instead of perpetuating cultural norms in the name of some allegedly objective and neutral hermeneutical or rhetorical science (Lachmann; Lentricchia; Loubser: Robbins, 1993; Wuellner, 1978b; see our chap. 2). In doing so, the new rhetorical critics will be participating in resistance from below to the prevailing norms of society.[53]

One further aspect of postmodern approach to the rhetorical tradition needs to be included, namely, a critique of rationality. . . . The power released by effective speech not only affects the hearers in ways the speaker could not anticipate; it also makes the speaker say things he never anticipated saying (the phenomenon of "getting carried away by one's own rhetoric").[54]

Finally, rhetorical performance takes place within many interpretive communities, each with its own institutional investments. . . . There needs to be a high degree of critical self-reflection about these rhetorical communities, but nowhere more so than in the academic community.[55]

My past work on the Corinthian correspondence exhibits a number of these characteristics of postmodern rhetorical criticism.[56] I will not reproduce that work here. Instead, I have chosen to illustrate some of these characteristics of postmodern rhetorical criticism by applying them to two key aspects of a brief passage in 1 Corinthians that is often understood to express Paul's entire philosophy of rhetoric or anti-rhetoric:

When I came to you, brothers and sisters, I did not come proclaiming the mystery of God to you in lofty words or wisdom. For I decided to know nothing among you except Jesus Christ, and him crucified. And I came to you in weakness and in fear and in much trembling. My speech and my proclamation were not with plausible words of wisdom, but with a demonstration of the Spirit and of power, so that your faith might rest not on human wisdom but on the power of God. (1 Cor 2:1–5 NRSV)

The first thing I would point out in light of Wuellner's characteristics of postmodern criticism is that most members of the academic rhetorical

---

[52] Ibid.

[53] Ibid., 167.

[54] Ibid.

[55] Ibid.

[56] Given, *Paul's True Rhetoric*, 83–137.

community who interpret this passage are also members of faith communities. In many cases, the institutions in which they teach and do research are church-related. Such scholars are particularly susceptible to a canonical bias, although since the Bible is a classic text in Western culture more generally, even "secular" scholars are not unaffected. The assumption is that if Paul says something, it must be intended to embody truthfulness rather than "truthiness."[57] This is surely one of the main reasons that it does not even occur to most classical rhetorical interpreters to ask if Paul is giving an entirely accurate account of his activities among the Corinthians or what "forms of power and performance" might cause him to give a skewed one.[58]

In the confines of this chapter, I cannot carry out a full analysis of the passage, but I will concentrate on two key aspects of it, because if one can demonstrate a reason to be suspicious of them, suspicion is cast on the whole thing as possibly being loaded with rhetorical hyperbole. Could the rhetorical situation Paul is addressing in 1 Cor 1–4 have caused him to "say things he never anticipated saying (the phenomenon of 'getting carried away by one's own rhetoric')"?[59] Paul claims he knew nothing but Christ crucified when he was among them, and, according to the usual rhetorical—or anti-rhetorical—interpretation of the passage, he did not rely on rhetoric to persuade them so that their faith would not rest on human wisdom.[60] But is it really likely that he relied on nothing but a message of Christ crucified? Furthermore, granted that he means to contrast human with divine wisdom, does he really want the Corinthians' faith not to rely on human resources at all? Before we can answer these questions, some further background is necessary.

---

[57] The second definition of "truthiness" in Merriam-Webster's dictionary is "the quality of preferring concepts or facts one wishes to be true, rather than concepts or facts known to be true." It was Merriam-Webster's word of the year in 2006. Although not coined by the comedian and political satirist Stephen Colbert, the word became extremely popular after he used it on the first episode of *The Stephen Colbert Report* in October 2005.

[58] Indeed, I suspect some interpreters of Paul continue to resist recognizing his training in and use of rhetoric since the "weapons of rhetoric" normally include the intentional use of ambiguity, cunning, and deception even by the "good man" fighting for a good cause. See Mark D. Given, "On His Majesty's Secret Service: The Undercover *Ēthos* of Paul," in *Rhetoric, Ethic, and Moral Persuasion in Biblical Discourse: Essays from the Heidelberg 2002 Conference* (ed. Anders Eriksson et al.; ESEC 11; Harrisburg, Pa.: T&T Clark International, 2005), 196–213.

[59] See above, p. 190.

[60] Some interpreters are not convinced that speech itself is the focus here, but rather its content.

Paul: Sophist or Sophos?

As already noted, in *Philo and Paul among the Sophists,* Winter provides a fascinating portrait of sophistic activity in first-century Alexandria
and Corinth. This provides an illuminating backdrop for reading Paul's
letters to the Corinthian church, most especially 1 Cor 1–4 and 2 Cor
10–13, but also for the Corinthian correspondence as a whole. In his book
(141–260), Winter uses the modifier "anti-sophistic" and the noun "anti-
sophist" dozens of times to describe Paul's rhetorical stance. Certainly in
many obvious ways, Paul was quite different from an ancient professional
sophist. However, as we shall see, on a deeper level there are striking
similarities as well.

Calling Paul a sophist is a perilous proposition.[61] The original title
of my dissertation, later published as *Paul's True Rhetoric,* was not *Paul
the Sophist* but rather *A Sophistic Paul.* I was careful to explain that while
Paul's rhetoric was somewhat sophistic, he was not technically a sophist.
I used the analogy that while a large number of previous studies have
established Greco-Roman philosophical influences on Paul beyond any
doubt, scholars still find it more proper to speak of Paul as philosophic
rather than as technically a philosopher. Similarly, I said my study would
demonstrate that Paul's rhetorical strategies show him to be rather sophistic, though not a sophist. Indeed, I chastened E. A. Judge—Winter's
dissertation advisor—for using the title "sophist" in so sloppy a way as to
apply it to Paul and other itinerant teachers who, as he admits, "would
have hotly rejected it."[62]

As H. P. Lee put it in his "Translator's Introduction" to *The Republic,*
the sophists "taught most things; but since success in life is what most men
[*sic*] want, and since the ability to persuade your neighbour is always an
important element in success . . . they all taught rhetoric, the art of self
expression and persuasion."[63] There are two characteristics of the Greco-
Roman sophistic profession as described here that do not fit Paul. First,
he does not charge a fee for his services. Indeed, he takes great pride in
offering his services to the Corinthians for free. Second, he does not teach
subjects relevant to success in life in the empire, or the type of rhetoric
that would promote such success in that domain.

Yet I would contend that there is still something rather sophistic in
how Paul went about his business. Paul seduced potential students with a
training for a much more glorious success in life, namely, success in the

---

[61] See p. 176 above for a basic definition of a sophist.

[62] Judge, "The Early Christians as a Scholastic Community," 125.

[63] Plato, *The Republic* (Harmondsworth: Penguin, 1955), 15. Also, see the
definition on p. 176 above.

life to come, in a new kingdom that was dawning and would soon appear in all its glory. Therefore, while I still stand by my critique of Judge's reasons for calling Paul a sophist, I now think that there are other reasons that justify it as long as one is speaking of a "sophist of the new age," a *sophos*, and some of them are found precisely where Winter finds his evidence for calling Paul an anti-sophist, 1 Cor 1–4.

Paul did not claim to be a sophist, but he did claim to be one who is *sophos* (wise): "According to the grace of God which was given to me, like a wise (*sophos*) master builder I laid a foundation, and another is building on it. But each man must be careful how he builds on it" (1 Cor 3:10 NASB). There is a well-known contrast running through 1:17–3:23 between the wisdom (*sophia*) of the world and the wisdom of God. "For God's foolishness is wiser than human wisdom, and God's weakness is stronger than human strength" (1:25 NRSV). Those who are wise according to worldly standards are fools. This leads to the paradoxical thought that "if you think that you are wise in this age, you should become fools so that you may become wise" (3:18b NRSV). But by what means does one become truly wise, in this age and the next?

Royal Seductions: The Rhetorical Power of Paul's Gospel

My purpose here is simple. I want to remind us that despite what Paul says in 1 Cor 2:1–5, there is evidence elsewhere that he was hardly persuading his audiences with nothing more than the scandalous and moronic paradox of a crucified Son of God (1:23) and the good news that they too are invited to suffer the same fate. It serves his rhetorical purpose in 1 Cor 1:11–4:21 to say that "I decided to know nothing among you except Jesus Christ and him crucified," but evidence that his message consisted of more than that is readily available.

First Thessalonians 1:9–10, for example, is often used as evidence for the type of message Paul must have used to persuade Gentiles. It would appear that Paul must have begun by arguing against idolatry and for belief in the one God of Israel. He then proclaimed that this God has a Son whom he raised from dead and will send from heaven to deliver people from God's coming wrath. There is good reason to accept this reconstruction since Acts 17:22–31 presents Paul making a quite similar appeal to a group of Athenian philosophers at about the time 1 Thessalonians was written. Intriguingly, and most revealingly for our purposes, neither the summary of 1 Thess 1:9–10 nor the sample of Paul's preaching in Acts 17 mentions the cross or crucifixion. Instead, both stress the resurrection and coming judgment. This type of argument is based on two types of invention, *logos* and *pathos*. Paul appealed to reason to try to persuade pagans that there is one God, and he appealed to emotion, that is, fear of judgment, to try to convince them that they should believe in this God and his Son. Who wouldn't want to avoid the wrath of God? This hardly appears to be a message that does not rely on rhetorical means of persuasion at all, if that is what 1 Cor 2:1–4 is taken to imply.[64] And it hardly consists of nothing but a crucified Christ.

But there is more. As Paul says only a little later, "You are witnesses, and God also, how pure, upright, and blameless our conduct was toward you believers. As you know, we dealt with each one of you like a father with his children, urging and encouraging you and pleading that you lead a life worthy of God, who calls you into his own kingdom and glory" (1 Thess 2:10–12 NRSV).[65] Here the appeal is to *ethos*. Even if on the basis of 1 Cor 2:1–5 one were to try to make the case that Paul did not use his *ethos* to persuade people of the truth of the gospel, which is doubtful, he is obviously appealing to it to maintain their continued allegiance. Moreover, Paul, no less than a typical Greco-Roman philosopher or sophist, is promising positive benefits from accepting his message. They may not attain glory in the kingdoms of this age, but they will have a much superior glory in the kingdom come.

It is not enough, however, simply to accept the message. One must live a certain kind of life to be worthy of the kingdom. That kind of life was modeled by Paul and his colleagues while they were among the Thessalonians, and he longs to be among them again to "restore what is lacking in [their] faith" (1 Thess 3:10 NRSV). Faith has definite content for Paul. It includes a way of life that when followed can, as he says, "strengthen your hearts in holiness that you may be blameless before our God and Father at the coming of our Lord Jesus with all his saints" (3:13 NRSV). Paul asks and

---

[64] This is where Winter's treatment of Paul's rhetoric becomes very unconvincing. Winter not only argues that 1 Cor 2:1–5 means that Paul was anti-sophistic in his presentation of the gospel but that he was anti-*ethos*, anti-*apodeixis* (i.e. anti-*logos)*, and anti-*pathos* as well (*Paul and Philo among the Sophists*, 159). However, from the standpoint of rhetoric, the notion that anyone can present anything without utilizing *logos* is absurd. For that matter, so is the notion that people could take themselves so out of the process of communication that *ethos* would not be utilized at all. It is quite clear that Paul would agree, as demonstrated by his discussion of tongues and prophecy in 1 Cor 14:1–25. Paul strongly prefers prophecy because it is intelligible and useful for such things as edification, exhortation, and consolation (v. 3). Prophecy can also convict or convince an unbeliever (v. 24), which sounds like a use of *logos*. *Ethos* is also a concern in this discussion: "If, therefore, the whole church comes together and all speak in tongues, and outsiders or unbelievers enter, will they not say that you are out of your mind?" (NRSV). Paul would prefer that they appear to be rational people.

[65] Cf. 2 Thess 1:5.

urges that "as you learned from us how you ought to live and to please God (as, in fact, you are doing), you should do so more and more" (4:1 NRSV). And he goes on to remind them of several specific instructions in the rest of 1 Thess 4 and 5. Since all of this can be accomplished by the power of God's Spirit working with them, Paul can conclude with the invocation, "May the God of peace himself sanctify you entirely; and may your spirit and soul and body be kept sound and blameless at the coming of our Lord Jesus Christ" (5:23 NRSV).[66] This is an intensely apocalyptic and intensely ethical letter from a sophist of the kingdom of God. As with the sophists of this age, imitating his example and following his instructions will produce a great reward.[67]

Did Paul depart from the rhetoric just described and use a different means of persuasion in Corinth, one focused entirely on the cross? It does not seem likely in light of 1 Cor 15. Here Paul reminds them of the message he proclaimed when he was among them, a message that included the cross *and* the resurrection (vv. 3–4). Did it also include the dawning of the kingdom, judgment, and the future reign of Christ (vv. 24–25)? Perhaps not, but is it likely? As 1 Cor 4 attests, in Corinth the hope of a coming kingdom and glory were not enough for some. Their powerful spiritual gifts convinced them that they were already reigning and participating in the glory to come. Paul chides them royally in 4:8 when he says, "Already you have all you want! Already you have become rich! Quite apart from us you have become kings! Indeed, I wish that you had become kings, so that we might [share the rule] with you!" (NRSV).[68] But a careful reader of the Corinthian correspondence could not fail to recognize that Paul is reaping what he had sown in Corinth. Indeed, he is still sowing it. In this very argument, Paul continues to encourage the thought that truly spiritual types are superior to others. In 2:15 he says, "Those who are spiritual discern all things, and they are themselves subject to no one else's scrutiny" (NRSV). Of course he means to claim the honor and authority of the title "spiritual" for himself and deny it to those Corinthians whom he immediately characterizes as "people of the flesh" (3:1 NRSV), but obviously this strategy could backfire. Some might see this statement as not only a reinforcement of the position that the rule of the "spiritual" ones

---

[66] Cf. 1 Tim 6:13–15.

[67] See Elizabeth Castelli, *Imitating Paul: A Discourse of Power* (Louisville, Ky.: Westminster John Knox, 1991).

[68] Cf. 2 Tim 2:11–12: "The saying is sure: If we have died with him, we will also live with him; if we endure, we will also reign with him; if we deny him, he will also deny us; if we are faithless, he remains faithful—for he cannot deny himself" (NRSV).

should not be challenged but also a reminder that by his scrutinizing of them, Paul is confirming that he is really not one of them.

Thus far, we have challenged the tendency to take Paul's word about his exclusively cross-centered message at face value. There is evidence in 1 Thessalonians, Acts 17, and 1 Corinthians itself to suggest that his message also included the resurrection and judgment, and that he used *logos, pathos,* and *ethos* to make his case. So is there a reason pertaining to "issues of power and performance" that could have caused him to make exaggerated claims in 1 Cor 2:1–5? Indeed there is.

The relationship between Paul and Apollos is crucial for understanding 1 Cor 1–4. As Paul says in 4:6, "I have applied all this to Apollos and myself for your benefit, brothers and sisters, so that you may learn through us the meaning of the saying, 'Nothing beyond what is written,' so that none of you will be puffed up in favor of one against another" (NRSV). What made this lesson necessary? The following reconstruction of the events could explain it. Paul started the church in Corinth. First Corinthians 1:26 suggests that he mostly worked among the poorer and less educated elements of the city. It is a basic rule of rhetoric that one adapts one's message to one's audience, so already we can see an additional reason why Paul would not have used "lofty speech and wisdom" among them. He would have been talking "above people's heads."[69] First Corinthians 1:26 could also suggest that Paul only had a little success with the educated and powerful. However, Paul was followed in Corinth by Apollos, a native of Alexandria, who is described in Acts as "an eloquent man, well-versed in the scriptures" (Acts 18:24b NRSV). Paul planted, and Apollos watered (1 Cor 3:6). Perhaps Apollos was a more impressive speaker than Paul was, but an overemphasis on this possibility is probably misleading. To judge from where Paul puts the emphasis throughout these chapters, what really attracted some to Apollos was his superior wisdom (*sophia*). In response to this situation, Paul pursues two strategies. One is to assert that he and Apollos are equals as God's servants and co-workers (vv. 5–9). The other is quite different and is especially relevant to viewing Paul as a *sophos*. Paul claims to have wisdom that only he can provide.[70] This is a powerful seduction. While he sticks with his claim not to preach the gospel "with eloquent wisdom, so that the cross of Christ might not be emptied of its power" (1:17b NRSV) until 2:5, he then makes a remarkable shift, stating that

---

[69] See discussion of *huperochē* (1 Cor 2:1) in Anthony C. Thiselton, *The First Epistle to the Corinthians* (New International Greek Testament Commentary; Grand Rapids, Mich.: Eerdmans, 2000), 208.

[70] For the probable apocalyptic Jewish wisdom aspects of this claim, see Robin Scroggs, "Paul: *SOPHOS* AND *PNEUMATIKOS*," *NTS* 14 (1967): 33–55.

> Yet among the mature we do speak wisdom, though it is not a wisdom of
> this age or of the rulers of this age, who are doomed to perish. But we speak
> God's wisdom, secret and hidden, which God decreed before the ages for our
> glory (1 Cor 2:7, NRSV).

Some have tried to read the following verses as if by "wisdom" here Paul
means only the message of the cross. But that interpretation runs aground
when one reaches 3:1–2, where Paul plainly claims that he did not give
them the meat reserved for "the spiritual" because they were people of the
flesh, mere babes. And he insists they are still not ready for it.

Here one can see how Paul is exercising rhetorical power over against
those who have become enamored with Apollos. If the Corinthians want
to become truly spiritual and experience Christ's power, they will have to
return to Paul's guidance, or, as stated later, they will have to recognize
that they have only one father (originator, authority figure), Paul. And so
he concludes by saying, "I appeal to you, then, be imitators of me. For this
reason I sent you Timothy, who is my beloved and faithful child in the
Lord, to remind you of my ways in Christ Jesus, as I teach them everywhere in every church" (4:16–17 NRSV). This will put them back on the
path to that secret and hidden wisdom that leads to glory.

There are yet more incentives for following Paul's ways. In 3:10–15
he builds up a scenario in which some believers' works will be burned
up on judgment day. These will "suffer loss" (v. 15a NRSV), although
they will be saved. Others, however, whose works are of the quality of
"gold, silver, and precious stones" (v. 12a NRSV), "will receive a reward"
(v. 14b NRSV). Furthermore, those who are truly spiritual are already
given the authority to judge others according to Paul's instructions in
5:12 concerning the errant brother. But this is child's play compared to
the much more powerful judging that will take place when the kingdom
comes. Paul asks,

> Do you not know that the saints will judge the world? And if the world
> is to be judged by you, are you incompetent to try trivial cases? Do you
> not know that we are to judge angels—to say nothing of ordinary matters?
> (6:2–3 NRSV)

Then he goes on to shame them by asking, "Can it be that there is no
one among you *wise* enough to decide between one believer and
another . . . ?" (v. 5 NRSV). Or, we might paraphrase, Is there no *sophos* of
the coming age among you? And all of this leads right into the same type
of kingdom language we encountered in 1 Thessalonians, where a long list
of wrong ways of life will bar entrance into the kingdom (vv. 9–10). As
1 Cor 15 makes perfectly clear, this would be a bad thing:

Then comes the end, when he hands over the kingdom to God the Father, after he has destroyed every ruler and every authority and power. For he must reign until he has put all his enemies under his feet. (1 Cor 15:24–25 NRSV)

In 1 Corinthians, Paul presents the way to glory and the kingdom as a difficult struggle, one that requires a good model to imitate, and Paul offers himself as that model.[71] Paul's rhetorical questions in 1 Cor 1:20, "Where is the one who is wise [*sophos*]? Where is the scribe? Where is the debater of this age?" (NRSV) invite another question: Where is the *sophos*, the scribe, and the debater of the new age? They are where Paul is, together with all those who will imitate him. The wisdom and knowledge he offers does not seduce potential students with the promise of a glory to be achieved in the kingdom of Rome, a glory like that desired by the *sophos*, the scribe, or the debater of this age. But it does seduce with the promise an eternal weight of glory in a far superior kingdom that is about to appear.

I conclude with G. B. Kerford's description of another kind of wise man, one perhaps not unworthy of comparison with Paul the *sophos:*

From the beginning *sophia* was in fact associated with the poet, the seer and the sage, all of whom were seen as revealing visions of knowledge not granted otherwise to mortals. The knowledge so gained was not a matter of technique as such, whether poetic or otherwise, but knowledge about the gods, man and society, to which the "wise man" claimed privileged access.

From the fifth century B.C. onwards the term "*sophistēs*" is applied to many of these early "wise men"—to poets, including Homer and Hesiod, to musicians and rhapsodes, to diviners and seers, to the Seven Wise Men and other early wise men, to Presocratic philosophers, and to figures such as Prometheus with a suggestion of mysterious powers.[72]

Paul, like Prometheus,[73] was a dispenser of mysterious knowledge and power for the benefit of humankind, but his true identity has often been bound by theological, academic, and rhetorical restraints: Paul was a *sophos* in the kingdom of God.

---

[71]"Do you not know that in a race the runners all compete, but only one receives the prize? Run in such a way that you may win it. Athletes exercise self-control in all things; they do it to receive a perishable wreath, but we an imperishable one. So I do not run aimlessly, nor do I box as though beating the air; but I punish my body and enslave it, so that after proclaiming to others I myself should not be disqualified" (1 Cor 9:24–27 NRSV).

[72]G. B. Kerford, *The Sophistic Movement* (Cambridge: Cambridge University Press, 1981), 24.

[73] For more on Paul and Prometheus, see Introduction, p. 1–2.

For Further Reading

Amador, J. David Hester. *Academic Constraints in Rhetorical Criticism of the New Testament: An Introduction to a Rhetoric of Power.* JSNTSup 174; Sheffield: Sheffield Academic Press, 1999.

Augustine. *St. Augustine's City of God and Christian Doctrine.* In vol. 2 of *The Nicene and Post-Nicene Fathers,* Series 1. Edited by Philip Schaff. 1886–1889. 14 vols. Repr. Peabody, Mass.: Hendrickson, 1994.

Betz, Hans Dieter. *Galatians.* Hermeneia. Philadelphia: Fortress, 1979.

———. "The Problem of Rhetoric and Theology according to the Apostle Paul." Pages 16–48 in *L'Apôtre Paul: Personnalité, style et conception du ministère.* Edited by A. Vanhoye. BETL 73. Leuven: Leuven University Press, 1986.

The Bible and Culture Collection. *The Postmodern Bible.* New Haven: Yale University Press, 1995.

Black, C. Clifton, and Duane F. Watson, ed. *Words Well Spoken: George Kennedy's Rhetoric of the New Testament.* Waco, Tex.: Baylor University Press, 2008.

Castelli, Elizabeth. *Imitating Paul: A Discourse of Power.* Louisville, Ky.: Westminster John Knox, 1991.

Eriksson, Anders, et al., eds. *Rhetoric, Ethics, and Moral Persuasion in Biblical Discourse: Essays from the Heidelberg 2002 Conference.* ESEC 11. New York: T&T Clark, 2005.

———. *Rhetorical Argumentation in Biblical Texts: Essays from the Lund 2000 Conference.* ESEC 8. Harrisburg, Pa.: Trinity Press International, 2002.

Given, Mark D. "On His Majesty's Secret Service: The Undercover *Ethos* of Paul," Pages 196–213 in *Rhetoric, Ethics, and Moral Persuasion in Biblical Discourse: Essays from the Heidelberg 2002 Conference.* Edited by Anders Eriksson et al. ESEC 11. Harrisburg, Pa.: T&T Clark International, 2005.

———. *Paul's True Rhetoric: Ambiguity, Cunning, and Deception in Greece and Rome.* ESEC 7. Harrisburg, Pa.: Trinity Press International, 2001.

Gowler, David B., et al., eds. *Fabrics of Discourse: Essays in Honor of Vernon K. Robbins.* Harrisburg, Pa.: Trinity Press International, 2003.

Kennedy, George A. *A New History of Classical Rhetoric.* Princeton: Princeton University Press, 1994.

———. *New Testament Interpretation through Rhetorical Criticism.* Chapel Hill: University of North Carolina Press, 1984.

Malherbe, Abraham. *Paul and the Popular Philosophers.* Minneapolis: Augsburg Fortress, 1989.

Martin, Dale B. *The Corinthian Body.* New Haven: Yale University Press, 1995.

Mitchell, Margaret M. *Paul and the Rhetoric of Reconciliation: An Exegetical Investigation of the Language and Composition of 1 Corinthians.* Hermeneutische Untersuchungen zur Theologie. Louisville, Ky.: Westminster/John Knox, 1993.

Porter, Stanley E., and Thomas H. Olbricht, eds. *Rhetoric and the New Testament: Essays from the 1992 Heidelberg Conference.* Sheffield: Sheffield Academic Press, 1993.

———. *Rhetoric, Scripture, and Theology: Essays from the 1994 Pretoria Conference.* Sheffield: Sheffield Academic Press, 1996.

———. *The Rhetorical Analysis of Scripture: Essays from the 1995 London Conference.* JSNTSup 146. Sheffield: Sheffield Academic Press, 1996.

Robbins, Vernon K. *Exploring the Texture of Texts: A Guide to Socio-Rhetorical Interpretation.* Valley Forge, Pa.: Trinity Press International, 1996.

———. *The Tapestry of Early Christian Discourse: Rhetoric, Society, and Ideology.* New York: Routledge, 1996.

Schüssler Fiorenza, Elisabeth. *Rhetoric and Ethic: The Politics of Biblical Studies.* Minneapolis: Fortress, 1999.

Stanley, Christopher. *Arguing with Scripture: The Rhetoric of Scripture in the Letters of Paul.* Harrisburg, Pa.: T&T Clark International, 2004.

Vanhoye, A., ed. *L'Apôtre Paul: Personnalité, style et conception du ministère.* BETL 73. Leuven: Leuven University Press, 1986.

Vos, Johan S. *Die Kunst der Argumentation bei Paulus.* WUNT 149. Tübingen: Mohr Siebeck, 2002.

———. "To Make the Weaker Argument Defeat the Stronger: Sophistical Argumentation in Paul's Letter to the Romans." Pages 205–31 in *Rhetorical Argumentation in Biblical Texts: Essays from the Lund 2000 Conference.* Edited by Anders Eriksson et al. ESEC 8. Harrisburg, Pa.: Trinity Press International, 2002.

Watson, Duane F., ed. *Persuasive Artistry: Studies in New Testament Rhetoric in Honor of George A. Kennedy.* JSNTSup 50. Sheffield: JSOT Press, 1991.

Winter, Bruce W. *Philo and Paul among the Sophists: Alexandrian and Corinthian Responses to a Julio-Claudian Movement.* 2d ed. Grand Rapids, Mich.: Eerdmans, 2002.

Wire, Antoinette. *The Corinthian Women Prophets: A Reconstruction through Paul's Rhetoric.* Minneapolis: Fortress, 1990.

Witherington, Ben. *Conflict and Community in Corinth: A Socio-Rhetorical Commentary on 1 and 2 Corinthians.* Grand Rapids, Mich.: Eerdmans, 1995.

Wuellner, Wilhelm. "Rhetorical Criticism." Pages 149–86 in The Bible and Culture Collective, *The Postmodern Bible.* New Haven: Yale University Press, 1995.

Index of Modern Authors

Index of Ancient Sources

Made in the USA
Lexington, KY
05 April 2016